The origins of Cheshire

general editor
Nick Higham

already published in the series

The origins of Lancashire   *Denise Kenyon*
The origins of Somerset   *Michael Costen*
The origins of Norfolk   *Tom Williamson*

The origins of
Cheshire

N. J. Higham

Manchester University Press
Manchester and New York
Distributed exclusively in the USA and Canada by St. Martin's Press

Published by Manchester University Press
Oxford Road, Manchester M13 9PL, UK
and Room 400, 175 Fifth Avenue, New York, NY 10010, USA

Distributed exclusively in the USA and Canada
by St. Martin's Press, Inc., 175
Fifth Avenue, New York, NY 10010, USA

British Library Cataloguing-in-Publication Data
A catalogue record for this book is available from the British Library

Library of Congress Cataloging-in-publication Data
Higham, N. J.
    The origins of Cheshire / N.J. Higham,
        p.   cm.—(Origins of the Shire)
    Includes bibliographical references and index.
    ISBN 0-7190-3159-1 (hardback).—ISBN 0-7190-3160-5
(pbk.)
        1. Cheshire (England)—Antiquities.   2. Land settlement—England—
Cheshire—History.   3. Man, Prehistoric—England—Cheshire.
4. Anglo-Saxons—England—Cheshire.   5. Romans—England—Cheshire.
I. Title.   II. Series.
    DA670.C6H48   1993
    936.2'71—dc20   93-15926
                                                                               CIP

ISBN 0 7190 3159 1 *hardback*
ISBN 0 7190 3160 5 *paperback*

Typeset by Best-set Typesetter Ltd., Hong Kong
Printed in Great Britain by Bell and Bain Limited, Glasgow

Contents

Contents

Tables

Figures

Plates

Plates appear between pages 125 and 126

Abbreviations

ASC (A, B, etc.)	*Anglo-Saxon Chronicle*, text 'A', etc.
DB	*Great Domesday Book*
DEB	Gildas's *Ruin of Britain* (*De Excidio Britanniae*)
HB	*History of the Britons*
HE	Bede's *Ecclesiastical History of the English People*

General Editor's preface

The shire was the most important single unit of government, justice and social organisation throughout the Later Middle Ages and on into the Modern period. An understanding of the shire is, therefore, fundamental to English history of all sorts and of all periods – be it conducted on a national, regional or local basis.

This series sets out to explore the origins of each shire in the Early Middle Ages. Archaeological evidence for settlement hierarchies and social territories in later prehistory and the Roman period is necessarily the starting point. The shire and its component parts are then explored in detail during the Anglo-Saxon period. A series of leading scholars with a particular regional expertise have brought together evidence drawn from literary and documentary sources, place-name research and archaeological fieldwork to present a stimulating picture of the territorial history of the English shires, and the parishes, estates and hundreds of which they were formed.

In some instances the results stress the degree of continuity across periods as long as a millennium. Elsewhere, these studies underline the arbitrary nature of the shire and the intentional break with the past, particularly where the West Saxon King, Edward the Elder, imposed his southern ideas concerning local organisation on the regional communities of the English Midlands.

These volumes will each be a great asset to historians and all those interested in their own localities, offering an open door into a period of the past which has, up to now, for many, been too difficult or obscure to attempt an entry.

Nick Higham

Acknowledgements

I am grateful to Dr Alan Thacker, Mr David Wilson and Dr Denise Kenyon for their many kindnesses, the stimulation which has come from contact and conversations over many years and for their unstinted assistance in providing access to work both published and as yet unpublished. Sarah Davnall's computerisation of Cheshire's Domesday and her MA thesis on Cheshire's early ecclesiastical organisation have been of unfailing assistance. Dr Jane Hawkes generously shared with me her as yet unpublished interpretation of the Sandbach crosses and all comments below on that subject are based on her work. Dr Paul Holder and the staff of John Rylands University Library have, as always, rendered much valuable aid, as has Mr Chris Perkins as curator of the Map Library of the Department of Geography, University of Manchester. I am grateful to Professor Barri Jones and Dr Andrew Wareham for the discussion of various aspects of this work over the last year. Comments on Wat's and Offa's Dykes depend heavily on conversations over many years with Dr David Hill and more particularly on recent discussions with Margaret Worthington, who kindly made available to me her own unpublished analysis of the historical context of Wat's Dyke.

This volume would never have begun without the Tatton research project, which first encouraged me to develop an interest in Cheshire's early history. To the many who have been involved with that project over the years, and to my many other Extra-Mural students, my grateful thanks. In a sense, this volume, even the entire series, stems from a distance learning package – 'Early Cheshire' – which I developed as a member of the Extra-Mural staff in 1988.

This book has only been rendered possible by the historical

and place-name studies already undertaken by other scholars, among whom pride of place must be accorded to the late and much lamented Professor John McNeil Dodgson, whose measured study of Cheshire's place-names underpins much of this work. Dr Margaret Gelling's *The West Midlands in the Early Middle Ages* only came into print after this text was submitted for publication but her views as expressed in earlier publications have influenced this volume profoundly.

I am particularly grateful to Dr Chris Lewis, who not only provided xeroxes of material which was difficult of access but also applied himself to the task of reading the first draft of this book. His magisterial judgements have led to major improvements in style and structure and discouraged the author from over-enthusiastic commitment to contentious theories. Where such still remain, it is in defiance of his advice rather than with his approbation.

Notwithstanding the weight of these debts, no one but myself is responsible for the opinions expressed herein concerning Cheshire's formative centuries.

I am grateful also to the University of Manchester for a term's sabbatical leave in the autumn of 1992, which enabled this book to be written. I have been ably assisted in bringing it to fruition by Richard Purslow and other staff at MUP but most of all by my family, Felicity and Naomi, without whose never-failing indulgence it could not have been written.

Introduction

This is a book which seeks to examine the evolution of Cheshire, its principal boundaries and its more important parts, such as its early parishes and hundreds – the internal administrative and judicial sub-divisions of the medieval shire. It is, therefore, a work which focuses on the study of territories – units of land defined according to social or governmental criteria. It is not an attempt to write a general history or archaeology of Cheshire. Such already exist in the now rather outdated series published by the Cheshire Community Council (e.g. Bu'lock 1970), as well as the very scholarly and full treatment of the shire in the recent and ongoing volumes of the *Victoria History*.

The particular pattern of evidence available for Cheshire has dictated the balance of this work: the poverty of Early Medieval archaeology and the lack of pre-Norman documents or literary references has forced the author to depend very heavily on Domesday Book. References to this important work are given throughout by folio and column, so as to enable readers to follow up specific points in the text of their choice. The Phillimore edition, edited by Philip Morgan, is the version which readers are more likely to own and use. An alternative and in some ways rather better edition is to be found in the final section of the *Victoria History of Cheshire*, I, by P. H. Sawyer and A. T. Thacker, which is to be found in most reference libraries.

Any work which seeks to explore territories and their boundaries before Domesday will necessarily stray into ill-supported hypothesis. If that is a sin, then this author must plead guilty, for the Roman and even the Early Medieval periods in Cheshire are in most respects as Prehistoric as the Iron Age. In mitigation, all that can be claimed is that the few sources which are available have been approached with as few preconceptions as possible, yet within the context of the wider study of Early Medieval Britain and western Europe. The resultant suggestions are frequently at odds with the views of other scholars but they do have a certain consistency, particularly when examined over the millennium or so under examination here. It is the investigation of social and political boundaries over this very long time span which is the hallmark of this volume. I hope that this justifies the particular interpretations it invokes, which are offered in the hope that they will contribute to some of the current debates concerning Early Medieval Britain, continuity across cultural divides and the genesis of England.

Felicitati,
toto amore nunc et semper

1

Structure and prehistory

By Natural Scituation, it lyeth low, nevertheless very pleasant, and abounding in plenteousness of all things needfull and necessary for mans use: insomuch that it merited, and had the Name of *The Vale-Royal of England.*

(Smith and Webb 1656, p. 16)

The medieval shire of Chester comprised a territory which, at greatest, measured *c.* 95 km east-west and 65 km north-south (Fig. 1.1). It was, therefore, a large area but one which was long inclined to be volatile as regards its western boundaries. At Domesday (1086), Cheshire was significantly larger than it was to be once Edward I re-ordered Wales (1284). Although its border with Wales then stabilised, there was renewed impetus to change in the modern era. In 1888, Birkenhead, Chester and Stockport were all made county boroughs and set free from the shire administration. By 1954 Cheshire had been reduced in size by a net transfer of land to its neighbours in excess of 28,000 acres (Harris 1979, pp. 94–5). In the debate concerning the future of county boundaries which was under way during the late 1960s, the more extreme proposals then aired would have entirely destroyed Cheshire. Although such dramatic change was successfully resisted, the county boundaries which came into effect in 1974 removed large areas of Wirral and of north-east Cheshire to new, albeit short-lived, metropolitan counties, with the old shire recompensed with Warrington and its environs, hitherto securely inside Lancashire. The modern map of the county (Fig. 1.2)

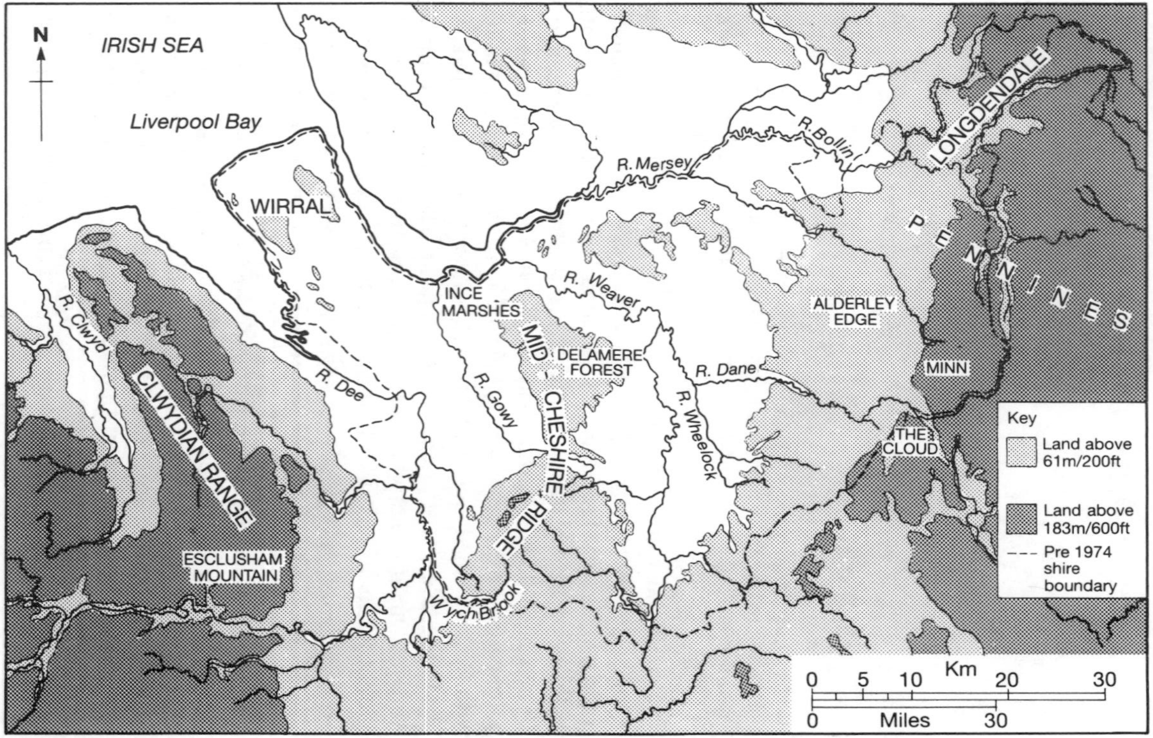

Fig. 1.1 The pre-1974 boundaries of Cheshire set against the topography and principal physical features

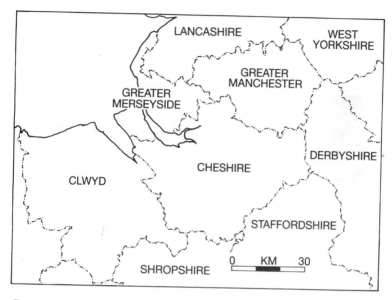

Fig. 1.2 Cheshire and neighbouring counties post-1974

differs dramatically, therefore, from Cheshire in its formative period, between the Scandinavian invasions of the ninth and tenth centuries and the conquest of Wales in the late thirteenth.

Government decisions were just one of several influences on the shire and its constituent parts. The landscape was also being fashioned by local landowners and by ordinary men, making numerous minor decisions concerning the use and descent of individual tracts of land. Their perceptions of the opportunities offered them as farmers by different types of terrain had a fundamental impact on the evolution of the landscape, and so on the parochial and manorial systems which drew their revenues from its use. It was such men too who worked the fisheries, peopled the market-place at Chester, and manned the salt works of the 'Wiches' – from all of which the aristocracy and government extracted profits. Collectively their influence may have been as important as that of the kings by whom Mercia was shired, who generally respected the systems of territorial organisation which they found in operation.

But neither kings nor local communities operated across a level playing field. The land which they worked or from which they drew their revenues was itself a consequence of powerful formative influences at work over a long time-scale. The basic landforms underpinning Cheshire's landscape resulted from geological processes, the consequences of which have been further moulded by climate and by early generations of man. It is with these more fundamental processes that any account of the shire must begin, to place its eventual evolution in an appropriate spatial and environmental context.

Landform and landscape

Notwithstanding that it is often treated for archaeological and historical purposes alongside Lancashire and southern Cumbria as a part of the north-west of England (e.g. Phillips and Smith, forthcoming), Cheshire comprises most of that part of the west Midlands Plain (or Plateau) of England which lies west of the Pennines (Clayton 1979, pp. 190–5; Goudie 1990, p. 140). This extensive lowland continues northward into Lancashire but is bordered to the west by the Millstone Grit and Holywell Shales of Flintshire with, beyond, the true upland of the Clwydian Range formed of Carboniferous limestone and Silurian rocks (Smith and George 1961, pp. 61–3). At its highest, at Moel Fammau, this upland rises to 554 m (1,818 ft). New Red rocks underlie the Cheshire Plain and the western boundary of the shire conforms closely to the boundary between these comparatively recent and level strata and the older, steeply folded and more resistant formations of north-east Wales (Clayton 1979, pp. 143–5; Fig. 1.3).

To the east, the Plain marches with the steep western edge of the southern Pennines, an upland dominated by deeply dissected plateau-like surfaces formed from limestone (the White Peak; Dalton *et al.* 1988) and deposits of mudstones and shales (the Dark Peak; Dalton *et al.* 1990), all of which were laid down in the Carboniferous period (280–345 million years ago). Within Cheshire, hills such as Shining Tor rise above 550 m (1,806 ft). Along the western edge of the Pennines, for example at Macclesfield, deposits of mudstone interface with later rocks – sandstones and shales overlying the coal measures which have been exploited commercially in east Cheshire, particularly in and around

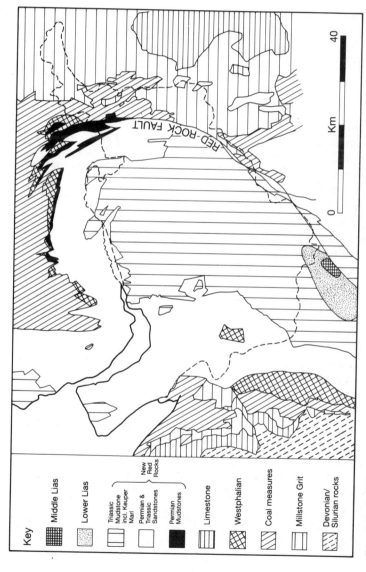

Key

▦	Middle Lias
░	Lower Lias
▢	Triassic Mudstone incl. Keuper Marl
□	Permian & Triassic Sandstones
■	Permian Mudstones
▤	Limestone
▨	Westphalian
▨	Coal measures
▥	Millstone Grit
▨	Devonian/Silurian rocks

New Red Rocks

RED-ROCK FAULT

0   Km   40

Fig. 1.3   Solid geology

Poynton. The edge of the Cheshire Plain here coincides closely with a major geological fault – the Red Rock Fault – which has helped create the significant landscape break of the western Pennine edge only slightly west of the east/west watershed. Along this edge are a succession of weak shales and more resistant sandstones laid north-south, with broadly parallel, eroded folds and faults. These have resulted in north-south valley systems such as that of the Goyt, steep elongated hills such as the Saddle of Kerridge, and high sandstone outcrops like Alderley Edge.

The Cheshire Plain overlies a structurally-defined basin which was already long-established 192–230 million years ago, when a series of newer sedimentary rocks, including the saliferous Keuper Marl and fine-grained Keuper sandstones, were deposited to a great depth. The area was later heavily glaciated, receiving successive ice-sheets which had travelled via Cumbria and western Scotland across the Irish Sea (Jowett and Charlesworth 1929). The last of these – the Devensian readvance – has left a marked impact on the region, pushing south as far as Long Mynd and completely filling the basin, although not all the high points of the underlying rocks were eroded away. A broken ridge of resistant sandstone was left, now known as the Mid-Cheshire Ridge, which reaches 143 m on its steep northern edge at Helsby Hill, and 211 m at its highest point on Bickerton Hill.

Glacial and fluvioglacial processes dominate the landform of much of Cheshire. The most widespread impact was the deposition of a layer of drift or till, up to c. 100 m thick, consisting of a confused series of clays, sands and gravels (e.g. Worsley 1970, p. 88; Fig. 1.4). This till covers the land surface up to around the 200 m contour along the Pennine edge, where it ends in a litter of glacial erratics. The ice-sheet was not, however, long static and a major terminal or 'retreat' moraine was left behind by the last readvance and subsequent retreat of Devensian ice, called the Whitchurch moraine, which approximates very roughly to the southern boundary of the medieval shire (Boulton and Worsley 1965; Worsley 1970). This moraine has created a landscape characterised by hummocky ridges interspersed with meltwater channels, eskers and outwash plains which can be clearly seen today around Malpas and Cholmondeley Castle. Similar morainic belts occur along the eastern boundary of the Plain against the Pennines between Congleton and Macclesfield, formed of sands

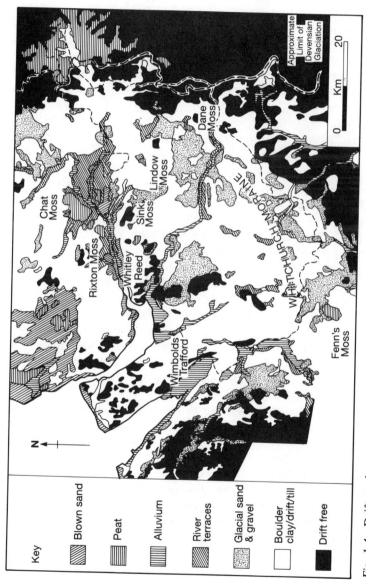

Key

Blown sand

Peat

Alluvium

River terraces

Glacial sand & gravel

Boulder clay/drift/till

Drift free

Chat Moss

Rixton Moss

Whitley Reed

Sink Moss

Lindow Moss

Dane Moss

Wimbolds Trafford

WHITCHURCH MORAINE

Fenn's Moss

N

Approximate Limit of Devensian Glaciation

0   Km   20

Fig. 1.4 Drift geology

with occasional beds of till. Much of this deposition was caused by meltwater trapped between high ground and the ice as it retreated northwards. Numerous outwash lakes were created during the late glacial and early post-glacial periods, beneath which were laid down extensive areas of sand in such areas as Delamere Forest. The resulting land surface is complex, with deep-cut streams draining sizeable valleys interspersed with enclosed hollows and intervening knolls. Elsewhere the ice-sheets left a comparatively level landscape, topped by the consistent and comparatively stone-free till which has resulted in the almost featureless plateaux of parts of Wirral, the Dee valley and central Cheshire.

Glacial and fluvioglacial processes have been the principal factors at work on the landscape of Cheshire. That influence has been far from uniform, so it may be helpful to subdivide the medieval shire purely on landform criteria. It will be obvious that the administrative geography has taken account of these physical characteristics, both in respect to the boundary of the shire and in internal divisions, but landform factors have rarely been the overriding influence in determining the shape and evolution of the medieval territory here under examination. Cheshire divides, in landscape terms, into five sub-regions (Fig. 1.5):

1   The largest is the Dee valley and Wirral peninsula, a low-lying but gently rolling and comparatively well-drained till plain broken by numerous low sandstone outcrops (including that on which Chester is sited), making up the entirety of the western part of the shire. It contained in 1086 the four hundreds of Willaston (Wirral), Atiscross (now very largely in Wales), Chester and *Dudestan* (later Broxton).

2   This is bounded to the east by the Weaver and to the west by the Mid-Cheshire Ridge, a discontinuous sandstone ridge fringed in places by fluvioglacial drift. This is widest in the north where it comprises the core of Delamere Forest but narrows to the south where it reaches Bickerton, with a further detached outcrop at Cholmondeley Castle. The steep outcrops support only thin heathy soils and moorland vegetation, while the surrounding fluvioglacial deposits support very mixed soils, some of high agricultural value but others which have become badly podzolised. Most of this region lies inside the Domesday hundreds of Ruloe and Rushton but it encroaches also on *Dudestan*, so emphasising

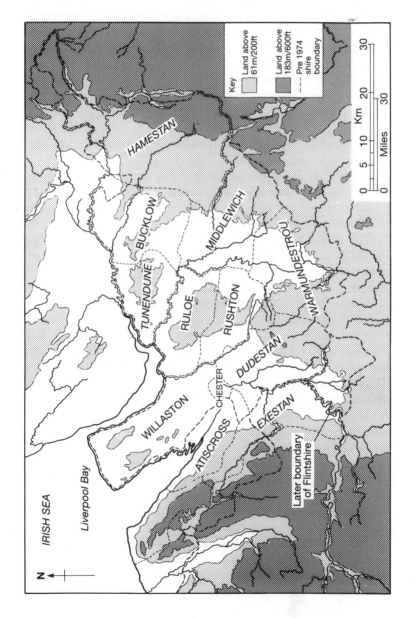

Fig. 1.5 The landscape and Cheshire's Domesday hundreds

Key
Land above 61m/200ft
Land above 183m/600ft
Pre 1974 shire boundary

IRISH SEA

Liverpool Bay

N

HAMESTAN

BUCKLOW

TUNENDUNE

MIDDLEWICH

RULOE

RUSHTON

WARMUNDESTROU

DUDESTAN

WILLASTON

CHESTER

ATISCROSS

EXESTAN

Later boundary of Flintshire

Km
0   5   10   20   30

Miles
0   30

the use made by administrators of this minor upland as a boundary between hundreds and the townships and estates of which they were composed, all of which were focused for governmental and parochial purposes on lowland sites.

3   Across southern Cheshire there stretches a landscape dominated by the Whitchurch moraine and the lesser glacial and fluvioglacial deposits to the north of it. This broken country lies between Malpas and Whitchurch (marginally inside medieval Shropshire) and Crewe and largely lay within *Warmundestrou* hundred (later Nantwich hundred) in 1086.

4   North of this moraine-littered landscape lies the flat and near flat plain of northern and central Cheshire, draining via the rivers Weaver and Bollin and their tributaries into the Mersey. Although there are occasional outcrops of pre-glacial geology, most markedly at and around Halton and at Bowdon, glacial till interspersed with low ridges of fluvioglacial origin cover the bulk of the land surface. This often poorly drained region comprised all of Bucklow and *Tunendune* hundreds.

5   The Pennine edge comprises both that narrow upland band which lies inside Cheshire and adjacent areas, which are characterised by the sandstone outcrops and fluvioglacial depositions that have created a highly irregular, if often attractive, landscape where the Plain meets the Pennines. This region corresponds closely to the Domesday hundred of *Hamestan*, later known as Macclesfield.

These regions have been differentially affected by later landscape changes. Successive adjustments in the relationship between land and sea levels have led to the formation of as many as four terraces along the major rivers, most particularly the Mersey. On the exposed tip of the Wirral peninsula, the sea has eroded the soft till, resulting in the loss of hundreds of hectares of land since Saxon times and the creation of extensive mud-flats and sandbanks in and between the Dee and Mersey estuaries. The submerged forest trees which have occasionally been noted along the estuaries of the Dee and Mersey imply that far lower sea levels were prevalent in the early post-glacial period than are now present. The same region has suffered from large-scale deposition of sand, forming extensive dune systems which have obscured earlier land surfaces, particularly at Meols on Wirral.

A more widespread feature of the landscape is the occurrence of peat. Peaty soils are a characteristic of the western Pennines, variously encountered upwards of *c*. 250–300 m above O.D., and some attain the depths of blanket bog found in Derbyshire (e.g. Hicks 1971; Tallis 1973a). More important are the lowland mosses which, if taken in association with those in Lancashire, constitute the largest concentration of lowland peat deposits in England north of the Wash. These began to develop during the early post-glacial period in drainage hollows, which were an important legacy of glacial and fluvioglacial processes. They are commonest in the north of the shire where the most extensive – such as Carrington Moss, Warburton Moss and Lindow Moss – grew upwards to become raised bogs. Initial peat growth was probably localised but then expanded laterally, particularly during periods of high rainfall in later prehistory, with the more active and closely spaced examples joining up to form extensive areas of mossland (Fig. 1.4).

Early modern writers reported the presence of forest trees within the peat in some mosses (e.g. Leland, see Toulmin Smith 1906–10, iv, p. 5), suggesting that mossland has spread at the expense of woodland. Medieval and later exploitation of these mosses as turbaries for fuel, improvement for agriculture or, more recently, conversion to industrial or residential uses has led to a dramatic decline in the area now recognisable as mossland. Many medium-sized examples, such as Sink Moss (High Legh), have been entirely converted to agricultural land, with only the blackness of the soil and characteristic field names now revealing the extent of peat prior to the nineteenth century.

Peat is, therefore, a feature of the landscape which was of far greater importance to patterns of land use and communication during antiquity than it is today. The reed-swamp peatlands and extensive alluvium around the river Gowy and Mill Brook in and below Wimbold Trafford (Shimwell 1985, p. 304) posed a serious impediment to travellers attempting to pass between the environs of Chester and central parts of the shire, and this is only one example of many. Extensive mosses on the Mersey's terraces much increased the difficulties of crossing between Cheshire and southern Lancashire. The scarcity of sites where firm ground is present on both banks has tended to concentrate fords at a very few locations, most particularly at and around Warrington and Runcorn (Kenyon 1991, p. 18). The mosses have, therefore, substantially enhanced the potential of the river Mersey as a social and political frontier over a very long time-scale.

These are, however, the more obvious minority of instances. Most mosses were far more local in their impact, influencing the precise route taken by trackways and roads and limiting the extent of intensive land use. Many are to be found on the periphery of parishes, townships and estates during the Middle Ages and seem often to have influenced the formation of such boundaries. Early communities clearly placed a comparatively low value on this type of terrain, particularly when compared with the better-drained soils which overlie the fluvioglacial deposits of the region.

Not all Cheshire's peat beds were extensive; most remained small, developing as mires along stream beds or in small basins, many of which still contain lakes, locally known as meres. These are so numerous that they invited comment by early travellers such as Celia Fiennes, who remarked on them at Betley, on the county boundary, and around Nantwich (Morris 1982, p. 156). The origins of these small meres and mosses have long been debated. The ever-interested John Leland opined that many were due to 'digginge of marle for fattynge the baren grownd there to beare goode corne' (Toulmin Smith 1906–10, v, 6) but such extraction was only responsible for the numerous small pools and ponds which still dot Cheshire's landscape (Axon 1884, pp. 239–42; Hewitt 1923), not the meres. Some originated as kettle-holes which were left when ice blocks melted within sand deposits during the late glacial period. At least two – Bagmere and Flaxmere – have base deposits which contain late glacial pollen (Birks 1965a; Tallis 1973b) but such an early date for others remains unproven. This may point to a later origin for some examples as a consequence of surface subsidence or even cratering over the salt beds of central Cheshire. Rock salt was exposed to a long process of natural erosion by underground water even before the commercial pumping of brine. Many small basin meres probably formed in solution hollows during prehistory, since a suspiciously high proportion overlie the upper saliferous deposits (as at Great Budworth, Oakmere and Rostherne). In some instances their lowest deposits have been dated to later prehistory. This process of subsidence was already at work before Henry VIII's dissolution of the monasteries since Leland recorded that 'in time of mind sank a peace of a hille having trees on hit, and after in that pitte sprang salt water, and the abbate ther began to make salt. . . .' (Toulmin Smith 1906–10, iv, 4). The intensive extraction of wild brine in the modern period led to an escalation of this process, with the appearance of new areas of open water, like Melchett Mere in Tatton Park, which is barely seventy years old.

Across the entire region, soils are today inclined to be acidic and this was probably the principal incentive to undertake marling – a common practice in Cheshire in the medieval and post-medieval periods, which has left numerous pits scattered across the rural landscape. Much liming also occurred in the late and post-medieval periods, although the absence of suitable materials rendered the practice expensive before the advent of the canals.

One influence on soils is the climate. That has varied considerably through time, even over the last two millennia (Lamb 1972–77), but recent figures at least provide a benchmark from which to estimate change and offer comparisons between different regions (e.g. Higham 1987a). Since the war, Cheshire has averaged an annual growing season of 241 days, a grazing season of 213 days, 29 days plant growth lost to drought and an annual rainfall of 714 mm (Smith 1975). By comparison, for example, with lowland Yorkshire, Cheshire is somewhat wetter and the growing and grazing seasons are slightly shorter, despite its lower latitude. It suffers from high summer humidity in consequence of its exposure to the Atlantic, and receives less protection from the rain-shadow of the Welsh mountains than other Marcher shires. This adversely affects the harvesting of hay and grain crops and encourages fungal infestations. It is the combination of comparatively damp conditions and poor ground drainage which has been responsible for the formation of the peats described above, and even where these have not developed, winter waterlogging inhibits ploughing across the Cheshire tills.

As Celia Fiennes remarked, she travelled into the county from the south by a 'deep clay way' and this description might have served for many of Cheshire's roads. Even so, the better-drained lowland soils, at least, produced crops of wheat, barley, oats and peas during the Middle Ages, and early fourteenth-century governments were sufficiently confident of the county's output to requisition large quantities of wheat, barley-malt and oats for their armies (Booth 1981, p. 5). The region was clearly able to feed itself but there is some doubt concerning an agricultural surplus. In the twelfth century, William of Malmesbury questioned the adequacy of its grain supplies in his *Gesta Pontificum* (Hamilton 1870, p. 308) but the early fourteenth-century Chester monk, Ranulph Higden, insisted that the region had a large supply of all kinds of commodities (Taylor 1966, p. 62). Later writers were similarly divided: in 1536 to 1543 Leland was impressed by the corn around Dunham but noted the improvements which had been made there to what 'sumtime was very fernny and commune grounde' (Toulmin Smith 1906–10, iv, p. 5). These improvements probably included underdraining and this was undertaken widely across Cheshire's tills during the eighteenth, nineteenth and early twentieth centuries (e.g. Phillips 1989, pp. 50–88; Aylett, forthcoming). In his *Britannia*, William Camden (1610, p. 606) noted of Wirral that 'the land beareth small plentie of corne'; the authors of the *Vale-Royall* reckoned in 1656 that Cheshire 'aboundeth chiefly in Arable Pasture, Meadow, and Woodland, Waters, Heaths, or Mosses'. If nineteenth-century parallels are relevant, yields may have always been low by national standards (Kain and Holt 1983, p. 40, but see also Phillips 1987). Medieval yields were universally low by comparison with modern levels.

Most commentators remarked on the relative abundance of other resources. Pasturing livestock was clearly an important component of the medieval economy and woodlands were extensively managed and exploited. Fisheries were also important. Several highly productive examples featured in the Domesday Survey and there have been frequent references to the abundance of salmon in the Dee. Numerous meres and lesser rivers also held large stocks of fish which can be shown to have been exploited during the Middle Ages. Rivers such as the Bollin contained trout in commercial quantities until industrial pollution destroyed them (Renaud 1876). Meres and mosslands also provided excellent feeding grounds for large numbers of wildfowl, which were probably widely exploited. Deer were common into the medieval period and wild boar were also present, if by then in steep decline. The region did, therefore, offer a rich and diverse range of opportunities to early man.

Significant climatic variations are to be found within the region, by far the most dramatic being the contrast between the Plain and the Pennines, where altitude and exposure are the dominant factors (cf. Parry 1978, pp. 74–5). Rainfall is half again as high, grain cultivation severely inhibited and the grazing season much reduced. Falls of snow and even drifting are common as late as May on Park Moor, Lyme, and Macclesfield Forest. There was very little agriculture along the upland edge during the medieval period (Plate 1). There are differences, too, between the north and south of Cheshire, with the north-eastern quarter sharing the higher humidity of south Lancashire's cotton belt. In contrast, the west and south are less moist, approximating more closely to the climate of Shropshire or Herefordshire.

The impact of man

Although stone implements have been found locally in glacial deposits, Cheshire has produced no *in situ* evidence of old stone age communities. The earliest evidence of human activity derives from the Mesolithic (Middle Stone Age), probably from the eighth millennium bc (uncalibrated), when hunter/gatherers using broad blade flint assemblages ranged across the Pennines and adjacent areas (Jacobi 1978). They followed the herds of red deer and aurochs from winter pastures close to the sea (e.g. Cowell 1990) to summer grazing lands on the uplands. A chipping floor of this period was excavated beside Tatton Mere during the early 1980s and has been interpreted as a temporary camp used by such a band (Cane and Higham, forthcoming). On ethnographic parallels, such communities probably had complex notions of communal rights over territory but, other than to postulate a west-east annual migration track, such early notions of territoriality in the region cannot now be reconstructed.

The Tatton band inhabited a comparatively open landscape, with tundra-type vegetation broken only by stands of birch and juniper, but the spread of deciduous woodlands across the region during the seventh and sixth millennia BC created very different conditions to which later Mesolithic communities were forced to adapt. There were attempts to maintain the last vestiges of open landscape through the use of fire at or near the upland tree line, as has been identified at Robinson's Moss, Derbyshire (Tallis and

Switzur 1990, p. 859). Certainly there are numerous find spots of later Mesolithic flints on both sides of Cheshire's upland boundary (Jacobi *et al.* 1976; Garton 1987; Longley 1987, p. 38). These suggest human activity on the uplands during the summer months, when prey species probably congregated in large groups on open pastures. Hunters perhaps continued, therefore, to migrate between the Cheshire Plain and the Pennines, in pursuit of the herds.

In the lowlands there have so far been few find-spots identified and no excavations of a Late Mesolithic site undertaken, but a scatter of finds on the Wirral coast may reflect one ecozone used by such communities in the winter, if not perennially (cf. Bonsall 1981). Recent fieldwalking in parts of central Cheshire has extended the density of find-spots on the Mid-Cheshire Ridge (Mayer 1990) and from the Weaver Valley (Cowell 1992) and isolated tools of the later 'narrow blade' type have been identified at Tatton (Higham, forthcoming (a)). This gradually accumulating evidence does suggest that Cheshire was occupied during the later Mesolithic, perhaps even in density sufficient to cause limited disruption to soils and the natural vegetation. There has, however, so far been insufficient carbon-dated research on vegetational history for this to be widely recognised inside Cheshire (cf. Tallis and Switzur 1990; Bartley *et al.* 1990, p. 631), where there are few signs of woodland disturbance before the elm decline of the centuries around 3000 BC (uncalibrated: e.g. Birks 1965b). Research on peat columns from Bagmere and Chat Moss did, however, suggest that the temperate forest characteristic of this region may have been less than uniformly dense (Birks 1965a), which may have had something to do with human agency.

It is with the advent of agriculture and of the domestication of animals in the Neolithic period (New Stone Age) that man began to leave behind artifacts sufficiently diverse and monuments sufficiently durable to invite speculation concerning the territories in which he lived and worked. Several different sites in the region have revealed levels of disturbance of the natural alder/oak/lime/elm woodland which can only have been the responsibility of man and domestic livestock (Birks 1965a, 1965b; Hibbert *et al.* 1971; Chambers and Wilshaw 1991). At Hatchmere, Norley, the first signs of clearance was carbon-dated to *c.* 3319 BC (calibrated) and the subsequent disturbance lasted over half a millennium.

Such findings are confirmed by comparable evidence from adjacent regions, most particularly from the central and southern Pennines (e.g. Hicks 1971; Bartley *et al.* 1990). The clearing of land and ongoing decisions concerning land use began the long process from which the territories, land units and estates of the early historic period eventually emerged.

Despite the reflection of this process in research on the vegetational succession, little progress has been made in the examination of later prehistoric communities via archaeology. Slight traces of early occupation were identified beneath the deserted village at Tatton, associated with flint tools of Neolithic type, and a post hole forming part of a small building was carbon-dated to 3500–2945 BC (calibrated). A rubbish pit yielded hulled 6-row barley, and this was carbon-dated to 3370–2945 BC (Higham, forthcoming). Within the limits of the methodology, these dates are identical and both features apparently derive from the same, perhaps rather brief, occupation by Late Stone Age farmers.

Such settlements may have been commonplace during the period but they are difficult to detect. It should be stressed that identification of the Tatton example was an accidental by-product of research into medieval settlement patterns. A scatter of stone artifacts and occasional finds of pottery imply that farming communities were widespread elsewhere. Yet even were more sites known, the scarcity of pottery made before the Late Neolithic/Early Bronze Age makes it difficult to form any meaningful judgements concerning the social or political groupings within which they lived (Longley 1987, pp. 51–2). In this respect, local finds compare unfavourably with the denser concentrations being found on Derbyshire's White Peak (e.g. Garton and Beswick 1983).

The location of the few larger monuments which have survived suggests territories which straddled Cheshire's boundaries. By far the clearest example is the Bridestones, a chambered long cairn, constructed as a complex tomb during the Early to Mid-Neolithic. This monument was largely intact when it first attracted the attention of antiquaries in the eighteenth century. It then comprised a long cairn measuring *c.* 110 m × 11 m covering a bipartite (or possibly tripartite) chamber constructed of large stones, with a semicircular facade of uprights at the eastern end (Longley 1979a, p. 44). Since then it has been dramatically reduced in size by the removal of stones both large and small, leaving only the uprights of the chamber (Plate 2).

The Bridestones lies at *c.* 267 m above O.D., on a low point on the apex of the ridge stretching southwards from the Cloud, the dominant landmark above Congleton, and was presumably constructed by communities exploiting the valleys of the rivers Dane and Churnet on either side. The latter lies in Staffordshire and the boundary between the two counties has long run lengthways along the cairn. An abrupt change of direction of the boundary at this point implies that those responsible for it saw the monument as a convenient landmark and pressed it into use as a boundary marker on the watershed, where the waterways which they generally utilised were unavailable. It may, of course, already have served as a boundary marker between estates and so naturally become the county boundary when those estates were allocated to different shires. Whether or not, it seems unlikely that the territory exploited by the builders of the Bridestones lay exclusively in any one of the later shires. Its location on the edge of the uplands may reflect the interest of regional communities in both lowland and upland resources and their seasonal movements between the two, in which cases its siting may parallel that of the several long cairns and somewhat later stone circles around the Cumbrian massif (Higham 1986, pp. 65–74). In all respects, the Bridestones is an outlier of a scatter of Neolithic monuments which centres on the White Peak (Marsden 1977), among which comparison with excavated examples, such as the Minning Low chambered cairn (Marsden 1982) suggests that it was structurally one of the less complex.

It has been suggested that an earthen ridge (*c.* 107 m × 25 m) at Somerford may be a Neolithic long mound but this has not been tested by excavation (Longley 1987, p. 47) and its location and shape more probably reflect glacial or fluvioglacial origins. A possible long mortuary enclosure found from the air at Churton in the valley of the Dee is the only other contender as a Neolithic ceremonial site in the county (Longley 1979b, 1987, p. 46), which, if authentic, may have served as a focus for communities west of the Mid-Cheshire Ridge. Other interpretations are, however, available and may eventually be preferred. Beyond the Clwydian hills a thin scatter of stone megaliths were probably outliers of a culture centred on or near Anglesey (Lynch 1969).

The scarcity of such sites is not peculiar to Cheshire but is shared by adjacent counties. It may be a consequence of poor levels of identification. Fresh finds are still being made (e.g. Barnatt *et al.* 1980). It may, alternatively, reflect the small numbers which were constructed, in which case Cheshire's population may already at this stage have formed the periphery of one or more regional communities centred outside the county. The region had no lithic resources which could be exploited in the Neolithic and, excepting only the use of glacial erratics, was dependent on the inflow of raw material, rough-outs or finished artifacts from outside. Whatever the mechanics of this exchange, such imports presumably had to be paid for with local produce, implying that this was a disadvantageous locality in which to settle.

Neolithic communites probably retained a seasonal interest in those upland pastures which had remained comparatively free of woodland since the Mesolithic. By felling and by concentrating livestock above natural carrying capacities, these early farmers had a significant impact on the natural vegetation. The effect was greater where woodland regeneration was already marginal, particularly on the uplands. Comparatively large numbers of Early Bronze Age burial mounds are known close to the Pennine edge of east Cheshire (Fig. 1.6), north-east Staffordshire and the Derbyshire Pennines, suggesting that the same terrain was particularly attractive to pastoralists in the second millennium BC. Further concentrations exist on and around the sandstone outcrops of central Cheshire. Examples have been identified in most areas which have free-draining sand or gravel based soils, sometimes in significant groups, as in the aptly named Seven Lows (or as Leland named them the 'vii Loos') and the groups at Church Lawton, Lower Withington (Wilson 1981) and Jodrell Bank (Longley 1987, p. 62). On the Pennine edge cairns consist of stones collected from the surrounding soil. On stone-free terrain, most probably consisted of sand, gravel and earthen dumps around primary structures of turf. Mounds might be successively enlarged or altered and some served as cemeteries over long periods (e.g. Wilson 1981; McNeil 1982a). A minority were structurally more complex, being set inside circuits of stone uprights, for example, or equipped with central structures which might be interpreted as mortuary buildings (e.g. Rowley 1975;

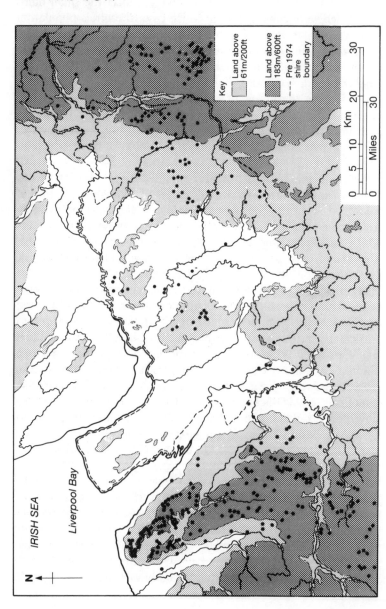

Fig. 1.6 Early to Middle Bronze Age burial mounds in Cheshire and adjacent parts of Clwyd and Derbyshire

Key

Land above 61m/200ft

Land above 183m/600ft

Pre 1974 shire boundary

IRISH SEA

Liverpool Bay

N

Km

Miles

McNeil 1982b; Wilson 1988). Where pollen has been sampled, barrows appear to have been constructed on cleared ground which had already been exploited for agricultural purposes.

Stray finds mostly derive from similar terrain, even including the hoard of bronzes recently found at Bridgemere (Turner 1985). There has been some discussion of the factors influencing this distribution, in case it has been heavily influenced by modern patterns of land use, but it does appear at present to be a genuine reflection of the pattern of discard (Longley 1979c). Of course, further examples of burial sites await discovery. Research into early field names, aerial photography and trial excavation continue to reveal new possibilities, but recent discoveries have tended to be located on similar terrain to those already known, merely extending the existing pattern to such ridges of fluvioglacial origin as make up the core of the medieval parishes of Rostherne and Runcorn. On this evidence, the till plains of central Cheshire appear to have seen only low levels of land use and settlement during the Bronze Age. Palaeobotanical research in the Craven area of Yorkshire provided evidence of a very localised land use history, with free draining soils overlying limestone around Eshton, for example, being cleared from the Elm Decline onwards, while the claylands around White Moss remained heavily wooded, if not entirely unused, until the early Middle Ages (Bartley *et al.* 1990, p. 631). This experience was probably comparable to that of Cheshire, excepting only the absence there of the highly prized lime-rich soils. Clearance arguably had little impact on the Cheshire tills, which retained ancient woodland or were used as woodland pasture throughout prehistory. Accumulating evidence of all kinds suggests two concentrations of activity during the period. That on the Pennine edge, largely between the 100 m and 300 m contours, was the western periphery of a larger concentration of monuments and finds which focus on the White Peak but extends also to the eastern edges of the Pennines (Hart 1976; 1981; Barnatt 1986). A smaller concentration lay on and around the Mid-Cheshire Ridge. Between them were wide expanses of poorly drained and still heavily wooded claylands, broken by partially cleared outcrops of sandstone or ridges formed from sands and gravels (e.g. Chambers and Wilshaw 1991, p. 32).

The political and social organisation of these communities and their territories may have reflected these patterns. Eastern

Cheshire should be considered part of the southern Pennine region and its peoples. The peoples of the Mid-Cheshire Ridge may have looked to the south – it is certainly in that direction that the affinities of the Bridgemere hoard lie (Turner 1985), and the region lay on the periphery of southern metal-working traditions during the Middle Bronze Age. It was, however, marginal to at least three regional traditions of metal working in the Late Bronze Age, each of which was centred outside the area (Cunliffe 1978, p. 58).

Of these two groupings of Bronze Age finds, that which lay on the Pennine edge experienced higher levels of rainfall and a generally harsher climate. Woodland clearance destroyed an important stabilising influence on soils and encouraged rapid erosion into the vigorous streams which are a feature of the region. Higher levels of rainfall during the Middle Bronze Age probably accentuated this process. If population levels rose during late prehistory and the Roman period, as is thought to have occurred nationally, it can only have worsened the situation. By late prehistory – at latest by the end of the Roman period – these upland soils had become degraded, incapable of woodland regeneration and supporting little more than the treeless heather and poor quality moorland vegetation of the present day (Hicks 1971).

This process was long-drawn-out but there is some evidence that communities in this region were already less able than those in central Cheshire to respond to changing social and political conditions in the Late Bronze Age. Impoverishment resulting from environmental degradation is the most likely cause, although significant downwash occurred also in central Cheshire.

This was a period in which societies throughout Britain invested heavily in weapons, in the metallurgical technologies which produced them and in defended settlements. Hillforts enter the archaeological record by around 1000 BC and early examples have been identified in Flintshire at Moel y Gaer (Guilbert 1976), on the Upper Severn at The Breiddin (Musson 1976, 1991) and in Derbyshire at Mam Tor (Coombs and Thompson 1979). Communities on Cheshire's Pennine edge presumably looked to the latter and its lesser near neighbours as foci of authority and for protection (Fig. 1.7).

A series of comparatively small fortifications was also constructed along the Mid-Cheshire Ridge. By far the largest is

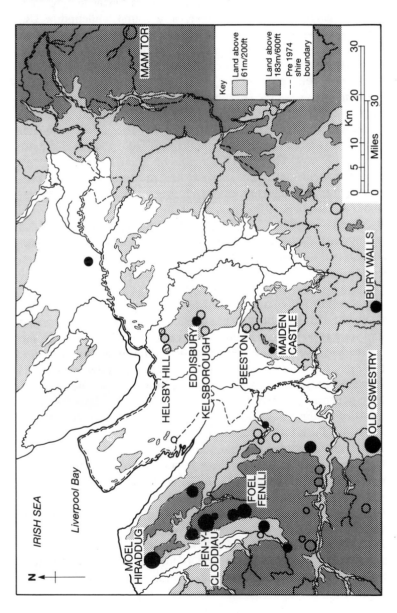

Fig. 1.7 Hillforts in the northern Marches. The size of symbol reflects the size of the defended area. Solid symbols are bivallate and open circles univallate

Within the figure:

N

IRISH SEA

Liverpool Bay

MOEL HIRADDUG

PEN-Y-CLODDIAU

FOEL FENLLI

OLD OSWESTRY

HELSBY HILL

EDDISBURY

KELSBOROUGH

BEESTON

MAIDEN CASTLE

BURY WALLS

MAM TOR

Key

Land above 61m/200ft

Land above 183m/600ft

Pre 1974 shire boundary

Km
0   5   10   20   30

Miles
0   10   20   30

Castle Ditch, Eddisbury (Plate 3), a 2.8 ha enclosure defended in part by a double bank and attendant ditches (Varley 1950; Longley 1987, pp. 110–11; Cocroft et al. 1989). Like Mam Tor, a palisaded enclosure preceded the earthworks so Castle Ditch may have originated in the first half of the first millennium BC. Refurbishment of the defences with stone revetting implies either comparatively lengthy occupation or more than one period of use. Little excavation has occurred in the interior but the identification of four post buildings at both The Breiddin and The Wrekin, and a planned setting of round-houses at Moel y Gaer imply that local hillforts were perennially occupied and were equipped with the capacity to store grain. The use of such sites may have differed little in general terms from that of the more extensively excavated site of Danebury (Cunliffe 1983).

Five further defended sites lie on the northern end of the Ridge, but although the largest (Kelsborrow; Plate 4) approximates in size to Castle Ditch, Eddisbury, they are characterised by simple defences, in many instances consisting only of a steep promontary cut off by a bank and ditch (Bu'lock 1956; Forde-Johnston 1962; VCH, I, 1987, pp. 111–14). On the southern end of the range, Maiden Castle is a double-ditched scarp edge site atop the Bickerton Hills, but its small size (0.7 ha) and the economy of labour implied by its siting render it less than equivalent to Eddisbury (Varley 1935, 1936). In between, traces of a hillfort were discovered during excavations on the castle site at Beeston. Although the extent of this site remains enigmatic, it has been established that it was in occupation by c. 910 BC (uncalibrated) and saw successive, apparently dense phases of use over several centuries (Hough 1982, 1984). At an early date bronze founding was taking place on site, producing artifacts in the Ewart Park tradition (c. 900–700 BC).

The Pennine edge communities, by contrast, seem barely to have invested in defenses. The sole site which might be relevant is Eddisbury Hill, Rainow, a small, univallate, hilltop enclosure which has not as yet been dated. At this stage, therefore, the archaeological record implies that the only focus of Late Bronze Age/Early Iron Age society which lay within Cheshire lay on the Central Ridge, primarily at Castle Ditch. Environmental research suggests that this region was heavily utilised both for agriculture and pasture throughout later prehistory (Schoenwetter 1982).

The surplus produced by the still unidentified farming settlements presumably provided the local elite with the means to invest in defences. An alternative interpretation would have the farmers themselves inhabiting hillforts (as argued by Stanford 1972) and this at least has the virtue of explaining away the apparent absence of undefended sites in the Welsh Marches. This solution is, however, incompatible with the growing evidence for wide-spread clearance in the region throughout late prehistory, which occurred at distances far removed from the Ridge (e.g. Chambers and Wilshaw 1991). It seems more likely that the defended sites acted as defensible centres for extensive territories running radially away from the Ridge across the lowlands on both sides, worked by a scattered population who inhabited open or palisaded enclosures which have not so far been identified archaeologically. Such central places may additionally have acted as food stores, as centres for metal-working under aristocratic patronage and for whatever long-distance exchange was occurring – hence the bronze-working and evidence for salt containers found at Beeston.

Despite the density of defended sites, those responsible con-structed only one fully-fledged hillfort, and this was small and weak by comparison with examples to the south, east and west (Fig. 1.7). Eddisbury should be compared with the 28 ha enclosure at Titterstone Clee (on the Clee Hills, Shropshire) or the double enclosure on The Wrekin, the inner and much smaller circuit of which encompasses 3 ha. If the influence of its builders was commensurate with the effort expended, then that did not extend outside the immediate territory which they controlled and may even there have been subject to the greater authority of those responsible for commissioning far more impressive fortifications in neighbouring territories.

A window on such relationships may be provided by recent research on 'very coarse pottery' (or VCP). Until the 1970s, this material was thought to be Dark Age pottery and its presence used as an indication of later reuse of prehistoric hillforts. It was then reinterpreted as oven fragments of prehistoric date, but it has since been associated with the nascent salt industries of Droitwich, in Worcestershire, and Cheshire. By around 500 BC, 'stony VCP' from the Nantwich–Middlewich region of Cheshire was reaching a series of major sites in the Upper Severn Valley (Morris 1985, pp. 352–79; Fig. 1.8). Although many scholars are

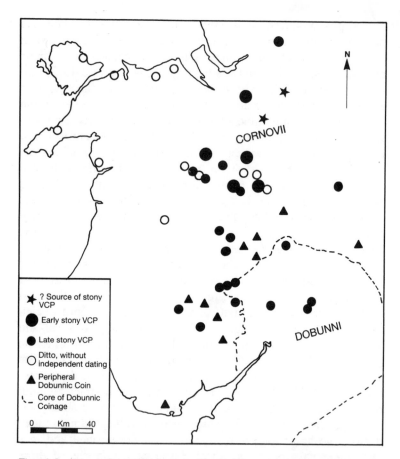

Fig. 1.8 'Very Coarse Pottery', Cornovian salt production and the influence of the Dobunni in the southern Marches

attracted by the concept of trade in pre- and protohistory, the movement of goods was probably controlled primarily by social and political mechanisms. The distribution of VCP may indicate a flow of goods inwards from the periphery towards the core of a nascent political community centred, as the Roman-period tribe was to be, on the Severn valley (Figs. 1.8, 2.1).

Speculation concerning political and social organisation in prehistory remains problematic until the last century before the Roman conquest, when the Roman presence in Gaul had revolutionary implications for the balance of power in Britain. In the south-east, a series of aggressive warrior kingships exploited their new-found access to Roman markets and consumer goods. Behind them, an arc of tribes supplied them with raw materials and slaves, probably extracted from their own neighbours to the north and west. In return, they benefited from limited access to the courts and exotic goods of the south-east (Nash 1987, pp. 118–42; Millett 1990, p. 32). These intermediate tribes were the Dobunni of the southern Marches, the Corieltauvi (or Coritani) of the east Midlands and the Iceni of East Anglia. All three copied their southern neighbours by producing coinages and these assist in the definition of their territories and their contacts (Allen 1963; Haselgrove 1978; Cunliffe 1981; Fig. 1.8). All were, by the Late Pre-Roman Iron Age, focused on sites defined by massive earthworks, generally known as *oppida*.

The peoples of the north-west Midlands were among the outer periphery of tribes which did not produce a coinage. Nor, as far as can be judged, did they construct *oppida*. Finds of Corieltauvian coins at Halton Castle and on the coastal plain of north Wales may reflect limited contact with that people, perhaps the result of local men returning from mercenary service. The Corieltauvi do not, though, appear to have had significant interests west of the Pennines, concentrating instead on their contacts in the Peak and north of the Humber, where their coins are relatively numerous. The few finds from the west may result from much later losses from collections. More important for Cheshire must be relations with the coin-minting Dobunni of the southern Marches, into the northern marches of whose territory 'stony VCP' penetrated extensively during late prehistory (Fig. 1.8). Although this process is poorly dated (Morris 1985), it does reflect a strong flow of goods from the north-west Midlands southwards in the Late Pre-Roman Iron Age. That salt was being carried so far in such inconvenient containers, rather than, for example, the packs or cartloads characteristic of the Middle Ages, emphasises the 'official' nature of this transaction. Pots were probably originally associated with the production and storage of salt. Then they perhaps became units of measure and so of official carriage and audit – perhaps of tribute. This is not, therefore, likely to have been part of some otherwise undetected, reciprocal trade between Cheshire and its southern neighbours but a response to political pressures brought to bear by a dominant and economically more sophisticated neighbour. If so, then Cheshire was by this stage a peripheral part of a tribal community which was itself subordinated to a wealthier and more powerful elite located at a considerable distance to the south. If local communities suffered perennial losses of wealth to their neighbours via such payments then the poverty of Cheshire's late prehistoric archaeology is the more understandable.

One much-publicised find that might be related to this debate is that of the body discovered in Lindow Moss in May 1983 (Stead *et al.* 1986). A young adult and, judging by his manicured nails, a man of high status, Lindow Man had been struck twice on the top of the head with an axe-like weapon and had received a blow in the back sufficient to break a rib before being killed with a garrotte. When dead, his neck was cut and his body dropped face downwards in a pool in the bog. When this occurred is as yet unclear, since carbon-14 dates offer two options, one in later prehistory and the other in the early post-Roman period; but this is only one, albeit the best researched, of several bog-bodies in the region. If Lindow Man was sacrificed, his death was arguably of a kind which was shared by other victims of late pre-Roman religious practices, but there is no particularly good reason to think him a local man, even if the deed was presumably done by members of the local community.

There is very little archaeological evidence to suggest that Cheshire's communities had adopted iron-working before the Roman conquest. They may have still been using artifacts characteristic of Late Bronze Age culture at that date, despite some signs of the more extensive clearance activity which is elsewhere associated with the advent of iron impliments. The region was distant from the principal maritime contacts which introduced many later prehistoric innovations in technology to British communities. The quantity of later bronzes found locally is not unimpressive and does include hoards, such as that from Congleton consisting of two spear-heads, two ferrules and a socketed axe. Hoards from Shropshire are none the less generally richer.

Copper ores on Alderley Edge were certainly being exploited and lead (an important constituent of late bronzes) was also locally available, although tin had to be imported if bronzes were to be manufactured. There is very limited evidence that this tribal community had made direct contact with the classical world: among the numerous finds from the beach trading site at Meols are three silver Carthaginian drachmnae of the period 220–210 BC, a handful of Greek and Armorican coins and a small gold coin from an unidentified British source (Hume 1863). Across the Mersey, Gaulish coins have been found at Liverpool. These finds may represent the arrival of sea-borne traders, voyaging up the Irish coasts of Britain from the tin-rich south-west, in which case Clwydian lead may have been their objective (Laing and Laing 1983; Carrington 1985b), although Meols seems an improbable landing place for trade focused west of the Dee. Alternatively seafarers may have been attracted by Cheshire's salt – a valuable item of trade as well as useful for preserving foodstuffs for the voyage.

Such contacts were clearly infrequent when compared with those taking place at sites along the south coast, such as Hengistbury Head, but they do herald a new era. Through Meols the elite of the region did enjoy some very limited access to maritime trade without the interference of other British communities. The day was approaching, however, when representatives of those same Mediterranean cultures as made token appearances at Meols were to have a far more intrusive impact on the region, in part as traders but more particularly as the colonialists, administrators and soldiers whose role it was to organise, sustain and defend the expanding Roman Empire. It is with that closer acquaintance with Mediterranean culture that our understanding of local territories begins its slow progress from inspired guesswork to historical reality.

2

Colonialism and community:
The Romans in the
north-west Midlands

Tribes and territories

Classical ethnologists and geographers had shown an interest in
Britain for centuries before the Roman conquest but it was only
with that event that they obtained access to information concerning the hinterland. Our only universal source, Ptolemy's
Geography, was written around the middle of the second century
AD but made extensive use of the work of Marinus, written
c. AD 100. There has been much recent doubt concerning
Ptolemy's attribution of *Brannogenium* (? Leintwardine, Herefordshire) and *Mediolanum* (Whitchurch) to the Ordovices of
northern Wales (*Geography*, II, 3, 11). This is not, however,
based on anything more than the geographical problems envisaged if Wroxeter (his *Viroconion*, otherwise *Viroconium
Cornoviorum*) and Chester (his *Devana, leg. XX Victrix*, otherwise *Deva*) lay in the territory of the Cornovii (Fig. 2.1). These
ascriptions are by no means impossible and modern scholars have
perhaps been overly hasty in discarding them without sufficient
cause (e.g. Rivet and Smith 1979, pp. 120–1, 143). The boundary
between England and Wales during much of the Middle Ages
was no less sinuous than that which his Ordovican/Cornovian
frontier implies. Indeed, it is possible that the former developed
out of the latter (p. 35), implying that the Marches had experienced a territorial structure over a millennium or more which

---

periodically fluctuated from one boundary to another, one of which predated the Roman conquest.

Like several other of Ptolemy's tribes, the Ordovices have more of the characteristics of a hegemony over several peoples than of a unitary tribal group. Difficulties in distinguishing their territory from that of the Cornovii derives from the close proximity of both in the valleys of eastern Wales, where the Ordovices may have had their most important foci (Jarrett and Mann 1968, p. 170).

The precise boundaries of the Cornovii are nowhere known (Webster 1991). More varied pottery industries and a tribal coinage help to distinguish the Dobunni to the south, in and around the valley of the central and lower Severn (Fig. 2.1) but the precise boundary (supposing that such existed) between these two tribes is a matter of guesswork. There has been much speculation concerning the northern limits of Cornovian territory and it has even been suggested that Cheshire was a sort of 'noman's land', outside all the tribal territories of the day (e.g. Strickland 1980, with some support in Carrington 1985). This does not, however, seem particularly plausible when viewed against what is known of Celtic tribal geography either in Britain or on the continent: tribal territories normally abutted those of their neighbours; Ptolemy's inclusion of the legionary fortress of *Deva* (Chester) in Cornovian territory implies that the moss-flanked Mersey was the frontier between this essentially south-facing tribe and the Brigantian hegemony beyond (Watkin 1974, p. 294; for the latter, see Higham 1987b). Ptolemy's name for the estuary – *Seteia* – is cognate with the Setantii of *Setantiorum Portus* at or about the Wyre estuary (Rivet and Smith 1979, pp. 456–7), who were surely part of the Brigantian hegemony. If the river was named by people to the south of it, it records the fact that Setantian territory began at this point, implying that the Mersey divided the Cornovii from their northern neighbours. That is not, however, a universally held opinion (e.g. Webster 1991, pp. 8, 21–2).

To the west and east, Cornovian territory cannot be distinguished on the basis of distinctive pottery or metalwork from its neighbours and we can offer no more than tentative hypotheses concerning its boundaries based on very limited literary and epigraphic evidence. Tacitus referred to a campaign of Ostorius

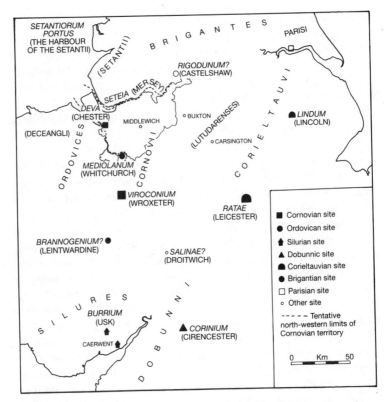

Fig. 2.1 The Cornovii and their neighbours at the Roman conquest

Scapula, in AD 47 or 48, against the *Decangi*, which brought
'Roman armies almost to the shores of the sea facing Ireland'
(*Annals*, XII, 32). Inscriptions on pigs of lead found, for example,
at Chester and Hints Common (Staffordshire), the fullest of
which reads DECEANGL (Webster 1953), suggest that their
name is more properly 'Deceangli'. Lead was already being extracted from their territory not much more than a decade after
this campaign, apparently even before the development of government mines under Vespasian. On the assumption that the lead
derived from the vicinity of Halkyn Mountain, Flintshire would
seem to have been Deceanglian (e.g. Frere 1978) and all of
Clwyd is generally assigned to them. Since no such tribe between
the Ordovices and Cornovii was acknowledged by Ptolemy,

they were presumably part of a larger tribal grouping under some other nomenclature during the first century. Given their belligerence in 47, this can only have been the Ordovices, whose resistance to Rome is well attested. Like the Brigantian hegemony to the north, that of the Ordovices encompassed several local tribes among whom the Deceangli and Gangani (of the Lleyn Peninsula) can be identified. This multiplicity of local loyalties is confirmed. When, in AD 50, the Ordovican tribesmen swore allegiance to Caratacus (or Caradog), each did so in terms appropriate to his own tribe (Tacitus, *Annals*, XII, 34). When the Ordovices then stood their ground against Roman armies, they probably did so at some vantage point overlooking the valley of the upper Severn (Jones 1991, pp. 60–3), so with Deceanglian territory largely behind them.

Although Ptolemy's Ordovices seem to refer to the tribal hegemony of the conquest period, this grouping was presumably being broken up during the later first century AD, both in consequence of local resistance and because imperial interests required the confiscation of large areas to form estates for the exploitation of mineral ores. The influence of the Ordovices is evidenced in place-names as far east as the Clwyd, where lies *Rhyd Oddwy* – 'ford of the Ordovices', though this was not necessarily named at this date, since this tribal name was one which survived the Roman period. So too did that of the Decanti, in *arx Decantorum* – Deganwy, on the estuary of the Conway – though this could be another minor tribe rather than a late reference to the Deceangli.

Reconstruction of the territory of the Deceangli has profound implications for our region: a major tribal boundary apparently existed between Chester (in Cornovian territory) and the Halkyn lead rakes (in Deceanglian/Ordovican territory). Iron Age tribal boundaries seem often to have followed major rivers, as for example the Humber, lower Severn and Thames. The broad estuary of the Dee offers just such a barrier. If it did divide two Ptolemaic tribes then the much later frontier between England and Wales may replicate a boundary between two prehistoric hegemonies; so of the very highest status. Indeed, if Whitchurch was Ordovican (or Deceanglian) at the conquest, the later boundary between Cheshire and Flintshire is foreshadowed by a major Iron Age boundary which distinguished southern Cheshire and northern Shropshire from Maelor Saesneg.

Ptolemy named no settlements in Derbyshire, so the boundaries of the Brigantes, Corieltauvi and Cornovii are far from clear. Brigantian territory pushed south as far as *Camulodunum* but that site is not securely placed (Rivet and Smith 1979, p. 295; Jones and Mattingly 1990, p. 20) and it seems most unlikely that the southern Pennines should be assigned to them (but cf. Hartley and Fitts 1988, p. 5). Most Corieltauvian coins have been found east of the Trent but examples have come from southern Yorkshire, Derbyshire and Nottinghamshire (Allen 1963). The southern Pennines lay beyond their circulation but this may have been concentrated in the core of the tribal territory, which certainly lay nearer the Trent.

Once again it is from inscriptions on pigs of lead that we obtain crucial information; at least twenty-nine lead pigs from Roman mining in Derbyshire have so far been discovered, several of which bear inscriptions referring to the LUTUDARE(N)SES. Although combination with, for example, *SOCII*, might imply that only the name of a business partnership is here being offered (Dool and Hughes 1976), these inscriptions are so numerous that they would seem to refer to a minor tribe rather than a particular enterprise (Rivet and Smith 1979, 403). The name derives from that of a river. Since the industry appears to have been focused on a cupellation plant at Carsington (near Wirksworth) this should probably be identified with the Derwent, or perhaps one of its tributaries, given that the latter name is also of Celtic origin and so may have been current in the Roman period. The river Dove is another possibility.

On analogy with the Deceangli, the Lutudarenses were probably another minor tribe whose territory became an imperial estate and whose name was used to mark the district of origin of pigs of lead destined for export from the immediate area. It arguably lay under military control during the late first and second centuries but was perhaps thereafter leased to civilians to continue exploitation (Branigan *et al.* 1986). It may be that this community was coterminus with a regional culture already defined (see page 21) on archaeological criteria, encompassing eastern Cheshire and Staffordshire but focused on the White Peak in Derbyshire. Given that the valley system of the Peak feeds into the Trent it is unsurprising that its lead was exported to other parts of Britain via that river and Humberside. This community

was arguably one which already looked to the east at the conquest, as its geography would tend to dictate. This is no more
than a tentative hypothesis, of course, but it allows us to raise
the possibility of another tribal boundary in or near Roman
Cheshire, this time between the Cornovii and the Lutudarenses,
a minor tribe which had perhaps been a satellite of the Corieltauvi.
One of the deities of this community – perhaps even their principal deity – was the goddess Arnemetia, whose name became
attached to the medicinal springs of Buxton (*Ravenna Cosmography*, 106) but which appears also on an altar at Brough-on-
Noe, in the High Peak (Collingwood and Wright 1965, No. 281).

The Mid-Cheshire Ridge with its defended sites seems, therefore, to have been the backbone of only a narrow finger of
Cornovian territory at the Roman conquest, defined to the west
by the Dee and to the east by an unlocated boundary with the
Lutudarenses. The tribal name is based on British *corn-* 'horn'. It
might refer to a specific site, such as the Wrekin hillfort; it might
allude to the unusually elongated shape of the territory; alternatively it might point to a horned god of the *Cernunnos* (stag-
god) type (Ross 1967, p. 143). The name occurs also in Cornwall
and Caithness and the former instance at least suggests that it was
the shape of the tribal territory which gave rise to the tribal
name.

No dedications to a tribal god have been identified in Cheshire
where the sole altar to a Romano-Celtic deity found so far is that
at Chester, commissioned by a Galerian army officer, which
associates the Roman Jupiter with the pan-Celtic sky-god Tanarus
or Taranis (Green 1982). However, *Deva* – the name given to
Chester but derived from the common British river-name meaning goddess – may imply a local water-cult on the western boundaries of the tribal territory. The shrine to Minerva at Handbridge
may have reflected a Romanised version of just such a cult. If
there are local shrines to a horned tribal god waiting to be
identified, these are more likely to lie on or near the Mid-Cheshire
Ridge, but such are by no means necessitated by the evidence.

The name Deceangli, by contrast, is of obscure origin, but a
major religious site is known within the tribal territory which may
already have been operative prior to the conquest. This was the
long-lived and popular shrine at Llys Awel, near Pen-y-Corddyn,
which centred during the Roman period (post-Domitian) on a

deity of healing associated with dog figurines and bronze votive leaves (Davies 1983, p. 82, footnote 29). This deity may earlier have had a wider scope as a tribal god.

In their names and in the deities to whom they looked for protection, these tribes emphasised their own separate identities. Boundaries between their respective territories must have existed and were probably both well marked and well known. They are now but shadows, yet shadows of great importance to the development of territoriality in the region.

Chester and the organisation of Roman Cheshire

The Roman occupation had an impact on the orientation of local society so profound that its consequences remain even today a powerful determinant of the political and social geography of the region. This impact is at its most marked at Chester.

Although prehistoric implements have occasionally been found within the city, there is no reason to believe that Chester was a site of any significance prior to occupation by the Roman military. Pre-Roman cultivation associated with a pottery scatter was identified on the Abbey Green site (McPeake *et al.* 1980) and underneath the parade-ground, so this island of well-drained land was apparently being farmed at some stage prior to military occupation. Ptolemy described Chester as a *polis*, a term he normally used for civilian settlements, but in this instance the characterisation seems improbable; his association of *Deva* with the twentieth legion demonstrates that his information on the site derived from official sources post-dating the removal of that unit to Chester late in the first century (see below) when it was primarily a fortress. That it took the river-name implies that there was no appropriate native place-name already in existence.

Despite enduring speculation concerning a pre-Flavian fort at Chester, there is little hard evidence for military occupation of the site before the 70s AD (Newstead and Droop 1936; Newstead 1939, 1948; Strickland 1980; Carrington 1985a). There is no record of Cornovian resistance to the Romans. In AD 43 they witnessed the ease with which Roman armies overcame more powerful tribes to the south and east of themselves, to one of which they may have been subservient. They are, therefore, strong candidates for inclusion among the communities which submitted to Claudius without fighting. Thereafter they seem to have given the provincial authorities little trouble. The presence of Roman troops in the valley of the upper Severn *c.* 48 should be associated with punitive action against the Ordovices and Deceangli, in part at least in their defence. A legionary fortress at Wroxeter in the heartland of Cornovian territory provided a base for the invasion of Wales via the upper Dee valley and Rhyn Park near Chirk – the route now followed by the A5 – and it was arguably by this road that Suetonius Paulinus attacked Anglesey in AD 60 (Carrington 1985a). Speculation in favour of a campaign via Cheshire and a Deeside port remains influential (e.g. McPeake 1978a) but is at best unproven.

Auxiliary forts were established to screen the base fortress of *Legio XX Valeria Victrix* but the most northerly was at Whitchurch, a site which in consequence became the nodal point for the road system of the north-west Midlands. If Whitchurch was in, or immediately adjacent to, Ordovican territory, its construction arguably had more to do with containing that people than in policing the Cornovii. During this period all that part of the Midland Plain which lies beyond the Severn–Dee watershed was ungarrisoned, presumably because its low levels of population and its political dependence on leadership within the core of the tribal territory rendered it quiescent without the necessity of a military presence. The evidence implies strong social ties between Cheshire and the Severn valley, not a tribal hiatus.

Even when Roman forces sought access to the coastal roads into north-east Wales, Chester was still not an inevitable choice of fort site. Indeed, there is some evidence for an earlier road system focused on the Dee crossings between Holt and Farndon. The immediate hinterland of Chester is dominated by extensive marshes, most noticeably to the north, east and south, which must have posed considerable problems to Roman road engineers.

The strategic situation changed, however, with the Brigantian ejection of Cartimandua's client administration in AD 69, after which Roman governors faced hostilities both in northern Wales and Britain beyond the Humber–Mersey. Chester was not only the lowest point at which the Dee could be easily crossed. It was also the highest point up-river which seaworthy ships could reach without difficulty. Roman governors needed a base from which to provision army units operating west of the Pennines, without having first to circumnavigate Wales. They sought, therefore, a port with access to the Irish Sea which could be supplied via the road-system from southern Britain. The twin factors of river-crossing and port determined the precise location of a fortress built by Frontinus or Agricola (Strickland 1980; Petch 1987, p. 118) or possibly even Petilius Cerealis. That the legion stationed there, II *Adiutrix*, had been raised from the Adriatic fleet in AD 69, made it an ideal unit for the role envisaged. Lead pigs dated to 74 have been found on the site and water-pipes from the fortress carry the date 79, by which year construction of the primary timber fortress was probably near completion.

Although both Wroxeter and Chester were held in tandem in the 80s, *Legio II Adiutrix* left Britain for the Danube at the end of the decade, never to return. After a period during which Chester may have been mothballed, the Wroxeter garrison, *Legio XX Valeria Victrix*, was relocated to the more northerly fort *c.* 88–90 and Wroxeter began its transformation into a purely civilian site, destined like so many other erstwhile legionary fortresses to become a *civitas* or tribal capital. The decommissioning of Wroxeter implies that Roman authorities expected little further resistance from north or central Wales but Roman control of the north was still problematic. With the abandonment of grandiose plans to extend Roman rule to all northern Britain under Trajan and Hadrian, the military establishment became increasingly entrenched in existing forts, many of which served primarily as barracks for units of a garrison little of which, below the Wall, was stationed against any specific threat.

The legionary fortress was, to this date, the largest and most impressive settlement sited in the north-west Midlands. It was initially equipped with a turf rampart which is still occasionally identified in excavation (e.g. Newstead 1948; Davey 1973; Strickland 1983), about thirty-five towers and a ditch. This defensive cordon was refurbished with gatehouses, angle and interval towers and a stone parapet, probably in the first quarter of the second century, enclosing an area *c.* 590 m × 410 m (24.33 ha: Petch 1987, p. 124). The defences were thereafter maintained and occasionally refurbished, with extensive work undertaken *c.* 200, in part using existing masoned stones many of which were inscribed, and again *c.* 300, when some sections were systematically redesigned and the curtain made free-standing by the inser-

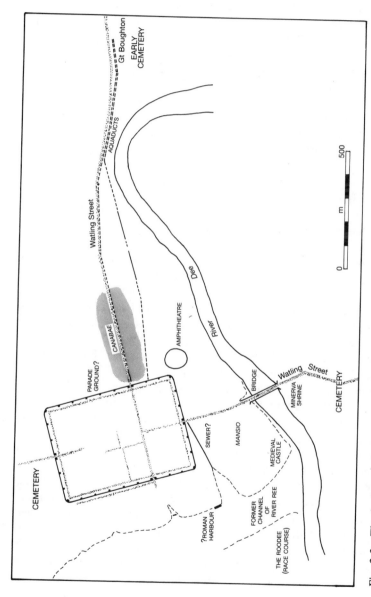

Fig. 2.2 The legionary fortress at Chester and its immediate hinterland

tion behind it of reused masonry (Strickland 1982, 1983: Fig. 2.2).

There has been much discussion of the levels of military occupation of the fortress. During the Hadrianic and Antonine periods much of the legion was active further north and this may account for the under-utilised and neglected appearance of the fortress. There were, however, even during the second century, episodes of building activity (Strickland 1978). The principal buildings of the fortress – the *principia*, *praetorium*, barracks, granaries and workshops – were built in stone early in the second century and the extensive rebuilding and refurbishment of existing buildings which occurred under the Severans effectively completed the complex to a very high standard.

The hinterland of Chester

From its inception, the fortress was equipped with a full range of amenities. Chester's well-known amphitheatre, discovered in 1929 outside the south-east corner of the fortress, was of late Flavian date (Newstead and Droop 1932) and the soldiers' water-supply was assured by the provision of an aqueduct consisting of a battery of pipes bringing water 1,500 m from springs equipped with a shrine and well-house at Broughton (Stephens 1985a). A parade-ground (outside the east gate) and several cemeteries competed with incoming roads, civilian occupation, the fort's sewers and a probable *mansio* (Mason 1978, 1980) for the limited amount of land suitable for building (Fig. 2.2).

This land was almost certainly controlled by the military authorities throughout the period and a certain amount of zoning seems to have occurred. The west side was given over to port facilities, a cemetery and a large and very substantial complex, equipped with a bath suite, which may have had some official function. If there were private residences here, then they were those of the richer classes, probably merchants or ship-owners, whose houses were equipped with hypocausts and wall-plaster. South of the fortress, where a probable *mansio* was erected c. AD 80, buildings seem to have been sparse and widely dispersed, suggesting that most were official. These apparently forced civilian occupation outwards to the south bank of the Dee where the Minerva shrine, numerous finds and Chester's principal cemetery have been located strung along Watling Street (Eaton Road in Handbridge). The main area of civilian occupation and craft activities lay to the east of the fortress, also along Watling Street but where that is eastbound. Over a distance of at least 300 m from the gates, numerous tradesmen and artisans presumably leased their narrow, half-timbered 'strip-houses' from the responsible officer acting for the legion (Mason 1987).

These roadside *canabae* ('cabins', generally used for civil housing associated with a fort) close to the walls existed primarily to service the varied needs of the military. Until the extension of Roman citizenship under Caracalla, it seems unlikely that they enjoyed an institutional existence separate from the fortress (Mason 1985; but cf. Birley 1948), although thereafter the civilian settlement may have attained the status of a *municipium*.

The exceptionally large establishment of citizen sodiers at Chester should be credited with a territory – a *prata legionis*, later a *territorium* – on a proportionate scale. On behalf of the state, the commander exercised proprietorial rights over this land which was commandeered from local owners primarily to provide pasturing for cavalry mounts, pack-animals and livestock but which also probably offered access to building stone, timber and other facilities.

When Ptolemy described *Deva* as being inside Cornovian territory he was technically incorrect since it lay by then within its own territory, the ownership, administration and use of which was entirely divorced from the *civitas* or tribe of which it had formed a part. His usage may imply that this military *prata legionis* had been carved out entirely from Cornovian territory and was still all but surrounded by it. Whether or not, the process clearly involved changes to the tribal territory of considerable importance. There are, however, major problems in attempting to define the boundaries of the new military estate with any precision.

This issue has been an important factor in recent speculation concerning the status of Roman Heronbridge (Mason 1986, 1988a, 1988b). This roadside settlement lies little more than half a kilometre south of the southern cemetery of the fortress at Handbridge. When first excavated, its presence so close to the *canabae* immediately outside the fortress walls led to its interpretation as a quayside site used by river traffic which was deemed

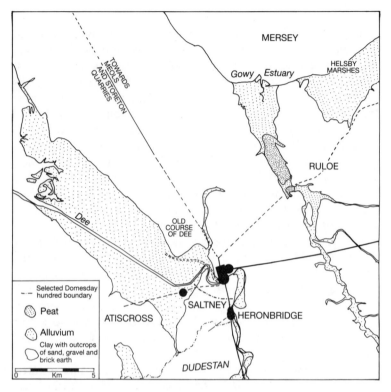

Fig. 2.3 The *Prata legionis* of the Chester fortress: problems of identification

unable to reach Chester via the Dee (Hartley and Kaine 1954). This argument is no longer credited and activity here does seem to duplicate that at the *canabae*, featuring small-scale manufacturing, bronze-casting and grain-drying, besides domestic activity.

An alternative explanation may be that this settlement grew up beyond the limits of the *prata legionis* and the constraints that military administration there imposed on civil settlement (Mason 1978, 1986, 1988a), in which case the presence of this site may help define the boundary of that military territory on its southern side (Fig. 2.3). Whether Heronbridge be considered inside Cornovian territory or inside a putative Deceanglian imperial estate is unclear but the latter may be more likely for a community on the west bank of the Dee, particularly given that the roads from the putative lead mines at Halkyn and Ffrith (Blockley 1989) are generally supposed to join Watling Street at this point. Heronbridge was, therefore, a meeting place for travellers and packtrains of lead from the Deceanglian hinterland, local shippers or officers based at Chester and traders operating across Cornovian territory. Its markets may have offered judicial and tenurial advantages to itinerants and residents alike, as well as a greater convenience for this particular trade than was available at the *canabae* further north. That Chester itself (including Handbridge, Netherleigh and Overleigh) was a hundred at Domesday separate both from the Heronbridge area (Claverton, in the predominately Deceanglian Atiscross) and both Pulford and Eccleston (in the predominately Cornovian hundred of *Dudestan*) may be a coincidence. If not, then these hundred boundaries could derive from those of the *prata legionis* of the Roman period.

Elsewhere the extent of the *prata* is little more than guesswork. The Dee remains the most likely western boundary, excepting only Handbridge itself. There is no indication whether the Romanised settlement at Saltney should lie inside or outside the *prata* but the latter may be the more likely. This ditch-defined settlement, now underlying the Lache housing estate along Cliveden Road, produced such large quantities of roof-tiles and pottery, including Samian (Newstead 1935), that it seems unlikely to have been a farming complex – particularly given its location on heavy clayland. It might better be interpreted as a further instance of the type of settlement represented by Heronbridge but this time close by the crossing of the road between Chester and the presumed centre of lead-mining at Pentre Farm, Flint (O'Leary and Davey 1976–77) and that from Heronbridge to Halkyn. Again, it lay in what would later be the hundred of Atiscross (Fig. 2.3).

The most plausible eastern limit lies on the Gowy. The fens and silted bed provide a natural frontier which was later to be an important hundredal boundary. The earlier name of this river, the Tarvin, survives today only as a name of parochial status at the point where the Manchester road out of Chester crosses the river but it means 'At the boundary river' (from British Latin **terminum**, Primitive Welsh **tervin**: Dodgson 1966/67– , III,

p. 281; Mason 1988a, pp. 179–80). If Dodgson's own (1967) interpretation of this name in the context of an English migration is set aside (see page 136), it may look back to a boundary between military and civilian administration which was a fact of provincial life from the late first century at least until the late fourth. This option certainly seems preferable to assigning the boundary to the Mid-Cheshire Ridge, which seems the only obvious alternative.

To the north the vitality of the beachhead trading site at Meols throughout the Roman period implies that the Wirral peninsula lay outside the *prata legionis* (but cf. the scenario preferred by Mason 1988a) but it is a matter of guesswork where its boundaries lay. The Neston–Eastham line speculatively proposed as an alternative by David Mason offers the chimera of a major Roman boundary approximating to the southern limits of the Scandinavian territory of Wirral beyond Raby, 'Village at a boundary' (from Old Scandinavian **ra-byr**: Dodgson 1966/67– , III, pp. 228–9) but this remains pure speculation. It may be that we should envisage that Storeton, with its important quarries, might have been included inside the military area.

Once more we can detect the presence of important boundaries between differing types of jurisdiction and land-ownership which will have had the most fundamental impact on communities and their lifestyles, yet without being able to define them precisely in the landscape. Whatever its boundaries, the legionary *prata* played an important role in the evolution of Roman Cheshire. So too did the exceptional purchasing power of its garrison, as is clear from a comparison of the dense pattern of deposition of Roman-style goods in the vicinity of the fortress with the sparse scatter elsewhere.

The influence of the legion was not restricted to the immediate environs of Chester. Its commander exercised oversight of the auxiliary forts across northern Wales as far as Caernarvon and throughout the north-west of the Midlands Plain, his authority stretching out along the Roman road system in all directions. Moreover, his highly trained soldiers were the principal agents of officialdom in the region. The products of the legionary tilery and pottery at Holt have been found in quantity at the industrial settlements at Pentre, Flint (O'Leary and Davey 1976–77), Prestatyn (Blockley 1985) and Ffrith (Room 1968; Blockley 1989), all of which are thought to have been centres for the government-controlled lead industry. Various buildings including the sophisticated stone bath-houses at the second and third of these may have been erected by legionary masons. Whether or not, the Holt factory certainly had contracts to supply some of the materials used. The legion was, therefore, central to governmental exploitation of the local economy and particularly to the extraction of minerals from Deceanglian sources to the west (Britnell 1991).

Communications, settlement and land use

The principal roads of Roman Britain were noted in the *Antonine Itinerary* – an official listing which may have had its origins as early the third century (Rivet and Smith 1979). *Iter* II began at Birrens, north of the Wall, and proceeded to Richborough on the Channel via Manchester, Northwich, Chester, and *Bovio* (probably a roadside settlement at or near Tilston), then along Watling Street to Wroxeter via Whitchurch. *Iter* X offered an alternative route from Whitchurch northwards, omitting Chester and passing to Manchester via Northwich. Chester was the eastern end of *Iter* XI to Caernarvon along the Welsh coast, which was the only route into northern Wales to be listed.

The *Itinerary* emphasises the importance of these roads to long-distance travellers, particularly official travellers, and this is an aspect of Roman road-building of particular relevance to the north-west Midlands. The road-system was designed for the rapid passage of troops and supplies from lowland England into northern Wales, but more particularly into northern Britain (Fig. 2.4). The local community was incidental to the network that developed, although it may well have been expected to assist in its construction with unpaid labour. We can be sure that Roman engineers were impervious to local property rights when laying out these routes.

Detailed fieldwork in recent years has done much to firm up our knowledge of these great trunk roads (e.g. Jermy 1965; Petch 1975; Waddelove 1983; Waddelove and Waddelove 1983). At the same time, it has demonstrated what has long been conjectured (e.g. Watkin 1974) – that these major routes were supplemented by lesser link roads, the alignments of which owe rather less to the ruler wielded by Roman officialdom (e.g. Hughes 1984). The

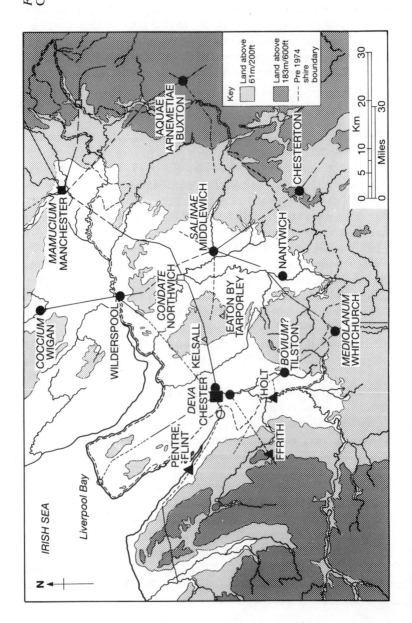

Fig. 2.4 Roman
Cheshire

construction of these minor roads was a more local responsibility, and perhaps even undertaken on local initiative, but all were arguably maintained by the regional community as part of their obligations to the Roman state.

Chester's role as a port for northwards and westwards traffic exercised a powerful influence on the developing road-system. Chester and its ford, along with its satellite at Heronbridge, became the focus of communications between the north-west Midlands and the military and industrial sites of northern Wales, playing an important role in the transportation and distribution of lead and other products from that region into the provincial lowlands. In return, various supplies and building materials for the Romanised community in Wales were presumably shipped from here. It was the most westerly point on Watling Street, which turns eastwards at Chester to pass via Manchester (itself a major route centre) towards York. Travellers wishing to journey from southern Britain by road towards Hadrian's Wall with no call to visit Chester were able to head northwards more directly from Whitchurch or Chesterton via King Street (Plate 6), crossing the Chester–York road east of Northwich and the Mersey at Warrington.

Most Romanised settlements in Cheshire were sited along these trunk roads and many of them developed to service travel along them. At Northwich (*Condate*), a fort was established late in the first century as a staging post for officials and soldiers travelling between Chester (17 mls : 27 km) and Manchester (20 mls : 32 km). During a phase of abandonment thereafter civilian activity within the fort suggests that a roadside market for pottery and smithing endured but a second military occupation intervened soon after AD 100. Lead pans found in the river valley indicate that salt was extracted from local brine springs but this industrial activity is poorly dated (Petch 1987, pp. 198–202).

Although there is little trace of direct military involvement at Wilderspool, the siting of this major settlement was dictated by a confluence of roads from Middlewich, Chester, and perhaps even Manchester, on the south bank of the Mersey. The precise location was determined by the presence of a patch of well-drained sand, in an otherwise peaty basin, which provided a dry approach to the river-crossing. Ribbon development grew up which may have stretched across 10 ha (Hinchliffe *et al.* 1992), within which different activities seem to have been concentrated in specific areas. Excavations on the Brewery Site revealed large-scale industrial activity based on kilns and furnaces, a hypo-caused building, ditched complexes and large timber-framed structures. Coarse pottery was manufactured here and elsewhere in the vicinity and locally made *mortaria* reached Hadrian's Wall. The inhabitants were using vessels from Holt, the Mancetter–Hartshull potteries and Wroxeter, which had clearly travelled via the road network. Activity on the site began late in the first century and continued to *c.* 160. Throughout, the movement of troops, officials and supply trains across the Mersey provided its economic *raison d'être*.

East of the Lumb Brook, excavations beside Loushers Lane revealed a series of enclosures and timber-framed buildings, including an early round-house. Roman-period occupation had apparently superseded an Iron Age farm. Industrial debris was generally lacking. The site was probably occupied by farmers – perhaps local men – who also engaged in fulling and dyeing cloth for the local market. Although the vast bulk of the pottery recovered predates AD 200, occupation did continue into the third century. Even so, the episodic deposition of manufactured goods on site reflected the variable market opportunities offered by passing trade.

Middlewich (Roman *Salinae* – 'Saltworks') developed at the confluence of roads from Wilderspool, Whitchurch, Chesterton, and a minor way linking Chester with Buxton. Its location 20 mls (32 km) from Whitchurch (and from Chester, but slightly more from Manchester and Buxton) implies that, once again, the 'dinner, bed and breakfast' trade was an important factor in its growth. Like Wilderspool, it offered travellers a wide range of products. Numerous timber open-fronted buildings along King Street and between the road and the rivers Croco and Dane offered the products of iron-working or bronze- and lead-casting, window-glass, woollen cloth and leather goods such as shoes. The site was occupied by the mid-Flavian period and, despite signs of contraction after the Antonine period, levels of occupation during the third century were far more buoyant than at Wilders-pool, continuing at least to the mid-fourth century (Petch 1987, pp. 202–8).

Roman Middlewich may have extended to 20–30 ha, making

this by far the largest settlement in the region outside of Chester itself. Had Chester not distorted the regional pattern of settlement and government, it might have become a regional centre for the northern Cornovii. Its name mirrors that of Roman Droitwich: both imply that brine-working was already an important activity at these sites when Roman occupation occurred. These two are, therefore, the most likely sources of the salt packed into VCP and 'stony VCP' in the very late prehistoric period (see above, p. 25). The fortunes of many minor Roman towns were based on a single commodity or resource, be it the medicinal springs at Bath or Buxton or the locally manufactured pottery at Mancetter (Todd 1970). Middlewich's continuing prosperity was probably based on the brine springs, which themselves provided an important commodity marketable to official and civilian alike. It was salt which gave Middlewich a competitive edge over some other roadside settlements in the region and the lead pans used in this industry and briquetage from its firings are prominent among finds from the site. However, the manufacture of such commodities as window-glass imply that Middlewich also had some local customers with Roman tastes and it may have been the principal market for a large region of southern/central Cheshire. Whether it was ever owned by the government is unclear but the discovery there of a *diploma* recording the discharge of an army veteran implies the presence of retired soldiers (Petch 1987, pp. 207–8).

Roman activity at Nantwich, a few miles from King Street, is evidenced by finds dating from the Flavian period to the mid-fourth century. Brine springs seem to have been the principal attraction of the site and lead pans and a plank-constructed brine-tank have been identified (McNeill 1985). Little excavation of Roman deposits has occurred but the principal occupation probably lies under the modern town, between Welsh Row and the river Weaver. That the site attracted neither the name *Salinae* (the Roman name remains unknown) nor the Roman road implies that its development had barely begun before the conquest.

Each of these settlements owed its development to the provincial or diocesan economy. Several were based on the production and marketing of an important local commodity – salt – which was distributed via the new road-system. All depended heavily on the density and affluence of road traffic, much of it official. When the movement of military personnel slackened and their wages declined, those roadside settlements which had failed to attract a sufficiently affluent local clientele to their markets were vulnerable to contraction or even abandonment. A microcosm of this relationship can be identified archaeologically: potters established themselves at Wilderspool, only to be left behind by their military markets. Their response was to relocate themselves to northern Cumbria (Hartley and Webster 1973). Other artisans, shopkeepers and hoteliers were presumably just as sensitive to market conditions.

There can be little doubt that officialdom, its expenses and its purchasing power were in retreat by the third century: changes in the way that Britain's garrisons were supplied drastically reduced the flow of goods into Britain and northwards via the roads or ports; Britain's soldiers were becoming fewer and their wages suffering from inflation; the flow of requisitioned grain which had subsidised the movement of manufactures over long distances was replaced by taxation in kind which arguably became increasingly regionalised during the later empire (Higham 1992a, pp. 51–3); the military presence in northern Wales was already massively reduced under Hadrian and most imperial estates and mineral-workings were probably in the hands of civilian lessees by AD 200; and more and more governmental contracts were being undertaken through *corvées* (compulsory labour) rendered by local men, rather than through the market.

In areas where most Romanised settlements were heavily dependent on the movement of goods and personnel from richer regions to the garrisons, this suite of social and fiscal changes necessitated large-scale contraction. Their difficulties worsened at the end of the century, when important developments occurred at Chester – the sole military establishment still extant in the region. A series of excavations have produced consistent evidence for the demolition of stone buildings within the fortress between about 280–300, giving way to pavements constructed of building rubble which were then used sufficiently to wear them smooth (McPeake 1978b). The losses included granaries, barracks and the water-tower but not the *praetorium*, *principia*, or large porticoed building under Northgate Street, all of which continued in use to the mid-fourth century. Alongside them, some stone structures remained standing, such as the granary under Hunter Street, although even this was arguably becoming derelict. Several timber-framed buildings were erected, perhaps during the consolidation of Britain's defences in 343 which is associated with Constans, but use of the fortress appears to have changed dramatically in the interim.

Legio XX is last attested in Britain by an inscription of the 260s found on the Wall and there seems little likelihood that their fortress base was capable of accommodating them after *c.* 300, despite its spendid walls. The walled area presumably remained in government ownership but its use thereafter is a matter of speculation. It might have passed to the procurator's staff or become a centre of provincial government. It may alternatively have been retained by the military and served as a supply depot or even a command post for the 'Irish Shore' defences from Anglesey to the Wall (see discussion in Dornier 1982). Barracks at Abbey Green and Princess Street revealed evidence of alterations during the fourth century so were then still in commission but the residential capacity of the fortress was much reduced from second-century levels.

Extramural settlement at Chester also reveals signs of contraction by the end of the second century. In parts of the *canabae* east of the fortress, abrupt abandonment occurred just before 200, although some plots were later reused (Mason 1978). Decay was far from uniform: excavations in Duke Street in 1983 demonstrated that occupation there lasted from the first century to the late fourth and Greyfriars Court revealed activity as late. After destruction by fire *c.* 290, the putative *mansio* or post-house south of the fortress was rebuilt and used up to the mid-fourth century, when it was systematically demolished (Mason 1980). Contraction and/or abandonment during the later Roman period were also characteristic of the settlements at Ffrith, Pentre Farm, Flint and Prestatyn, in Chester's hinterland to the west.

The picture which emerges is a confused one but none the less indicative of a long-term run-down of governmental activity at Chester itself. Fewer soldiers and their reduced pay-packets meant even fewer merchants, artisans and tradesmen. Governments successively retreated from direct exploitation of mines. The northern garrisons of Britain consisted of lower-paid frontier troops (*limitatenses*), numbering, perhaps, no more than a few thousand men (James 1984). With such factors in play, the proliferation and growth of *vici* (settlements outside forts) and road-side settlements, which characterised the second century, was bound to be reversed.

When Roman forces moved on from their first-century bases in southern Britain, many of the *vici* which had developed to supply them were able to become towns. Such centres had social and governmental roles to play and their markets facilitated the exchange of goods for coin which was needed for purposes of taxation. In their *fora*, local and regional produce could be traded for more exotic goods, which, even before AD 100, began to find their way into the countryside.

In Cheshire, there is, in contrast, little evidence that the local population were much attracted by Roman culture or affluent enough to invest in its outer trappings. Only a single villa site has so far been recognised with any degree of certainty, at Eaton-by-Tarporley (Mason 1983; Petch 1987, pp. 210–13), providing a distant outlier to the main concentration of Cornovian villas around Wroxeter (Webster 1991, pp. 97–103). By the late second century, the initially timber-built villa-house had been reconstructed in stone, in a modest, winged-corridor style. Its wall-paintings, bath-suite, *opus signinum* (mosaics), mortared floors and hypocausts suggest that this was more than an affluent farm: it is comparable in most respects with other Cornovian examples, all of which are modest by comparison with the palatial residences being built in the Cotswolds, for example; although other examples may await discovery (at Kelsall, perhaps), the very uniqueness of the Eaton villa militates against this being a common settlement type in the region; no farm-buildings are known to have been associated with it, despite excavation in some adjacent areas.

Its proximity to the Mid-Cheshire Ridge and the forts along it may imply that the Eaton-by-Tarporley villa represents the home of an indigenous aristocratic family who had abandoned their ancestral hillfort for a Romanised residence still within the core of their own kin-based system of patronage and exploitation. Its siting implies an interest in running water – for the bath-suite – and a preference for south-facing slopes in the wind-shadow of higher ground to the west. If its inhabitants were supported by rents of various kinds, rather than by farm work, they were under no obligation to site the house according to land use criteria.

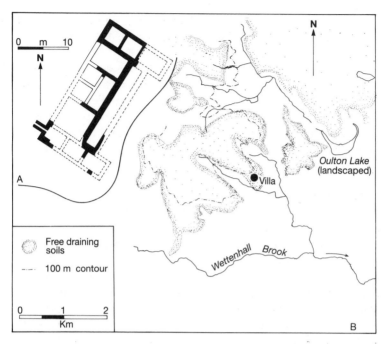

Fig. 2.5 Eaton-by-Tarporley Roman villa: A: The villa. B: The villa in the landscape

Even so, it is worth noting that it was sited close to the eastern side of the well-drained, loamy soils which are a feature of the Mid-Cheshire Ridge, with extensive sands and gravels to the north yet access to the pasturelands of the poorly drained Wettenhall Brook to the south and east (Fig. 2.5). If a home farm was worked from an adjacent yard, the site was well-chosen to act as a focus for mixed farming. Alternatively, it was well-placed as a focus from which to manage an estate within which both arable and pasture were important.

Another Romanised settlement is indicated by coarse ware and Samian associated with a cobbled surface revealed in small-scale excavations on the Lower Green below Beeston Castle (Hough 1982, 1984). The precise nature of this site must await further investigation but it is possible that it reflects the presence nearby of another villa-house. The location of this site so close to the hillfort would, in that case, reinforce the view that such sites represent a Romanising, but indigenous, aristocracy. Other examples have on occasion been suggested (e.g. Watkin 1974, pp. 305–7) but the evidence is in no instance compelling.

Fields in use during the Roman period have barely been recognised in Cheshire. A small area of lyncheted fields of 'Celtic' type at Longley Farm, Kelsall, may, on analogy, have been used during this period. A similar group may have existed on Pale Heights, Eddisbury, before recent agricultural destruction, Most of Cheshire's few lynchet systems are, however, probably medieval (as at Cotebrook, just north of Eaton). In East Anglia, south-east and eastern England, Roman roads can often be seen to cut across large enclosure systems, suggesting that these were already in existence when the roads were constructed (Riley 1980; Williamson 1984, 1987; Higham 1992a, pp. 130–4). Despite detailed examination, Cheshire's field systems do not betray this characteristic; even where Watling Street survives only as a field boundary – as, for example, where twin road-lines mark the boundary between Churton-by-Aldford and Coddington (Waddelove and Waddelove 1983) – it shows every sign of being the primary element in the enclosure system now extant. The relationship can at times be reconstructed: between Middlewich and Northwich, King Street runs through Rudheath. This area was unenclosed until after its reorganisation as the comital manor of Drakeslow, some time soon after 1347 (Booth 1981, p. 4) and there is scant evidence of earlier alignments (Plate 6).

Possible field-systems identified by aerial photography are few in number, undated and small. Perhaps the best example is that at Somerford Hall (near Congleton), comprising what way be a complex of ditched enclosures or fields, on a plateau of coarse, loamy and free-draining soils beside the river Dane (Plate 7), but the site has not as yet been investigated in detail and these cropmarks could easily represent later drainage cuts. It may be that few ditches were dug, enclosures being demarcated by hedges with or without banks, which do not lend themselves to identification from the air. Much of Cheshire today lies under permanent pasture, with medieval and post-medieval ridges obscuring large tracts of land, but observation of widespread cereal crops planted over a variety of soil types in central Cheshire have revealed very few sites which are even potentially of the Roman period.

Despite these rather negative results, there is plentiful evidence that Cheshire's landscape was comparatively open during the Roman period. Pollen analysis on cores from various of the region's mosses have revealed widespread clearance for pasture and cereals and a decline in tree-cover. Although localised evidence such as that from Tatton suggests that farming decreased during the period, this was not thought to be indicative of the general condition even of this township. Pollen from a sample of turf taken from the ditch flanking Watling Street at Eaton (on the Dee) suggested that there was little local woodland: a single grain of cereal contrasted with a high count of weed pollen suggestive of cleared but waste ground in the vicinity (Buchanan *et al.* 1975). The demand for wood for fuel for the salt industry and for heating the larger settlements implies heavy pressure on local woodland resources and probably necessitated widespread management. Coppicing must be a possibility at this stage.

Spelt, heavily infested with rye, was grown and processed at Wilderspool (Hinchliff *et al.* 1992) and corn drying ovens were among the last features to be inserted into the Eaton villa. There was nothing novel about local cereal cultivation; Iron Age farms had been present at Chester and Wilderspool, and not far distant from Tatton's deserted medieval settlement. It is against this backdrop of mixed farming that we should examine land use in the Roman period.

Although originally interpreted as a military site (Newstead and Droop 1937), a 1.4 ha, sub-rectangular ditched enclosure at Halton Brow (Runcorn) should probably be thought of as a civil settlement (Brown *et al.* 1975). Pottery of early second- to early fourth-century date was deposited in the ditch. It could represent a large farmstead. Alternatively, if it be deemed rather too large for a typical farm, this enclosure may have served some function associated with the summer pasturing of cattle in the Mersey basin.

Recent aerial photography has identified a few small ditched enclosures of a kind which generally prove, upon excavation, to have been occupied by farmers during the Roman period. Although most are curvilinear, a rare rectangular example was located on the upper terrace of the Mersey between Winwick Church and the Sankey Brook (now Cheshire but historically Lancashire). Trial excavation demonstrated that all archaeological surfaces had been destroyed by modern agriculture and this would seem to be a general problem in the region. The bivallate promontory site at Great Woolden Hall (Irlam, marginally on the Greater Manchester County side of the modern county boundary) revealed Roman pottery. Other examples south of the Mersey include a possible bluff-top site at Heyesmere (near Sandiway) which may have traces of associated fields. At Legh Oaks Farm, High Legh, a small oval enclosure has been tested by excavation and second-century sherds recovered from the upper levels of the ditch (Nevell 1991). This farmstead lies on a south-facing slope at the interface between clay and the Keuper Marl and sands and gravels from which the ridge is formed. This siting was probably deliberate, since it facilitated access to two different terrains while interposing the settlement between livestock grazing on unenclosed moss-edge claylands and crops, which are likely to have been sown on the ridge (Fig. 2.6). A Roman road only *c.* 800 m from the site provided contact with Romanised markets at Wilderspool and Northwich (each about 12 km by road).

By the standards of the upper Severn valley (Webster 1991, pp. 103–7) or the Solway Plain and Eden valley (Higham and Jones 1975; Higham 1986), Cheshire's Romano-British peasantry are poorly represented. This is in part due to problems of identification of their settlements caused by modern agricultural practices. It may also reflect widespread reliance on other types of settlement; in Northumberland farms built of timber and enclosed by palisades were commonplace at the Roman conquest (e.g. Jobey 1978), only being replaced by ditch and bank or stone walling when local timber became less plentiful. If much of Cheshire's widespread claylands retained woodland throughout the Roman period, it may have been convenient as well as cost-effective to use timber in large quantities on rural settlement sites, as the slightly later Tatton site implies (see below, p. 66). Building stone was never plentiful and would everywhere have required quarrying if it were to have been used. It is not therefore surprising that masoned farmsteads are absent. We might expect to see ditches and banks being constructed most extensively where woodland resources were under greatest pressure, and so around the *wiches* and Chester itelf. If farming occurred at Saltney (as it did at Wilderspool), then it may reflect the latter,

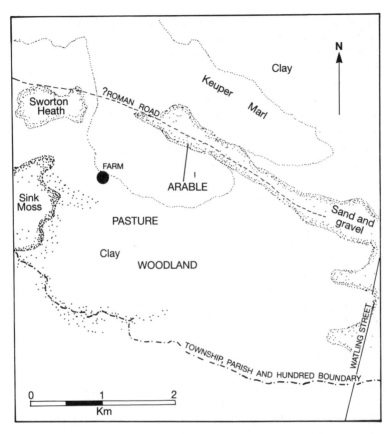

Fig. 2.6 Legh Oaks Farm Romano-British farmstead in its environmental context

but the evidence is at present too idiosyncratic to offer significant distributions.

Another of the problems of locating such sites is the small number of artifacts which they produce. Outside the principal Romanised settlements, very little residual Roman pottery has been found in excavations. At Tatton, for example, the total excavation of a hectare of prime farmland revealed no Roman wares at all, and only a single glass bead came from the nearby excavation of a Mesolithic site. Recent fieldwalking of farmland has revealed little concerning the Roman period. This pattern reflects that found in other parts of the so-called 'Highland Zone', such as northern Wales and the north west of England, where only very small quantities of cheap Romanised goods reached the bulk of the indigenous community. In consequence, few broken vessels found their way from the midden (muck-heap) on to the fields. This pattern contrasts with the high density of such pottery scatters on arable land across much of southern Britain.

The scarcity of manufactured goods in Cheshire's countryside is mirrored by the distribution of coinage. As in other areas without a pre-Roman coinage, Roman coins only dispersed very fitfully and seem never to have reached farmsteads in significant numbers. If locals saw cash very largely as a medium of taxation, rather than exchange, the continuing dependence of the region's markets on soldiers, officials and their suppliers is explicable.

Eaton-by-Tarporley represents the outer limit of the distribution of villas in Roman Britain, suggesting that in Cheshire they will have been the preserve of only a small class of landowners who were exclusively able to afford to participate in the incoming cultural and economic system. The principal centre to which this class looked lay well to the south, at Wroxeter – *Viroconium Cornoviorum*, the capital of the *civitas* to which they were attached. In this respect, at least, there seems little discontinuity between the pre-Roman and Roman tribal systems, although Roman protection and taxation had replaced whatever hypothetical inter-tribal dependence and exploitation had previously held sway. If Cheshire's sparse aristocracy had town residences, these were presumably at Wroxeter itself, rather than in the low-status, roadside settlements within Cheshire.

The region, therefore, gives every sign of being an economic hinterland, with obscure peasant farms forming the most numerous type of settlement, the surplus from which went largely in compulsory outgoings to landowners and the state (cf. Slofstra 1983). The social structure probably remained family or kin based and the culture of the majority determinedly British, with few concessions to, or borrowings from, the colonial power. Its exports were raw materials – minerals perhaps and livestock – and so of low value compared with manufactured goods. They may also have included men and women: an ornate early Roman tombstone at Ilkely of a thirty-year-old woman records that she was a *civis Cornovia* ('a citizen of the Cornovii': Collingwood and Wright 1965, No. 634); an army unit listed in the *Notitia Dignitatum* as being stationed at Newcastle-upon-Tyne bore the name *Coh. Prima Cornoviorum Ponte Aeli*. If they had not been recruited from beyond the Wall, its founder members at least may have come from the north-west Midlands. If the Roman mines of Derbyshire and Wales were manned with slave labour, the Cornovii may have contributed their own convicts to the gangs, via the courts presided over by the tribal aristocracy at Wroxeter.

3

The aftermath of
Empire

By the fourth century, major structural shifts within the Roman Empire were affecting the very fabric of society (Williams 1985; Esmonde Cleary 1989; Higham 1992a). To an extent, these trends foreshadowed fundamental changes which culminated only after the demise of imperial authority in Britain. For example, urban life was in retreat during the fourth century (Reece 1980, but see also Brooks 1986) and society was increasingly focused on the households of great men, normally in undefended villas in the countryside. At the centre of this process were the strategies adopted by late third- and fourth-century governments to reimpose their authority on the Empire and to halt the slide towards chaos and insolvency. These measures included increasing and reorganising the armed forces, swelling the bureaucratic base of government, raising taxes and recourse to taxation in kind (including labour). The Empire was reorganised into approximately twice as many provinces, now grouped in dioceses and prefectures. Provincial governors were divorced from control of the armed forces by which they were defended. To these changes was added an Empire-wide and imperially sponsored religion – Christianity – the organisation of which replicated in the world of faith the authoritarian regime of the Empire. These changes had important repercussions for the nature of Roman culture in Britain as a whole, and Cheshire was no exception. In the most general terms, it fostered a culture of dependency among the leaders of civil society which rendered the provincial community dangerously dependent on the armed forces of the state.

Late Roman Cheshire

Cheshire had always been a peripheral part of Roman Britain but this characteristic was accentuated as the province was divided and then subdivided. Throughout the third century, the Mersey is generally assumed to have been the frontier between *Britannia Superior* in southern Britain and *Britannia Inferior* in the north and north-east Midlands. If Corieltauvian territory was attached to this northern province, then the ill-defined eastern boundary of the Cornovii was probably also a frontier of provincial status, with the Lutudarenses of the Peak beyond it. It may be that the structure of the new Roman provinces was influenced by patterns of dependence which were then already ancient (Figs. 1.8, 2.1).

Cheshire's marginality was enhanced by the subdivision of the provinces in the fourth century. Their precise boundaries cannot be reconstructed. Indeed, little more is known concerning them than their capitals. It is, however, generally supposed that the two existing provinces were simply subdivided along existing *civitas* (tribal) boundaries (e.g. Salway 1981, map VII; Barker 1990). Given its long association with military and governmental activities in northern Wales, there can be little doubt that Chester lay in the western province of *Britannia Prima*. The boundaries of the Cornovii may now have served to divide that province both from *Britannia Secunda* to the north and *Flavia Caesariensis* to the east. If so, then the Wirral coastline, the Mersey and a more shadowy eastern boundary of Cornovian territory along the Pennines were frontiers of provincial status. Regions peripheral to three provinces were few in late Roman Britain and this circumstance can only emphasise the frontier nature of Cheshire and reinforce its status as a remote hinterland, distant from the capitals of both the tribe, at Wroxeter, and the province, at Cirencester in the territory of the Dobunni.

The early Roman period had witnessed a high level of subsidy paid by richer areas of the province, and even continental communities, to sustain a large army in northern and western Britain. In Wales, this subsidy declined in the Hadrianic period as most western garrisons were withdrawn. It was reduced further during the third century as troop numbers and army pay shrank and fort provisioning became progressively more regionalised within the Empire. By the second half of the third century, military units were being positioned along the Channel coasts (later termed the 'Saxon Shore'). The town-centred bureaucracies and field army units of the fourth century competed with garrisons on the outer edge of Britain for scarce resources. One result was the cessation of that flow of resources from the lowland core to the upland periphery, which had earlier conditioned the economy of Roman Britain, leaving garrisons in the west and north dependent on local produce and taxation.

This process is clearly reflected in the archaeology of Cheshire and neighbouring shires. As already noted, most roadside settlements here and in north-east Wales flourished between c. AD 80–200. Thereafter the deposition of Roman goods slackenend or even collapsed. What had apparently been official complexes at Ffrith, Pentre Farm (Flint) and Prestatyn ceased functioning and local mining was turned over to civilian contractors. Only Chester, Middlewich and, to a lesser extent, Nantwich survived as market centres, the last two presumably buoyed up by salt extraction. The extent to which most such sites were wholly abandoned is debatable but they certainly lost most traces of Roman culture before the collapse of Roman Britain.

Chester's role in the fourth century is obscure, although the continuing deposition of coins and the working of gold in the *praetorium* both imply that it remained a site of high status. With the legion apparently absent from about 300, diminishing parts of the site remained in use, despite some refurbishment which might be associated with Constantine I. General abandonment has been variously dated from the mid-fourth century onwards (Mason 1987, p. 167) but coins were still reaching Chester in the period 368–78, with a few strays even later (Shotter 1979, p. 4). It is by no means certain that the site was ever entirely abandoned.

Elsewhere, little trace of later Roman occupation has so far been identified. At the villa at Eaton-by-Tarporley, as at many British villas, artifacts were being deposited towards the end of the century if not beyond (Mason 1983), but the problems of dating in and after the late fourth century render the late period obscure and the date of abandonment is impossible to calculate. At Dove Point, Meols, coins recovered from the beach trading site during nineteenth-century erosion span the years from Claudius to Magnus Maximus (383–88) with little sign of oscillation in the numbers from any one period (Hume 1863; Thompson 1965, p. 99), suggesting that trading continued throughout the Roman period. A tiny corpus of early Anglo-Saxon artifacts hints at some continuing activity, if at very low levels, in the fifth–seventh centuries.

During the late fourth century, the military presence in the west of Roman Britain was still further reduced. The *limitatenses* (frontier troops) at Caernarvon (*Segontium*) seem to have been upgraded to the status of field army troops and withdrawn from the diocese, emerging as the *Seguntienses* in Illyricum (Stevens 1940, p. 134). The territory of the Cornovii was without a permanent garrison in the late Roman period but the large numbers of throwing darts (*plumbatae*) found in Wroxeter's *basilica* (Webster 1991, pp. 120–1) may imply the presence of units of the diocesan field army (*comitatenses*), stationed so as to be able to react against Irish raiders before they could strike at the lowland heartland of the southern provinces.

If it does not reflect the loss of sections of the text, the total omission of the western command from the *Notitia Dignitatum* suggests that all fort garrisons had been withdrawn even before the demise of Roman authority. The role of Magnus Maximus as putative founder of several Welsh dynasties and his high reputation in early insular poetry may mean that this occurred as early as the 380s but it need imply only that Magnus Maximus was the best-remembered general of late Roman Britain, perhaps because of his exceptional, if undeferential, treatment by Gildas (DEB XIII, 1, 2). Coins continued to reach Welsh forts in small quantities up to the mid 390s. The ultimate cessation of coinage at this time may represent the final withdrawal of the garrisons, perhaps for service under Arbogastes against Eugenius (392–95: Casey 1989), but it need mean nothing more significant than the failure, for the future, to pay the soldiery.

Interpretation of this evidence is particularly problematic both because it is essentially negative, so vulnerable to periodic revision as new finds are made, and also because the final collapse of the supply of coins to Roman Britain occurred so soon after, during the period 402–10. All that can be said without fear of contradiction is that garrisons ceased to be paid in Chester's command area within a decade of 400.

With the demise of artifacts of Roman manufacture in the late fourth and early fifth centuries, archaeological evidence shrinks away and all but disappears. It was not to recover in this region until the thirteenth century, when pottery again began to be deposited in some quantity on sites of sufficient diversity to enable the archaeologist to define periods of occupation with some confidence. In the interim, evidence of varying calibre can be extracted from a small number of documents and literary references, place-names, finds of ecclesiastical masonry and a tiny number of excavations, but interpretation of this material is necessarily very hypothetical. The best that we can hope to achieve is a consistent use of the available evidence, but it will always be possible for scholars to approach the very limited body of source materials from different perspectives or with different value judgements, and then offer hypotheses which differ dramatically one from another.

Tribal society after Rome

Among the Cornovii the sole evidence for literacy is a reused tombstone, recovered from plough-soil in 1967 at Wroxeter. This reads: CUNORIX MACUSMA QUICOLINE – 'Cunorix ["Hound-King"] son of the son-of-the-Holly' (Wright and Jackson 1968). His name and the effort made to commemorate him would suggest that Cunorix was a man of Irish extraction and high standing, and so probably a warrior, when he died at or near Wroxeter. The stone was found just inside the defences but close to the eastern cemetery of the Roman town, and so adjacent to ground where a sub-Roman community may still have felt that honourable burial was appropriate.

This stray inscription, akin to the ogham text found at Silchester, may imply the presence of a settlement of the highest status still occupying the site of a major Roman centre in the north-western lowlands in the later fifth century. On other grounds, Wroxeter's role in the sub-Roman period has been shown to have been a focal one (Barker 1975, 1979, 1990; Pretty 1989; White 1990). An occupation dated to c. 450–550 centred on a massive timber structure reminiscent of a Roman villa, surrounded by large numbers of lesser buildings. Despite the lack of associated artifacts, the complex is on a scale which requires it be viewed as a centre of high status and it is at least arguable that this site continued in some form the administration of the late Roman tribe, eventually re-emerging as the central court of a British kingdom (White 1990). Whatever its precise role, its material poverty points to a British occupation, as opposed to an Anglo-Saxon one, although its function within local society may have differed little from the high-status hall complexes of early England.

Other parts of the old tribal capital have yielded graves, some at least of which appear to have been deposited in an organised fashion and aligned, so the presence of a Christian church and cemetery seems possible. Pretty (1989) has drawn attention to the siting of what may be a very early English church on the site (see also Moffett 1990; Bassett 1990), which may have served to maintain continuity of worship and burial from the British to the Anglo-Saxon periods. Carbon dates which post-date the abandonment of the sub-Roman complex centre on *c.* 610 (calibrated), suggesting that it was deserted by *c.* 550–650. Crop-marks which have been tentatively interpreted as a complex of great halls of Anglo-Saxon type at nearby Atcham (Gelling 1989, p. 174) may signify the building of a new palace complex to replace that at *Viroconium*, perhaps when Anglo-Saxons first took direct control of the region, but firm interpretation must await excavation.

In Cheshire, in what has here been interpreted as the probable northern reaches of Cornovian territory in the Roman period, only two sites have so far revealed evidence of sub-Roman occupation. At Chester itself, excavations at Abbey Green demonstrated the presence of a large timber-framed building constructed on dry-stone sleeper walls *c.* 11 m × 5 m and with a flooring of flags and gravel, which appears to have been aligned on the Roman street. The presence of class B IV amphorae and red colour-coated vessels imported from the Mediterranean implies an occupation broadly similar to that dated to *c.* 450–550 at Wroxeter (McPeake 1978b; McPeake *et al.* 1980). Since these finds were made, re-examination of the pottery from other excavations in Chester has revealed a further scatter of sub-Roman imported wares. This occupation and the pottery associated with it is of prime importance, particularly since these imports are so far unique in Cornovian territory. It suggests that ships from the

Mediterranean or Gaul were still visiting the port of Chester. That they departed with fewer containers than they had brought implies that they either traded or deposited gifts here, perhaps in exchange for lead and silver, salt, animal products or slaves. Whoever controlled this 'trade' was presumably of high status and the Abbey Green site may have been part of a 'court' of some sort. If the high proportion of *amphorae* among these finds had brought wine, this would be consistent with the presence of a Christian Community, but any sub-Roman court is likely to have enjoyed wine when it was available. That these vessels did not reach Wroxeter may imply that Chester's rulers enjoyed status sufficient to keep the benefits of their overseas contacts to themselves. This might reinforce the case for a senior churchman, Chester's claims to a sub-Roman church otherwise rests on later literature (Thacker 1982; see below, p. 79) but it is possible that the detritus uncovered by archaeology reflects the presence of a sub-Roman bishopric based on late-Roman Chester or its immediate hinterland.

This occupation was succeeded by evidence of metal-working, probably in both bronze and iron. Such activities, too, are characteristic in the sub-Roman period of British sites of high status. Elsewhere, archaeological evidence shows that Roman occupation at Chester was succeeded by agricultural activity. Around Lower Bridge Street, excavations revealed ploughing in 12 m wide strips which long continued between slight ditches, but dating was no more precise than *c*. 400–850 (Mason 1985b). The width of these strips may imply the use of the heavy plough characteristic of the second half of the Anglo-Saxon period, so this evidence is more likely to belong to the eighth or ninth centuries than earlier.

The second occupation of putative Dark Age date is that at Tatton. Here excavations designed to examine medieval and early post-medieval activity on the site of a loosely nucleated settlement revealed a fenced or palisaded enclosure *c*. 44 m across. Within this had stood a large timber-framed building (over 24 m × *c*. 5 m; Plate 8) built on the post-in-construction-trench principle (Fig. 3.1). Associated with it was an ancillary building of similar construction, the foundations of which were much better preserved, a putative threshing-floor and several pits appar-

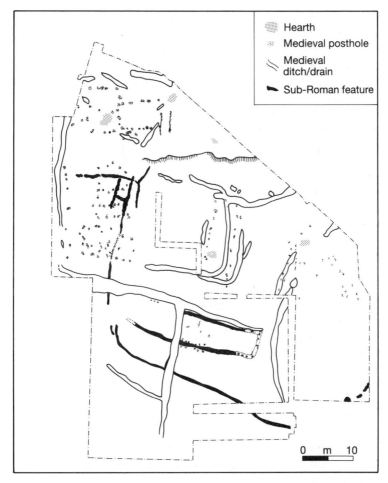

Fig. 3.1 Excavations at Tatton Deserted Village: the Early Medieval and Medieval Phases (c. AD 400–1500)

ently serving as the bases of storage structures (Higham, forthcoming, (a)).

This complex had been severely affected by later activity, including ploughing, and this may be one reason why no diagnostic artifacts were identified. Dating was therefore dependent on carbon dates, which centred in the Roman period. However, the total absence of Roman artifacts inclined the excavator to an early sub-Roman date, on the assumption that its buildings were constructed from mature, hardwood trees which would consistently provide carbon dates which were earlier than the period of occupation. Associated research identified a clearance episode characterised by cereals comprising seven per cent of the total pollen counted and including rye, dated (after calibration) to AD 430–670 (HAR-8408: Chambers and Wilshaw 1991) and the complex identified archaeologically should probably be linked with this activity. Again, the material poverty would suggest a British rather than an Anglo-Saxon community, but the large size of the principal building may imply that the complex was superior to a peasant farm in status.

If this site was typical of the sort of settlement and the levels of artifact deposition which we should expect from this period, it is not surprising that so few have so far been identified here or elsewhere in western Britain (e.g. Edwards and Lane 1988). It does seem clear that the area was one which, in comparison with those yielding evidence of early Anglo-Saxon settlement, had a very impoverished material culture, despite access to varieties of mineral ores in the locality. This discrepancy is so marked that it is difficult to explain merely by reference to cultural differences such as contrasting funeral practices. Indeed, it may imply that other factors, such as political dependency, were in play.

The *Wrocen sǣte*, Powys and Anglo-Saxon England

There is no further documentation of the Cornovii after the *Notitia Dignitatum*. Like many other names current in Roman Britain, the tribe's official title apparently failed to outlive the Empire. Its disappearance need not, however, be of any particular significance. The Roman tribe had been administered for more than three centuries from *Viroconium Cornoviorum*, and that site certainly continued as a place of the highest status into the early Middle Ages. The place-name (otherwise *Uriconio*, *Viriconio* or *Viroconion*) is of obscure origin (Jackson 1969; Rivet and Smith 1979), but Wroxeter derives directly from it (Jackson 1953, pp. 601–2; Gelling 1990, pp. 330–1).

When the name occurs in Anglo-Saxon texts (*Wreocen*, *Wrocen*, *Wocen*) it has generally been assumed to refer in the first instance to the hillfort (e.g. Gelling 1989) but (admittedly limited) excavation of the prehistoric site revealed no evidence of Roman, sub-Roman or Anglo-Saxon settlement (Stanford 1984). The names of several Early Medieval kingdoms derive from Roman sites; Lindsey, or *Lindesfaran*, for example, is from Lincoln (*Lindum*), its focal palace and church site (see the discussion in Bassett 1989b) and the *Magonsǣte* of Herefordshire derives from *Magnis* (Roman Kenchester; Rivet and Smith 1979, p. 407; Gelling 1988, pp. 102–5; Pretty 1989, pp. 178–9). In these examples it was the walled enclave which was the centre from which the kingship and people were named. These instances may suggest that Wroxeter, rather than the Wrekin, was the eponymous centre of the early sub-Roman *Wrocen sǣte*. Roman defences and a long tradition of government on the town site may have offered both greater security and a more valuable tradition of authority which could be advantageous to a sub-Roman ruler, who may have had little to gain from reoccupation of the long-derelict ramparts on the hill above. Uniquely, it is Wroxeter which has provided archaeological evidence of just this period of occupation.

Although both the Wrekin and Wroxeter lie outside, the nature of the *Wrocen sǣte* and the extent of the territory administered from Wroxeter is of crucial importance to our understanding of Cheshire in the Early Middle Ages. Although the stem is pre-English, the name occurs exclusively in Anglo-Saxon contexts and is an Old English compound, the suffix being *-sǣte* (or *-sǣtan* in the plural) – 'inhabitants' (literally, 'those sitting'). It was long in use, being last documented as *Wreocensetun*, a province or district of Mercia in which the Vikings were reported to be active in 855 (Birch 1885–87, No. 487).

The origin of this name is obscure but it occurs first in the *Tribal Hidage*, a tribute list which is normally dated to the seventh century, albeit only surviving in the vernacular in a single copy of *c*. 1000 (Dumville 1989). It has been variously attributed to any one of several Mercian kings but recent re-examination has suggested that a Northumbrian origin might be more appropriate (Brooks 1989), in which case Edwin of Deira (616–32) is a possibility (Higham 1992a, pp. 148–9, 1992b and forthcoming (b)). It is in two parts, a primary list with a correct total of the hidage, to which secondary material, and an (incorrect) grand total had been appended. Whoever compiled it, the basis of the primary list of nineteen hidations (but twenty peoples) would seem to have been a list of Mercia's tributaries, to which Mercia had itself been added, with an exceptionally high hidation and in pole position.

If Mercia be temporarily excluded, then the *Wrocen sǣte* headed this tribute list, followed by the *Westerne*, *Pecsǣte* and *Elmedsǣte*. The 'Peak-dwellers', in the Peak District (see p. 176), and the 'Elmet-dwellers', in Elmet (in the West Riding of Yorkshire; Higham 1993), are easily placed (Fig. 3.2). The 'Peak-dwellers' would seem to carry the social distinctiveness of the Peak (and so perhaps of the territory of the *Lutudarenses*) into the Early Middle Ages, and Elmet is known to have been under British kings until Edwin's reign (HB, LXIII). Both may, therefore, in origin have been sub-Roman British territories.

Definition of the territory of the *Wrocen sǣte* depends heavily, however, on interpretation of the *Westerne*. The location of this people has been much debated, with scholars traditionally opting for either Cheshire and northern Staffordshire (Stenton 1971, p. 296) or Herefordshire (e.g. Davies and Vierck 1974, p. 231; Hill 1981, p. 76; Yorke 1990, p. 13; Sims-Williams 1990, p. 18). Both options have significant drawbacks: the first preserves the consistency of the clockwise circuit around Mercia, which seems such a clear characteristic of the list, but requires that an otherwise unknown kingship capable of paying a very high tribute (7,000 hides) existed in this thinly populated and economically impoverished backwater; the second avoids this problem but destroys the ordering of the list, the very consistency of which, in this sector at least, otherwise requires that it should be maintained at all costs (Fig. 3.2).

Given these objections, an alternative solution might be appropriate. This is not a tribal name (such as the West Saxons) nor one derived from a specific place (such as the *Wrocen sǣte*), but an indication of location meaningful only from a particular, and external, perspective. As a name it has parallels with the directional place-names which are common in the western Midlands (hence Astbury, Weston, and so on) but there is no reason to think it is the name that was used by the people so designated at the court of the tribute-taking king. From either Deira or Mercia, those who best warranted the term 'Westerners' were the British

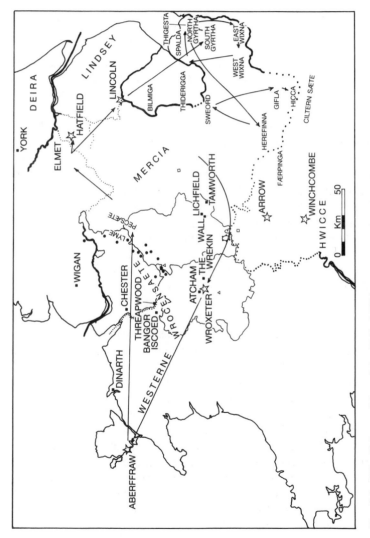

Fig. 3.2 The Primary List of the Tribal Hidage: a tentative reconstruction

kings of Wales beyond Wroxeter and its territory (Higham 1992c).
A similar usage occurs in Ptolemy (1883–1901, II, 3, 18): 'farthest
to the west live the Ordovices . . .'. In this instance it may refer to
the kings of Anglesey or Gwynedd, whose regional 'overkingship'
in the west is implicit both in the much earlier *De Excidio Britanniae* of Gildas and in Bede's *Historia Ecclesiastica*.

This identification has the merit of associating the *Westerne*
with a well-known and powerful kingship which was interactive at
this date with English kings – it was Cædwallon of Gwynedd who
rebelled and killed Edwin in 633 (HE, II, 20). It also maintains
the clockwise ordering of the circuit. It may, therefore, be preferable to the other identifications so far offered.

This 'overkingship' in the west can, to an extent, be reconstructed from the *De Excidio* of Gildas (XXVIII, XXXVI), albeit
for a date which is about a century earlier (Higham 1992c).
Gildas referred by name to the rulers of Dumnonia (Devon and
Cornwall), southern Wales and *Din Eirth*, in terms which imply
them to have been of lesser status than Maglocunus, the 'Dragon
of the Island' (Anglesey), *Din Eirth* was probably Dinarth, near
Llandrillo-yn-Rhos and Degannwy on the east side of the lower
Conway (Winterbottom 1978; Jackson 1982). It belongs, therefore, to northern Wales east of the river Conway. If this king had
responsibility for a kingdom roughly equivalent to that of his
peers (Cornwall and Devon, for example), it presumably encompassed the bulk of north-east Wales, and so the Deceangli of the
Roman period.

Although the name 'Deceangli' may have survived in Medieval
Tegeingel and Englefield (and even this is debated), by the eighth
century a new kingship and tribal name had come into being:
Powys. This is a Welsh form of the Latin *Paganses*, 'country-folk'
or 'rustics' (Jackson 1953, pp. 91, 443), later 'pagans', from
pagus, 'village' or 'rural district'. The name would have been
particularly suited to a territory which is not known to have been
recognised as a self-governing tribal territory, and so had no
urban centre in the late Roman period. Nor did it have a prominent military site. It was, therefore, of necessity ruled from the
countryside (unlike Anglesey – where a Roman fort was reoccupied, the *Wrocen sǣte* or *Magonsǣte*) and Gildas's *receptaculum
ursi – din eirth*, so 'bear's den' – would seem to reflect this. The

Powys of the central Middle Ages is fixed by the 'Pillar of Eliseg', an early ninth-century monument erected at Llanthysilio-yn-Ial, near Valle Crucis (Nash-Williams 1950, pp. 123–5); but even then the extent of its territories is unknown. Powys in the sixth and seventh centuries is even more obscure, although later Welsh poetry and annals associate its rulers with Flintshire and Shropshire west of the river Tern.

There are two possibilities: either early Powys encompassed both the Cornovii (subsequently the *Wrocen sæte*) and adjacent areas of north-east Wales (as implicit in Morris 1973, supported by Webster 1991), or it corresponded broadly with the Deceangli (or even in some sense the Ordovices) of Roman Britain. Apparent links between the kings of Powys, the monastery of Bangor Iscoed and the battle of Chester (presumably fought in what had been Cornovian territory) has hitherto encouraged this author to give support to the former solution (Higham 1992b), on the assumption that Bangor was necessarily inside Cornovian territory, and subsequently in that of the *Wrocen sæte*.

This assumption seems less secure if the region is examined over a longer time-scale. If *Mediolanum* was correctly attributed by Ptolemy to the Ordovices and the interlocking tribal geography which this implies was then frozen by the dead hand of Roman administration, then their territory necessarily included the detached portion of Flintshire (Maelor Saesneg), as well as Denbighshire. If sub-Roman kingships then perpetuated pre-existing boundaries, then Bangor Iscoed lay under the protection of the sub-Roman kings of north-eastern Wales, rather than Wroxeter. The terms *Wrocen sæte* and Powys were in contemporary use in virtually irreconcilable contexts as late as the ninth century, when the Mercian conquest of the latter was closely associated with the fall of Degannwy, only a stone's throw from the putative palace site of Gildas's King Cuneglasus at Dinarth. A definite solution is impossible on so little evidence but continuity of tribal territories seems the more likely option. It will here be suggested, therefore, that the *Wrocen sæte* were a continuation of the Cornovii of Roman Britain, with Powys succeeding the Deceangli to their west. That the latter extended south of the Severn seems clear from the survival of the name as a Marcher lordship south and west of Oswestry, and from the observation by Gerald of Wales in the late twelfth century (Thorpe 1978, I, 4) that three of the cantrefs of Powys lay in Shropshire in his day.

That the old tribal name of the Cornovii should have given way to that of its principal centre may reflect the shift from oligarchical to royal government, with the principal palace site supplanting the old organs of tribal government under the Empire. In the form in which it has come down to us, the new name is one which was coined by outsiders, whose business was not with the people as a whole but with its rulers. The literal meaning of the name is 'those dwelling at *Wrocen*'. It may refer quite specifically to the court itself, in the first instance, and only by extension to the territory administered from that court. That its rulers governed a large territory is confirmed by the hidation allotted them in the Tribal Hidage (7,000 hides), which distinguishes the resources of this kingship from the petty territories on Mercia's northern and eastern borders, with hidations of 300, 600 and 1,200 hides. The *Wrocen sǣte* should, therefore, have encompassed Cheshire, as well as much of both Shropshire and at least western Staffordshire.

The principal counter – argument derives from the location of both Wroxeter and The Wrekin close to the south – western extremity of Cornovian territory as here defined. Their location has been thought too marginal for the name to be valid in Cheshire (e.g. Gelling 1989, p. 192) but this case rests partly on the assumption that it is the hillfort which is significant. If the name refers not to a landmark but to a seat of government, then the extent of the territory is not restricted to the immediate vicinity of the Wrekin. Wroxeter was no more marginal to its putative territory as a sub-Roman royal capital than it had been for centuries as a tribal centre. At least one other peripheral site had given its name to a people listed in the Tribal Hidage – hence *Lindesfaran*. Such marginal locations are by no means uncommon among Early Medieval palace sites: Aberffraw, Dumbarton Rock, Edinburgh and London (sometime *metropolis* of the East Saxons) all lie on the edge of the territories administered from them during the same period. Numerous later English sites were equally marginal to their administrative areas (e.g. Chester, Southampton). When placed in a wider context, this argument therefore loses much of its impact.

The *Wrocen sǣte* of the early seventh century may, therefore, very tentatively be equated with the Cornovii of Roman Britain. The geography of this corner of Britain in the sub-Roman period need have evolved little from that already in place under Rome. The order enshrined in the Tribal Hidage suggests that their territory was coterminous with that of the *Westerne*, and so the Deceangli and later Powys, with their neighbours to the west. Links between Powys and the monastery at Bangor Iscoed have already been mentioned. Bangor lay marginally inside Maelor Saesneg, which consisted of just three great manors in 1086, when it formed an integral and hidated portion of *Dudestan* Hundred in south-west Cheshire (Fig. 3.3), but the pattern of its land tenure at that date was exceptional, being far closer in organisation to the hundreds west of the Dee than other parts of *Dudestan*. There were none of the small manors held by little-known thegns which are characteristic of other parts of the hundred. Although it was clearly in English hands under Canute (DB, 264b), it was perhaps a late addition, never fully integrated into the pattern of English tenure, where it was felt advisable that all estates should remain in the hands of the highest secular authorities. Although a priest was noted at Bettisfield in 1086, parochial organisation earlier probably oriented on Bangor, which was unnamed in Domesday Book but was perhaps part of Earl Edwin's estate of Worthenbury. In the early modern period, Bangor's parish included four townships in Denbighshire, Bangor and the dependent chapelry of Worthenbury. The bishop's claims in 1086 may signify his interest in the property of this church, which, if it had been as large as Bede suggested (HE, II, 2) could have encompassed, *c.* 600, the entire sub-region. The recurrence of Isycoed as a place-name between the Dee and Wrexham may reflect Bangor's early authority throughout *Exestan* Hundred but its components are common elements, **coed** meaning 'wood'. Threapwood – 'disputed wood', an anomalous, extra-parochial and extra-jurisdictional district (Dodgson 1966/67– IV, pp. 61–2) lies between those parts of *Dudestan* Hundred which were more conventionally part of Cheshire and those which comprised Maelor Saesneg and may hint at early uncertainties about Iscoed and Bangor's borders, but a later origin is at least as likely. These factors affecting Maelor Saesneg may reflect the Ptolemaic ascription of *Mediolanum* to the Ordovices but the early medieval

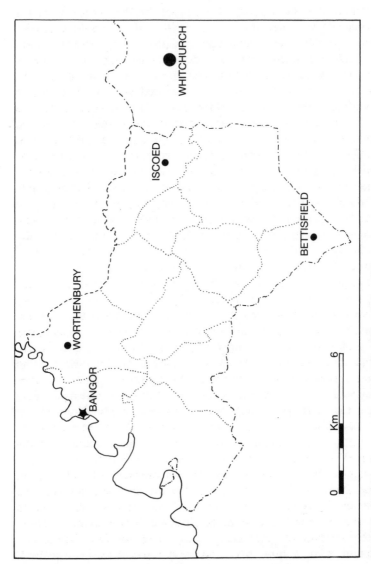

Fig. 3.3 Maelor Saesneg, based on the first edition OS

organisation of this region is fatally obscured by its marcher status in the twelfth and thirteenth centuries.

The lower Dee may have continued as the tribal boundary. If so it had now become the frontier between Mercia's satellites and kings who at least periodically recognised the leadership of Gwynedd (Higham 1992c). Further north, the Mersey river – a frontier of provincial status in later Roman Britain – attracted a name in the early Middle Ages implicit of a frontier of the highest status: OE *(ge)mǣre – ēa* – 'boundary-river' – as befits the boundary between the Mercian and the northern Anglian (Northumbrian) 'overkingships'. It was probably the Mersey that Bede had in mind (HE, II, 5) when he referred to the boundaries adjacent to the Humber which helped define the lands of the Northumbrians. The *Pecsǣte* were listed separately in the Tribal Hidage, confirming that an important boundary lay in or near eastern Cheshire, where arguably the tribal and provincial boundaries of later Roman Britain had been. This obscure Early Medieval boundary may have followed the pre-existing one. All that lay between the *Westerne* and the *Pecsǣte* is perhaps best thought of as the northernmost districts of the *Wrocen sǣte* – the peoples ruled by the 'Wroxeter-dwellers'.

Culture and ethnicity

If sub-Roman Wroxeter was a British court, there seems every reason to envisage that the entire tribal territory remained under British control, with an indigenous population, at least up to the early seventh century. This would seem to be confirmed by the total absence, to date, of pagan Anglo-Saxon cemeteries from Shropshire, Cheshire and western Staffordshire (Meaney 1964; Fig. 3.3). Although English folk movements into parts of the western Midlands prior to the conversion have retained some supporters (e.g. Sims-Williams 1990), it is difficult to justify such a view where archaeological evidence is entirely negative. Attempts to explain the eventual supremacy of the English language in such areas by the influx of Germanic families who converted to Christianity on entry to powerful British kingdoms in what is now the western Midlands of England (e.g. Bassett 1992) are far from convincing. That the notion of a British conversion of the English was vigorously rejected by Bede (HE, I,

22) must count against such models. So too must the lack of any evidence of militarily significant British leadership east of Powys. This region fell to the Romans without a struggle. It seems most unlikely that kings based here kept the English at bay or controlled their entry to the region through military prowess.

Pagan English burials might be slightly more in evidence than is generally thought. A case has been made for the -**hlaw** place-names of Cheshire being isolated pagan burials under mounds (Dodgson 1967; see also Gelling 1988, pp. 134–7) but no such site has so far produced material evidence in support of this thesis and alternative interpretations are generally preferable: some certainly represent prehistoric burial mounds (as in 'The Seven Lows'); others are natural prominences (e.g. Werneth Low); others may be man-made meeting-places of a later date (e.g. possibly the Hundred centres at Bucklow Hill, Ruloe, or Mutlow – 'Moot-hill' – in Marton). The common association of -**hlaw** with personal names need not indicate the burial place of that person. A proprietorial interest is at least as plausible.

If this category of evidence be set aside, therefore, as at best inconclusive, the absence of pagan Anglo-Saxon graves is a consistent feature of the entire territory, in contrast, for example, with the Peak to the east. So too is the absence of non-English types of memorial in stone: excepting only the exotic example with Irish associations found at Wroxeter (above), these occur exclusively west of the valleys of the Severn and Dee, in what was already evolving into Wales. Between these two distributions is a broad region along the Welsh Marches and the western Midlands which offers practically no archaeological evidence diagnostic of culture or ethnicity throughout the Early Middle Ages (Fig. 3.4).

One indication that Christianity survived up to the conversion of the English is the occasional presence of place-names formed from Latin *ecclesia* – a 'congregation' or 'church', via an Old Welsh version of Modern Welsh **eglwys** and Old English **eclēs** (Cameron 1968; Gelling 1988, pp. 96–9). Only one example is extant in Cheshire, Eccleston (*Eclēstūn*, 'church-settlement'). Its location only 3.5 km south of Chester on Watling Street has been seen as implicit of early Christian organisation in the hinterland of that focal site (e.g. Barrow 1973; Thacker 1982) and traces of a bank or *vallum* have been identified associated with the ancient church site which lies behind the modern one (Laing and Laing, undated). Eccleston lies south of Heronbridge. If that site lay in the Roman period on the borders of Deceanglian and Cornovian territory, ossification of those same boundaries in sub-Roman Britain might suggest that Eccleston lay in the territory of the *Wrocen sæte*, albeit on the periphery. It is possible that the church referred to was at Chester, in which case the place-name acknowledges the dependency of this settlement on a prominent church site at a little distance, but the precise meaning must remain speculative and a church on this site remains a possibility. Later legends concerning an early church at Chester dedicated to Saints Peter and Paul might be pertinent (Thacker 1982), and it is possible that a British mother-church occupied the site of the Roman settlement and sustained its focal role into the Middle Ages, but this remains unproven and the literary evidence is of the most dubious historicity. The Staffordshire manor of Eccleshall may represent a second **eclēs** place-name in the same territory.

Wells with early Christian associations are widespread throughout Wales (e.g. Jones 1954). In many instances these arguably reflect centres of pagan worship which at some stage were Christianised, whether that occurred in the Roman period or thereafter. The powerful spring at Holywell was close to the borders of Domesday Cheshire but none on the English side of the border can be associated with cults earlier than the tenth century – the earliest possible date for St Plegmund's Well in Barrow.

Sub-Roman cemeteries in Wales were clearly attracted to pre-existing prehistoric earthworks, some of them graves, which may have had a ritual significance (e.g. Brassil 1987; James 1992). Recent excavations at Tandderwen have provided tantalising glimpses of a complex British site very close by, but in Cheshire there has been very little archaeological investigation of such sites. Many medieval churches are sited close to springs and streams, some of which are striking natural features (e.g. Lymm). Others lie on the banks of major rivers (as do Warburton, Runcorn, Weaverham, Chester, Farndon) or close by standing water – as at Rostherne, where a 'Celtic Head' and local legends could (but need not) reflect the cult of an earlier pagan god(dess) (Crowe 1982). Yet more medieval churches occupy ridge-top or hilltop sites (e.g. Bowdon).

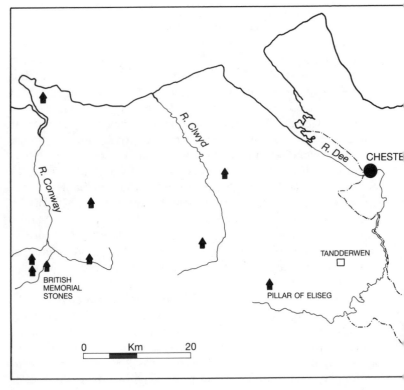

Fig. 3.4 Anglo-Saxon burials and British memorial stones in the north-ern Marches

These are precisely those categories of site which Gildas singled out in the late fifth century as characteristic of pre-Christian, British paganism (DEB, IV, 3): 'nor shall I invoke by name the very mountains, hills or rivers which were in times past so deadly, but which now are useful to the needs of mankind, at which divine honours were heaped up by a blind people'. River deities are a commonplace in Roman-British place-naming and it would be attractive to postulate some association between the cult of a British river deity, *Deva*, and the religious sites on the Dee at Bangor Iscoed, Chester, Eccleston or Farndon, but there is no evidence by which such a thesis can currently be tested.

The size and shape of churchyards has long been considered a

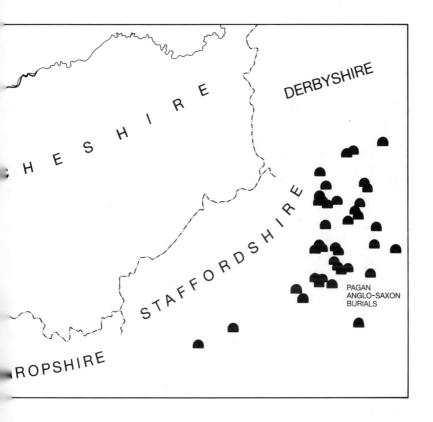

possible indicator of their antiquity (e.g. Thomas 1971, 1981).
A recent survey of the southern Marches has suggested that
numerous curvilinear cemeteries in what eventually became western England may have originated in the British past (Brook
1992), with their size relating primarily to their importance.
For Cheshire, this category of evidence was examined by Alan
Thacker (1987, pp. 286–92), who has identified eighteen churchyards which could be described as curvilinear (Fig. 3.5). With
only seven exceptions, these lie in that third of the county which
lies west of the Mid-Cheshire Ridge, with two actually west of the
Dee and another (Farndon) on its banks. That this category of
site can be significant finds a little support in the place-name
evidence: one is that same Eccleston which has already been
noted as a potential early church site on place-name evidence

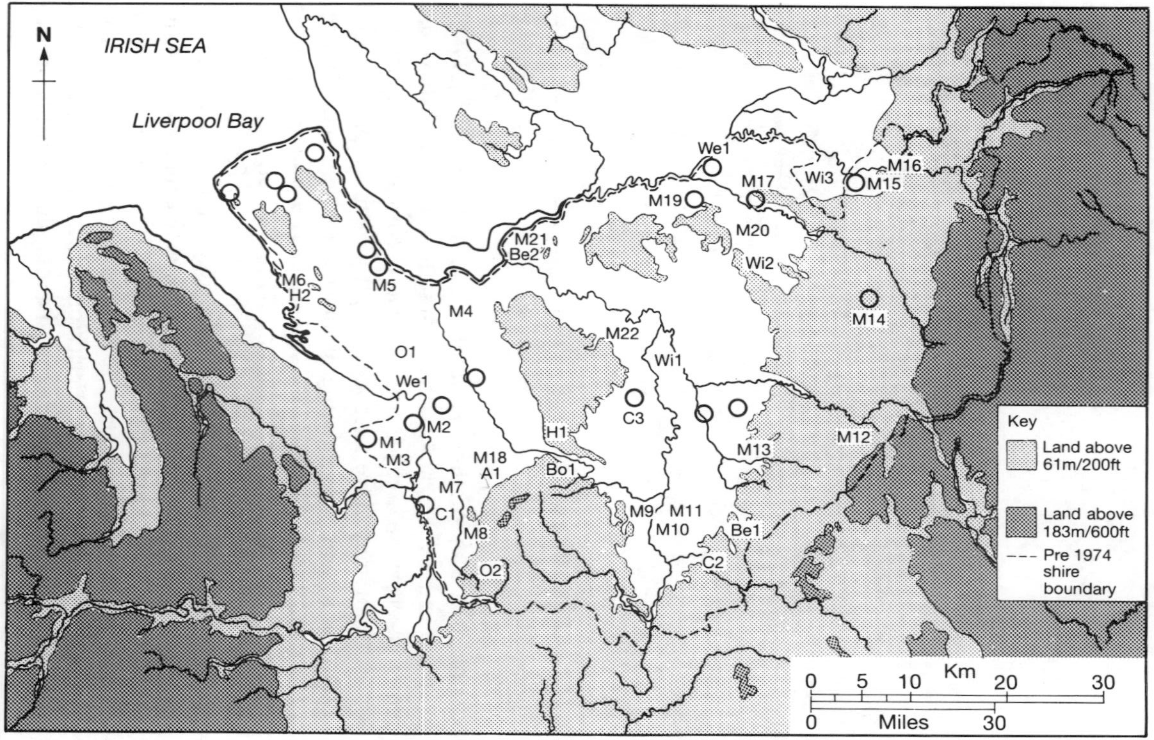

Fig. 3.5
Curvilinear
churchyards and
selected
dedications in
Cheshire

alone; another (Woodchurch) was known during the Anglo-Saxon period as Landican, a place-name which is wholly Welsh in origin and which incorporates *lann – 'church', in combination with a Welsh personal name (see the discussion in Dodgson 1966/67– , IV. pp. 266–7; Roberts 1992). However, curvilinear churchyards are present in all parts of England and need indicate neither British origins nor exceptional antiquity. Cheshire's examples seem to include both ancient and less ancient, medieval church sites, not all of which are likely even to predate the Norman Conquest.

Some church dedications could be comparatively early but none certainly predate the conversion of Mercia; of the eighteen churches which make up this sample, none is dedicated to a British saint and only three to English saints of the period 650–875. Some of even these are suspect; Warburton's association with St Werburgh is unlikely to predate the Norman Conquest (for that of Chester Abbey, see below, p. 105) and the remaining two (Farndon and Over) are to St Chad, fifth English bishop of Lichfield and a dedication common throughout the diocese, particularly on episcopal estates. Farndon's tenure by the bishop in 1066 is a matter of record, so the dedication could have been adopted at any date after *c*. 700. Of the remainder, six are to St Mary. These are perhaps the best candidates for a seventh-century date, since dedications to the Virgin Mary were widespread by 731 and included the first church at Lichfield (HE, IV, 3). Her monastery at Chester is documented in Domesday, but her popularity was rekindled in the Norman period and was never entirely lost, with post-medieval dedications continuing to appear (e.g. Poynton). Even so, the dual dedication to St Beuno and St Mary at Whitford (Clwyd) may imply that this dedication was popular in the region as a substitute for pre-existing Welsh dedications. Dedications to St Mary may, therefore, include early church sites but they are very far from being diagnostic and should barely even be considered a significant indicator of possible antiquity.

St Helen was the dedication at Tarporley, Witton and Neston (with St Mary) but there is no evidence that these allusions to Constantine's mother were of Roman or British origin. Nor is the isolated reference to St Alban at Tattenhall likely to be of early provenance. Other churches were dedicated to various apostles, none of whom were exclusively early in use, despite the role of St John at Chester. The otherwise unknown St Tegan enshrined in the place-name Landican is the only pre-English saint so far identified with any degree of certainty in a region which probably had several (perhaps even numerous) shrines and churches in the fifth and sixth centuries.

The concentration of curvilinear churchyards west of the Mid-Cheshire Ridge need not imply any greater commitment to Christianity there than elsewhere, nor a westward retreat of Welsh territory (as postulated by Dodgson 1966/67–), although it could reflect the more extensive Romanisation of this region as a focus of late Roman and sub-Roman administration. Throughout the Middle Ages, churches were to be more thickly clustered in precisely the same area, leaving much of southern, central and eastern Cheshire in very large parishes comprising numerous townships. The distribution may relate as much to social and economic factors, therefore, as to cultural ones.

Before the seventh century, Cheshire may, then, have been part of a comparatively large sub-Roman British kingdom within which Christianity had survived the collapse of Empire as the official religion. That its rulers paid tribute to English kings in the early seventh century is a matter of record. Gildas's comments on the tribute being paid by British congregations in his own day (DEB, I, 5–6) may imply that many British communities were already paying tribute to the Saxons a century or more earlier. He drew an analogy between the fate of the Britons and the Babylonian captivity of the Jews following Nebuchadrezzar's sack of Jerusalem, as lamented by the prophet Jeremiah, and elsewhere represented the majority of his countrymen as 'slaves not of Christ, who is God, but of the devil' (XXVI, 4). The latter was probably intended both literally (the Devil) and metaphorically, to be equated with the Saxons whom he had already asserted were 'hated by man and God' (XXIII, 1). Gildas's testimony is obviously very generalised and that of a distant observer (he arguably lived south of the Thames; Higham 1992d) but his is the fullest description now available of the spread of Saxon dominance across the British lowlands and as such carries some weight.

It is also consistent with an even earlier, but far briefer, reference, written by a chronicler in Gaul (Mommsen 1892), perhaps only shortly after the middle of the fifth century, who noted against the year 441 that 'The Britains [i.e. the British provinces] . . . have been handed over across a wide area . . . to the jurisdiction [or "rule"] of the Saxons'. The territory of the *Wrocen sǣte* was peripheral to areas where archaeology attests that Saxons established themselves, where Christianity was surely doomed. However, if this account is literally true and this 'wide area' encompassed the north-west Midlands, then the *Wrocen sǣte* were subordinated to Germanic rulers from *c.* 441 onwards. It may, in other words, have been a region of England that fell to the English by some diplomatic solution, as opposed to conquest (Lloyd 1939, p. 195; Finberg 1964). That unequal relationship may, perhaps, solve the conundrum posed by the material poverty of the region when compared with areas under more direct Anglo-Saxon control (see above, p. 68). It may also help explain why its rulers made so little use of the type of inscribed memorial stones through which the rulers of more independent British dynasties further west recalled their dead.

There are several indications that British kingships were still widespread in the Midlands at the start of the seventh century. One is the occurrence of those -sǣte names already referred to; they are particularly common along the western edge of England (e.g. Anderson 1934, p. xxvi; Gelling 1989, p. 200). They also occur elsewhere in England but only in areas characterised by a scarcity of pagan English burials before *c.* 600 (e.g. Rutherford Davis 1982). They may in general have been recognisably British rather later than some of their neighbours.

A second indication is the synod of the British church which was held at Chester *c.* 600. This meeting was occasioned by pressure exerted by Augustine of Canterbury on those British churchmen further south who were vulnerable to the influence of his patron, King Æthelberht of Kent, at the first Augustine's Oak Conference. The Britons responded by calling their own council to discuss Augustine's demands. This synod was noted in the *Annales Cambriae* against the year 601 (supposing that *Urbs Legionis* does refer to Chester), although it is not certain that this reference is independent of Bede. His account is the longest which survives (HE, II, 2) but it is undated, highly subjective and reflects his own anti-Welsh prejudices. It was apparently based solely on oral sources but what is relevant here is the choice of location.

At first sight Chester may seem to have been an unlikely venue, so its selection has important implications. We have already elaborated several hypotheses which may have a bearing on the synod. Chester was probably a site of high status but close to a major frontier, marginally inside the territory of the *Wrocen sæte* but near Powys across the Dee. The first Augustine's Oak Conference had then just occurred on the borders of the West Saxons and Hwicce. This location implies that a frontier location might offer significant advantages for a meeting of this kind. At Augustine's Oak the protecting 'overking' was King Æthelberht. At Chester it is tempting to imagine that it could have been the pagan Mercian king but the synod lay under the immediate protection of the rulers of the *Wrocen sæte* and adjacent to the authority of the British kings of Powys and Gwynedd.

Chester was an important Roman site, parts of which were arguably still standing *c.* 600 and capable of giving temporary shelter. There may still have been a settlement present (particularly given Bede's use of *civitas* for the site). There may also have been a sub-Roman cemetery church (perhaps St John's). Indeed, the synod almost requires the existence of an important church. If not there were probably several churches within an hour's ride and barely further away was the large monastery of Bangor Iscoed, the monks of which reputedly played a prominent role in the debate. The site was distant from King Æthelberht's territory and his influence. It was, however, a focal point on the Roman road system which still linked Christian and British clergy in the north of central England (such as Elmet) with Wales and western England. It was also a port in the sixth century.

Chester's attractions in this context were therefore considerable, both in terms of routes and political systems. Its use demanded that the rulers who were immediately responsible for its protection were Christian but behind them loomed the greater power of the pagan Mercian king – possibly King Cearl. The synod could be seen as a facet of a competition between two of the greatest kings of the day – the Mercian and Kentish 'overkings' of central and southern Britain, respectively. From the Mercian viewpoint, Augustine's claim to authority over all the British clergy represented an attack on their own political influence among the more numerous British and Christian kingships in central and western Britain. The siting of the synod reflects the interests of the kings of Wales and the Midlands in jointly resisting Æthelberht's expansionism. The subsequent rejection by the British clergy of Augustine's demands implies that they were assured of far more powerful political support before they attended the second conference that had been available to them at the first.

Such reasoning implies once more that Cheshire was characterised by its frontier location, just as it has been in the later Roman period. This view is reinforced by the political context of the Battle of Chester. This was one of only a handful of decisive engagements fought in the first half of the seventh century, but it is our misfortune that the only account of it which survives is the highly coloured version given in the *Historia Ecclesiastica* (II, 2). Bede presented this victory over Welsh forces and the butchering of British clergy by a pagan Bernician king as the fulfilment of the curse uttered by Augustine at the termination of his abortive second meeting with the British clergy. The relationship between these two events is entirely apocryphal and Bede perhaps even adapted his account of the battle to make it more appropriate to the context in which he deployed it (Higham, 1992b). To him it was a contest between Æthelfrith's pagan Anglians from the north (whom he invested with Old Testament analogies) and the 'treacherous' (or 'heretical') Welsh, yet several factors imply that Cearl's control of the Midlands collapsed at about the same time. Æthelfrith's aggression should probably be linked with Cearl's commitment to Edwin of Deira, an *ætheling* who had fled following Æthelfrith's usurpation of the Deiran kingship in Yorkshire and who had married Cearl's daughter (HE, II, 14), but whom Æthelfrith was determined to kill. Æthelfrith's campaign southwards via the Mersey crossings and Chester may imply that his strategy was to interpose himself between Welsh and Mercian forces and destroy them separately before they could unite against him, as they were later to do against his son Oswiu (HE, III, 24).

The death-toll was probably high, although only British casualties are named. Bede referred to one Brocmail as the protector of the Bangor monks. That the name occurs on Eliseg's pillar in an eighth century context is consistent with his inclusion in a later genealogy of the Powys dynasty (Bartrum 1966, p. 14), as the grandfather of Selyf son of Cynan whose death was registered in the notice of the battle entered in the *Annales Cambriae*. King Iago of Gwynedd, Cædwallon's grandfather, was also reputed to have died in this year and he may have been another casualty. Other names occur in later Welsh literature (Bromwich 1961, pp. 321–2, 436, 507). Some might even refer to leaders of the *Wrocen sæte* but none need be historical.

After this campaign, Æthelfrith's 'overkingship' may briefly have encompassed the Midlands (as hinted at by Kirby 1991; Higham 1992b). It was destroyed by Rædwald of the East Angles (HE, II, 12) who apparently replaced him in his northern and central kingships with that same Edwin, his own protégé, who later defeated the West Saxons and attained universal 'overking-ship' in England and Wales (*c.* 626–33; HE, II, 5, 9). The old alliance between Mercia and the Welsh kings was restored by Penda, who defeated and killed his rival, Oswald of Bernicia, in 642 at *Maserfelth* (HE, III, 9), otherwise known as *Cocboy* (*Annales Cambriae*) or *Maes Cogwy* ('Field of Cogwy', Welsh poetry) – possibly Wigan (? Roman *Coccium*) in Makerfield, on the north side of the Mersey frontier (Kenyon 1991, p. 77). When the Bernician, Oswiu, in turn defeated and killed Penda, he took the opportunity to ravage Mercia's Welsh allies (*Annales Cambriae* 1980, 658), so confirming the importance to the Mercian kings of Welsh support.

If these armies regularly used the Roman road system, most passed through Cheshire. The geography of this region, set against the power politics of the day, meant that it was particularly vulnerable over a long period to hostile armies marching against enemies whose core territories lay some distance away.

It is far from clear when the separate (but tributary) kingship of the *Wrocen sæte* was finally suppressed and its people incorporated into Mercia. The complete absence of pagan burials may imply that this change occurred not long (if at all), before Mercia's rulers espoused Christianity in 655. A later reference in Welsh literature to a retaliatory raid following Penda's encroachment on British Powys mentions a bishop and monks at *Caer Lwytgoed* (Bromwich 1961, pp. 321–2), which should probably be identified as *Letocetum* – Wall (Staffordshire). If this has any historical reality (and it may not), it implies that even eastern

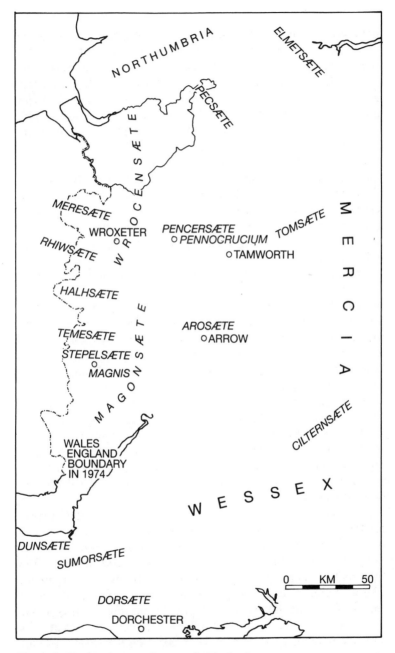

Fig. 3.6 Regional names in **-sæte** in England

Staffordshire still contained Christians and a diocesan clergy as late as 642–55. This area was the territory of two Mercian sub-groups, the *Pencer sæte* and *Tomsæte*, in the ninth century (Hooke 1983). The *Pencer sæte* should be associated with Penkridge, hence the river Penk, and *Pennocrucium* (Water Eaton; Rivet and Smith 1979, pp. 436–7). The name *Tomsæte* is cognate with the river Tame and the first element of the Mercian palace site of Tamworth (Fig. 3.6). The pagan cemeteries which seem to denote the English core of Mercia do not spread south of the upper Trent and so stop short of these territories, though not of Breedon-on-the-Hill (Leicestershire), which was later to be described as 'of the *Tomsæte*'. Both these minor peoples or kingships may, therefore, have constituted part of the *Wrocen sæte* in the early seventh century for the purposes of tribute payment.

The subsequent transfer of the first element of *Letocetum* to the new, Mercian bishopric at Lichfield (*Letocetum – feld*) may suggest that the Mercian kings took advantage of the existing estates of a well-endowed British church in this same locality to establish their own religious centre at minimal expense. Parallels between this place-name, Hatfield, Sheffield, *Maes Cogwy*, Makerfield and *Campodonum* ('Field – Doncaster') imply that it was already a significant focus. Lichfield was hardly a convenient centre *de novo* for a diocese which initially extended not only to Mercia but also to Lindsey and Middle Anglia, suggesting that some pre-existing factor influenced the choice of site. Even after subdivision of the Mercian diocese, the north-west Midlands remained in the jurisdiction of Lichfield and this church was increasingly associated with the north-west Midlands as the Saxon period wore on.

Christianity may, therefore, have survived in this region throughout, in which case British government of the *Wrocen sæte* presumably persisted until the last decade or so of Penda's life. It may be relevant that Bede's account of the conversion of the English had nothing to say concerning missions to this people, whom he never mentions, nor their neighbours along the Marches. His *Historia* referred elsewhere to British bishops in areas under the ultimate protection of English kings (HE, III, 28), albeit ones who were nominally Christian. He recognised the Hwicce as part of the English church by *c.* 680 (HE, IV, 13) but, in contrast to the clearly Anglo-Saxon kingships of southern and eastern England, had nothing to say concerning their conversion from paganism. It seems likely that his comments concerning the correction of Britons subject to the West Saxons by Roman clerics in the late seventh century (HE, V, 18) would have been as relevant in the Marches (Bassett 1992). Beyond, the Britons in Wales (HE, V, 22) and the south-western *Dumnonia* (Aldhelm 1884) still adhered in 731 to the British tonsure and dating of Easter (the Welsh finally adopting the Roman dating of Easter in 768).

The demise of several neighbouring kingships is better understood: British rule in Elmet was suppressed by Edwin of Deira (616–33), who also took over Lindsey and Hatfield, although the ruling dynasty of Lindsey survived for a while longer. Rich pagan burials of exclusively late date in various of the Prehistoric *tumuli* of the Derbyshire Peak suggest that that area had an aristocracy with pagan Anglo-Saxon tastes and aspirations under Penda (Ozanne 1962–63). The arrival of southern English metalwork there suggests that they were well-rewarded followers of a powerful leader. It may be the proximity of this territory to Northumbrian-controlled Elmet that led Penda to take control of it rather earlier than the *Wrocen sæte*. There is, however, little evidence that the cultural preferences of the warrior elite in the Peak had time to disseminate very widely among the local community before paganism was abandoned. The *Magonsæte* (of Herefordshire) were apparently ruled c. 650 by one Merewalh ('illustrious Welshman'; see Finberg 1964; Pretty 1989), whom later and far from disinterested writers related to the large body of saints spawned by the Mercian royal family. His reign may more realistically be viewed as the interface between British kingship and the transfer of this territory from Powys to the Mercian hegemony, again under Penda. The various small kingships of the south-east Midlands were amalgamated under Penda to create the Middle Angles for his son, Peada, by the early 650s.

The minor kingdoms around Mercia do, therefore, seem to have become provinces of more powerful neighbours during the period c. 616–50. On the evidence available, the *Wrocen sæte* were probably among the last to receive this treatment, but only excavation at Atcham is likely to shed further light on the date. In only one instance is a putatively British kingdom listed in the Tribal Hidage known to have resisted this process – the *Westerne* being the only exception. This brought to an end a period during which many local communities had paid a high price for the commitment of their leaders to a religion and culture different from that of their ultimate protectors. The capacity of tributary kings to protect their own people was severely inhibited by 'over-kingship' and their powers of patronage undermined by tribute payments. Where local aristocracies had no expectation that their own dynasties would achieve supremacy – so enriching them by an inflow of tribute at the expense of their neighbours, incorporation into the more central parts of the patronage system of a successful king offered tangible advantages.

Those aristocracies may have been inclined to adopt some aspects of English culture even before the final demise of local kingship. The only basis for discussion of this process is the formation of place-names. In Cheshire, place-names of Old English origin are dominant. Despite its propinquity to Wales, pre-English place-names are barely more numerous as a proportion of the whole than in any other part of England.

The retention of pre-English names has been greatest among river names but that again is characteristic of much of England. On the basis of the prevalence of pre-English survivals nationally, the late Professor Kenneth Hurlstone Jackson (1953, p. 220) proposed an oft-reproduced, fourfold division of southern Britain, but his interpretation of this map in the context of an east–west push by Germanic settlers over several centuries can no longer be accepted uncritically (Higham 1992a). The divisions were, in any case, highly subjective and based on a data-base too small for statistical analysis.

The most recent survey of pre-English and related place-names in this region (Gelling 1989, p. 197) reveals just how flimsy this evidence is (Fig. 3.7). Place-names in neither *walh-* nor *cumbra-* need be relevant (Sims-Williams 1990, p. 24), since both may contain nothing more significant than personal names of Old English usage (e.g. Walton, Wallasey; Comberbach, Combermere – all of which are Old English compounds). The second most common group of pre-English place-names nationally are topographical and there are several examples in Cheshire: Werneth ('Alder Swamp'); Minn ('Mountain'); several minor names containing Primitive Welsh, **bryn** or **penn** ('hill') and the problematic district name, Lyme (see below). Otherwise there are three Crewe

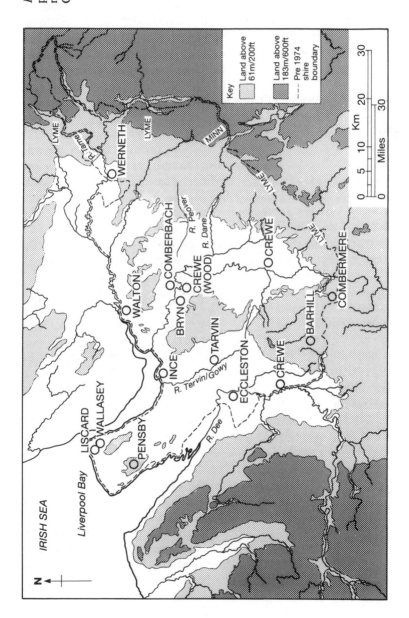

Fig. 3.7 Possible
pre-English place-
names in
Cheshire

place-names ('fish-trap' or 'weir'), the element **bar-** in Barhill, Tarvin – a backformation from a now disused name for the river Gowy, Ince ('The Island') and the Old English compound, Eccleston. Cheadle contains the Old Welsh ***ced** – 'wood' to which Old English **leah** – 'wood' or 'clearing' has been added, suggesting that the pre – English element was not understood when the compound was created, despite the consistency of the landscape to which it referred. Only two Old Welsh compound names survive, Liscard (***lisso-carreg**; 'Hall at the rock') and Macefen ('Boundary field') but neither was of manorial status in 1086. Indeed, only three of these names were. Pre-English names are generally characterised by their lowly status and peripheral distribution in the later Anglo-Saxon period, both as regards topography and estate structure. Among names known to have fallen into disuse during the Middle Ages, Landican is the only certain compound name formed in Old Welsh.

For a border shire from which Welsh – speakers were never far distant, this is an unimpressive collection. It is not a particularly satisfactory data-base on which to postulate an 'English Settlement' stemming from the east and pressing towards the west (but cf. Dodgson 1966/67–). Dodgson's interpretation was put forward at a date when place-name evidence was almost universally explained in migrationist terms. As Margaret Gelling recently remarked (1989, p. 197), the success of the English language is likely to have here been 'due not to the numerical superiority of English farmers' but 'to the social and administrative superiority of a relatively modest number of Mercians'. Behind them stood the Mercian kingship which, during the seventh century, became an increasingly pressing, yet also an increasingly attractive, source of patronage in the region and to whose service the local aristocracy presumably sought access. Acculturation was a necessary first step in this process (Higham 1992a) and this presumably occurred first at the political focus of the *Wrocen sǣte*, thence disseminating outwards via existing social contacts and hierarchies. That the erstwhile British *Wrocen sǣte*, eventually adopted Anglo-Saxon culture (including language and thence place-names) from self-interest is at least as plausible as arguments which rely on large but otherwise unevidenced English immigration. Those pre-English place-names which survived probably did so for reasons which were idiosyncratic. Within

Cheshire, anglicisation probably spread from the political focus of the region, in the Dee valley, towards the periphery, and so in the reverse of the direction so often postulated.

Ethnocentric explanations of language replacement have a long history, beginning, by implication at least, with Bede. William Camden (1586) offered in an early but extreme form the same thinking as many later writers (such as Smith and Webb 1656; Ingham 1920, p. 13; Dodgson 1967) have brought to their interpretations of the Dark Ages in the western Midlands:

> the English-Saxon conquerors, altred the tongue which they found here wholy: so that no British words, or provinciall Latine appeared therin at the first: & in short time they spread it over this whole Iland, from the Orcades to Isle of Wight, except a few baren corners in the Westerne parts, whereunto the reliques of the Britans and Scots retyred, reserving in them both their life and language.

The scatter of pre-English place-names in Cheshire is sufficient to disprove such catastrophe theories of population replacement and demonstrate a degree of contact between language groups, but rarely more. Most place-names have very little to tell us about the creation of England. One pre-English name does, however, apply to an extensive district. This is Lyme (otherwise Lime, Lyne), which occurs in, or as a suffix attached to, numerous place-names stretching from Ashton-under-Lyne (Lancashire) on the river Tame to Market Drayton (Shropshire. See Figs. 3.2, 3.7, 4.5). Its common association with terms indicative of forest or woodland suggests that this was a heavily wooded area and the derivation may be from British **lemo-**, 'elm' (Dodgson 1967–   , I, pp. 3–6). What may be the earliest surviving reference is in the Irish Annals of Clocmacnoise, describing the *Brunanburh* campaign of 937, where the battle was said to have occurred 'on the plaines of othlynn' (Campbell 1938). If 'oth' is Old English *oð* ('up to'), this is a reference to the Cheshire plain 'within the Lyme'.

As Dodgson noted, 'Lyme' is associated with the steep western edge of the southern Pennines and the hills which continue that line and constitute the borders of Cheshire, northern Shropshire and Staffordshire. Given its pre-English nomenclature, its international currency and its linear, but extensive, distribution, it seems reasonable to suggest that the role of the Lyme as a boundary zone was already ancient by the tenth century. If so, then it may offer the means to define the eastern periphery of the northernmost core territory of the *Wrocen sǽte* versus the *Pecsǽte*, *Pencer sǽte* and *Tomsǽte*, and perhaps even of the Cornovii before them.

More localised place-names only emerge as of use to the historian in the Anglo-Saxon period, when they offer tentative lines of enquiry into the structure of estates and local land use. Before moving on to that subject, however, it may be appropriate to refer very briefly to a number of misleading myths concerning Cheshire in the British period. Some of these are of considerable antiquity but none are of any independent historical value.

It has become common practice to postulate that the 'Halleluia Victory', reputed to have been won by St Germanus, may have occurred in the region (e.g. McPeake 1978b; Laing and Laing, undated). If it ever occurred (and it should be remembered that this is a miracle story incorporated within a work of hagiography written at a distance both in space and time from the events it purports to describe) then it should be placed somewhere in south-east England (Thompson 1984). The removal of St Germanus to Wales is a purely literary device which post-dates the creation of England and is known to us from no source earlier than the *Historia Brittonum*, a Gwynedd-centric work which has no independent historical value for the fifth century. The ascription of a battle at *urbs legionis* to Arthur has the same derivation and is no more historical. Nor has the historical 'proud tyrant' (probably Vortigern) of Gildas (DEB, XXIII, 1) any real link with the Welsh dynasty of Powys (as e.g. Hooke 1983, p. 10). The propagandist purposes of the *Historia Brittonum* are once more to blame, since it served the interests of the Gwyneth dynasty to paint their eastern neighbours as descendants of the villainous British anti-hero who brought in the Saxons. The victory of a 'Roman Captayne', Gormundus, over the Saxons is recorded no earlier than the Diary of John Dee, dated 1574 (Harleian MS, 473) and is no more historical than the claim by Henry Bradshaw, a monk of Chester Abbey (*c.* 1500), that his house had been founded in the time of Lucius (a king ascribed to Roman Britain by Bede (HE, I, 4) and before King Arthur (see discussion in Tait 1920, p. xiv). Bradshaw followed Ralph Higden (*c.* 1350; Taylor 1966, p. 62) in speculating on the origins of Chester itself (Hawkins 1848, p. 148):

> The founder of Chestre, as sayth Polichronicon
> Was Lleon Gauer, a myghty stronge gyaunt
> Which buylded caves, and dongions many one
> No goodly buyldyng, propre ne pleasaunt
>
> But the Kynge Leil, a Briton sure and valiaunt
> Was founder of Chestre, by pleasaunt buyldyng
> And of Caerleil, also named by the kynge.

Both suggestions are clumsy attempts to write history on the basis of the place-name recorded by Bede (*Legacæstir*) and an awareness of ruinous masonry in the city.

There have been recent suggestions that the Chester area be a possible location for Gildas (Thompson 1979, followed by Thacker 1982), admittedly on rather more scholarly reasoning than lies behind the antiquarian association of Pelagius with Bangor Iscoed (e.g. Camden 1610, p. 602), but neither stands up to critical analysis (for the former, see Higham 1992d).

Such speculative links between Cheshire and prominent Dark Age figures – be they fictional or historical – must, regretfully, be set aside. Cheshire's history throughout the period is characterised by its very anonymity. Yet it was a vital period in the region's development, albeit one during which it is possible to do little more than hypothesise concerning the political and cultural conditions under which local men and women lived their lives and the boundaries by which local kingships were constrained.

4

Politics and the shire

The Mercian take-over

Despite the obscurity of Mercia's western frontier in the seventh
century, it does seem clear that King Penda caused his Welsh
allies or tributaries such offence that they deliberately betrayed
him to his death at Northumbrian hands in 655 (HE, III, 24; HB,
LXIV, LXV). If this rift had been caused by Mercian territorial
aggrandisement, then this was probably at the expense of Powys,
from Herefordshire to Deeside. His victories in the 640s over
Oswald of Bernicia and Cenwealh of the West Saxons much
reduced Penda's dependence on Welsh support and he may thereafter have felt less constrained to respect British territory. This
would seem to be the period during which he reorganised many
of his tributaries, such as the various small Middle Anglian
peoples whom he marshalled into a single large dependency ruled
by his own son. In the process he presumably dispossessed many
erstwhile royal dynasties, although some may have survived as
ealdormen, as seems possible among the southern Gyrwe (HE,
IV, 19).

If the rulers of the *Wrocen sæte* were the victims of similar
treatment, Penda arguably found along the borders of their lands
a chaotic interlocking of territories with Powys which he may
well have decided to 'rationalise' at the latter's expense. Further
south, Penda probably exploited his victory over the West Saxons
to establish his own control of the Hwicce (who had been part of

the southern English *imperium* in the 620s) and to seize control of parts of southern Powys, where he perhaps inaugurated the short-lived and dependent kingdom of the *Magonsǣte*. This westward expansion was ultimately at the expense of the ancient 'overkingship' of Gwynedd (Higham 1992c). It may have occasioned the Welsh raid into the West Midlands referred to in the Cynddylan Cycle (p. 88). It surely led Cadafael ap Cynfedw of Gwynedd to desert Penda on the eve of the battle of *Winwǣd*, in 655.

It has already been suggested that direct Mercian rule of the *Wrocen sǣte* began not long before the Mercian conversion (post 655), so a date after 642 would seem reasonable. The immediate reason may have been instability on the northern Welsh frontier occasioned by Penda's territorial expansion further south. Once their long alliance with the Welsh kings was in question, the Mercians could no longer afford the luxury of tributary British kings among the *Wrocen sǣte*.

This border was eventually stabilised by the construction of massive earthworks, each comprising a ditch and bank, known as dykes. There are two near parallel dykes north of the Severn, Offa's Dyke, which culminates in the vicinity of Mold, and Wat's Dyke which reaches the Dee estuary at Basingwerk, near Flint (Fox 1955; Hill 1977, 1981, p. 75; Fig. 4.1). That the Wat's Dyke was not continued south of the Severn implies that it was constructed in response to a political and military context which was specific to the northern Marches. Although there has been some dispute, it is generally agreed that Wat's predates Offa's Dyke and it is both the better built and better sited of the two (Worthington 1986 and pers. comm.). The persistent association of the latter with King Offa (757–96) and Asser's later attribution of a dyke to him (Keynes and Lapidge 1986, p. 71) confirm that it should be dated to the second half of the eighth century. Wat's Dyke could be dated to the earlier eighth century (e.g. Varley 1936) but it could equally be as early as the mid- to late seventh century. Excavation has demonstrated its post-Roman date but has not otherwise established its provenance. That it belongs to the period of Mercian retrenchment and stabilisation after a rupture with the Welsh and the disaster of *Winwaed* (655) finds some support in the late medieval claim that King Ethelred (675–704) founded St John's at Chester early in his reign. If that

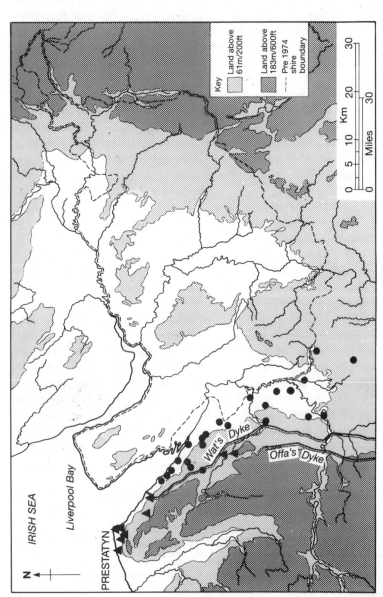

Fig. 4.1 The Mercian dykes and the limits of hidation in western Cheshire

Key

Land above 61m/200ft

Land above 183m/600ft

Pre 1974 shire boundary

IRISH SEA

Liverpool Bay

PRESTATYN

Wat's Dyke

Offa's Dyke

N

were true, it at least provides a terminal date for direct Mercian control of the Dee valley, but it need not be historical. Oswiu of Northumbria was reputed to have raided Wales (*Annales Cambriae*, 658) but his motive may derive from the role of the Welsh kings in his discomfiture in the 'Distribution of Iudeu' (HB, LXV). It seems unlikely that the dyke was his idea, yet its termination on the Severn could be equated with his direct rule specifically of the northern Mercians. There is one even earlier option; Penda apparently dealt with southern Powys by establishing a client kingdom there (the *Magonsǣte*), but he seems to have been the first Mercian king to take personal responsibility for the northern Marches. After 642, he arguably had both the authority and the resources to build a dyke from the Severn to the sea and may have seen fit to do so, in which case Wat's Dyke was his initiative.

Whatever its precise date, the Wat's Dyke provides a formal boundary to north-west Mercia, the importance of which lasted to the Norman Conquest. It was to be the western limit of hidation and geld payment in 1066 (Fig. 4.1), which reached as far as Bagillt and Eyton. It was necessarily, therefore, already built and active as a frontier when Cheshire was hidated. Hides were the standard method in early England of assessing the renders due from an estate, based on the goods necessary to support a household of free status (probably in origin that of a *ceorl*: Higham 1992a, p. 144). By the seventh century, the hide was the normal unit for determining the value of estates granted to the Church and was to remain so in western Mercia into the ninth century and beyond (e.g. Birch 1885–87, No. 462). The territory of the *Wrocen sǣte* was probably hidated shortly after it was taken under direct Mercian rule. When that occurred, Wat's Dyke had already been constructed and was functioning as a frontier. Wat's identity is a mystery but the absence of this personal name from local place-names may imply that he lived at an early date.

If the territorial structure of British Cheshire was taken over little changed by the Mercian kings (Thacker 1987, p. 268 and see below, pp. 178–81), then the renders which had been paid to the central courts of local territories presumably now approximated to standard English units. That some sort of parallel existed seems clear from Bede's use of 'the land of a family' (i.e., the hide) in assessing the renders supporting the British kings of Anglesey and Man (HE, II, 9). This change was probably, therefore, more one of nomenclature than substance. Hides replaced the sort of renders recorded in the Domesday Book for unhidated Bistre, where King Gruffydd had been in receipt of 200 loaves, a barrel of beer and a firkin of butter for each plough in use whenever he should be present (DB, 269b). Renders in kind were still commonplace in Shropshire at Domesday.

Mercian Cheshire

The minting of silver coins in Mercia on a vast scale during the eighth century implies that royal finances were then shifting towards a cash economy, perhaps with taxation in coin. This development appears to have made little, if any, impact on Cheshire. The bulk (perhaps all) of the Mercian coinage was minted at London, the principal Mercian *emporium* (commercial centre). The absence to date of this *sceatta* coinage from Chester must count against the site functioning as a Mercian port of any consequence. The obvious contrast is with York, where stray finds of pre-Viking Northumbrian coinage long preceded the archaeological identification of an Anglian *wic* or port at Fishergate.

Two early eighth-century coins and various other artifacts found at Meols imply that it was that site which monopolised Mercia's slight contact with the sea-borne trade of the Irish Sea (Hume 1863; Bu'lock 1960; Thacker 1987, p. 289). The complete absence of Mercian coinage elsewhere in the north-west Midlands suggests that the region continued to contribute to royal revenues more through renders in kind than coin (see Hill 1981, p. 123), in which case what local trading occurred was almost certainly conducted by barter.

As in earlier periods, therefore, Mercian Cheshire displays symptoms of having been an economic backwater, answerable ultimately to a secular and episcopal hierarchy which was normally resident outside it. The apparent resilience of its early organisation and territorial structure (see Chapters 5 and 6) suggests that it changed comparatively little during the eighth and ninth centuries. It may also imply that the Mercian crown long retained a proprietorial interest in many of its estates, particularly in the western half of the medieval shire.

The recurring volatility of the Welsh March certainly gave the Mercian kings good cause to secure resources in the region which could be used to man and supply forces on campaign. The early ninth-century 'Pillar of Eliseg' refers to Welsh successes against Mercia in the preceding century (Nash-Williams 1950, pp. 123–5). The *Annales Cambriae* recalled a battle between the Britons and Saxons at Hereford in 760 and it may be following this that Offa ordered his dyke to be constructed. If so it did not solve his problems for long. He devastated southern Wales in 778 and wasted British territory again in the summer of 784. Indeed, each of the five entries in the *Annales Cambriae* between 778 and 798 (inclusive) detailed conflict with the Mercians. Where any details are given, fighting occurred beyond the dykes. Mercian expansionism lapsed temporarily after Offa's death and the subsequent succession crisis in Mercia but the same annals record Mercian penetration of Snowdonia in 816 and the destruction of Degannwy and loss of Powys to the English in 822. That Gwynedd was experiencing its own long-drawn-out succession crisis at this time is probably relevant and there are signs that the Mercians intervened in this struggle to their own advantage.

Royal tenure of territory in the Dee valley was perhaps as necessary to these conflicts as Edward I's hold on Chester would be to his own attacks on Wales, more than four centuries later. Such factors may help to explain the apparent strength of royal landholding in western Cheshire, in comparison with areas east of the Mid-Cheshire Ridge and river Weaver. Earl Edwin's estates in 1066 probably derive in large measure from the estates of the Mercian crown before the Viking Age. If so, they bear silent testimony to royal determination to provide men, resources and accommodation along Watling Street (Fig. 6.1).

Triumph over northern Powys in Clwyd came too late for Wales beyond Wat's Dyke to be incorporated permanently into Mercia's north-western province. A prolonged succession crisis during the 820s enabled Mercia's southern neighbours to challenge for supremacy and Egberht of the West Saxons briefly established his own control of Mercia in 829 (ASC(A)) – a deed which encouraged later West Saxon annalists to append his name to the list of *imperium*-wielding kings which Bede had constructed so as to lend credibility to the lacklustre Æthelberht of Kent (HE, II, 5). Mercian kingship was restored in 830 but it would never again be the dominant force in Britain that it had been under Offa and Coenwulf. Although later Mercian kings retained a degree of political supremacy over northern and central Wales, there were no further attempts at total conquest and western Powys probably slipped once more from English control.

Cheshire and the Vikings

By the 850s the region was under threat from a new direction. Ireland had experienced Norse raids since the last years of the eighth century and Gwynedd suffered major attacks *c.* 850 and 853. Our knowledge of Viking raids in England is largely dependent on the Anglo-Saxon Chronicle, the West Saxon weighting of which leaves attacks elsewhere largely unrecorded, but Mercia seems most unlikely to have escaped attack. London was sacked in 851, although the Vikings then turned south into Surrey. Among the few Mercian charters which survive is one of 851 granting assets to Croyland Abbey referring to 'the violence of the Pagans (Birch 1885–87, No. 461) and a second of 855 which recalled a grant at *Oswaldesdun* 'when the pagans were in *Wreocensetun*' (*Ibid.*, No. 487). Although this is generally taken to relate specifically to the vicinity of the Wrekin, the arguments rehearsed above (pp. 68–77) imply that this could refer to any or every part of central or eastern Shropshire, Cheshire and west-central Staffordshire.

The region was not, therefore, immune from Scandinavian raids. If some of these were launched against Mercia from the Irish Sea, Cheshire was necessarily the first area to experience any attack and it may have suffered severely in consequence. In 893, Chester was described by a contemporary chronicler as deserted (ASC(A)). It may only recently have fallen into ruin. Among the richer but less adaptable victims of the Vikings may have been the clerical communities staffing the two putative minsters at Chester itself and the minster at Sandbach, along with any other Church communities which were easy of access from the estuaries or via the road system.

The major dynasties did what they could to oppose the Vikings and *détente* between Mercia and Wessex may have stemmed from their need to work together. King Burgred of Mercia married Æthelswith of Wessex (daughter of King Æthelwulf, and so sister to Alfred) in 853 and Alfred married Ealhswith, an obscure Mercian princess, in 868, but even concerted action in that year was insufficient to contain the Danish army which arrived in 866. This was the *micel here*, often known today as the 'Great Danish Army'. It crushed Northumbria's kings in 867 and withstood a joint Mercian and West Saxon investment of its headquarters at Nottingham the winter following. In 870 East Anglia was conquered. In 872 the Danes overwintered in London, then in 873 in Torksey (Lindsey). On both occasions King Burgred made peace. The following summer the host marched on the core of Mercian power and occupied Repton, driving Burgred into exile (ultimately to Rome) and appointing a rival Mercian prince, Ceolwulf, as client-king of Mercia. In 877 the Danes returned and 'shared out' some of the kingdom, leaving the remainder in the hands of Ceolwulf.

Although the Anglo-Saxon Chronicle made no attempt to distinguish the new Danish territories, they presumably included the core of English Mercia which would, in the tenth century, become the Mercian Danelaw or the Five Boroughs (for illustrations, see Hill 1981, pp. 60, 98). Derby, and the territories dependent on it, was the most westerly of these and probably marks the periphery of Danish land seizures in 877, excluding only temporary and ultimately unsuccessful attempts to settle at Gloucester which were noted by Ealdorman Æthelweard (Campbell 1962, p. 42). It was probably the intention of the Danish leadership that the western periphery of Mercia should be ruled on their behalf by Ceolwulf. If later medieval chroniclers are to be believed, it was during the 870s that St Werburgh's remains were removed from Hanbury (Staffordshire) to Chester, the walls of which may have been considered a safer haven, more remote from the Danish settlement.

Cheshire, therefore, falls within the English rump of the old kingdom. Re-emphasis on the ancient boundary between Cheshire and the Peak at this stage implies that the division of Mercia was far from arbitrary, being undertaken along such pre-existing boundaries as were appropriate. Danish dispositions were challenged by Alfred of Wessex, whose connections with the dispossessed branch of the Mercian royal family offered a lifeline to those Mercian leaders who were less complacent towards the Danish hegemony. By 886, when he granted London to his Mercian allies, Alfred had established an alternative Mercian leadership under his own son-in-law, Ethelred, Æthelflæd's husband. Their regime was probably *a priori* based on Gloucester, which they seem to have rebuilt as a planned town, but it eventually exercised authority as far north as Chester. Although West Saxon chroniclers consistently withheld the title from him, there can be little doubt that Ealdorman Ethelred was perceived by his own people, as much as by his Celtic neighbours, as king of the Mercians. It was in this capacity that he was campaigning on the Conway against Gwynedd *c.* 880, where he presumably sought to restore Mercian 'overkingship' and perhaps even control of Powys.

By the 890s, a mint was operating in the north-west of Mercia. It has been suggested that this was in Chester (Dolley 1955), although there are several alternative candidates which might be preferred, given Chester's decayed condition in 893. Even so, archaeology has revealed signs of new activity at Chester during the later years of the ninth century. On Lower Bridge Street, the Dark Age ploughing which has already been referred to was superseded by roasting-pits and a small oven or kiln, then, late in the century, by a sub-rectangular timber building associated with a 'sunken featured building' (Mason 1985b). Comparison of this occupation with Coppergate and other excavations at York implies that this represents the beginnings of a more urban occupation of the site. These deposits presage more widespread activity during the next century.

In 893 the backwater of north-west Mercia was caught up in the general contest between English and Danes. A large Viking force concentrated in Essex in that autumn. Reinforced from East Anglia and Northumbria, it raided deep into English Mercia as far as the Severn but was besieged and then defeated at Buttington. Retreating to Shoeburyness, the host raised fresh reinforcements from the same quarters and made a rapid sortie into English territory which brought it to Chester. The Viking force was pursued by a Mercian and Welsh army led by several ealdormen and thegns, headed by Ethelred, but reached the Roman walled enclave before it could be overtaken. If this objective was deliberate (Higham 1988a), then it may have intended to detach this narrow northern corridor from Mercian territory and carve out a new Viking lordship based, like most others, on a pre-existing fortification. If so, the tactic failed. Some of the raiders were caught outside and killed and the English drove off the cattle and destroyed the corn 'in all the surrounding districts'. In the aftermath, the Danes withdrew into Wales, starved out of the Dee valley. When they returned to Viking territory, they did so via Danish Northumbria, and so probably crossing the Mersey at Runcorn or Warrington, for fear of the Mercian army. Neither side forgot these crossings thereafter.

With this raid contained, West Saxon sources lapse back into silence concerning northern Mercia until 907, when the only event recorded was the restoration of Chester. English interest in this remote corner of Mercia was rekindled by events in Ireland. The Annals of Ulster (Hennessy 1887) recorded against the year 901 the 'Expulsion of the Gentiles from Ireland, from the fortress of Ath-cliath [Dublin], . . . where they left a great number of their ships, and escaped half-dead, after having been wounded and broken.' The precise date of this event is debated but the Norse were expelled from Ireland in the early years of the tenth century and sought new bases across the Irish Sea. They fled in several groups, among which the largest probably sailed direct to Northumbria, but the best documented was led by Ingmund, who attacked Anglesey (*Annales Cambriae* 1980, 902), then, having been repelled there, sought an accommodation with Ethelred and Æthelflæd (Wainwright 1975, pp. 81–7, 131–61; Radner 1978).

That they granted him lands on which to settle may suggest that Viking damage in 893 had caused significant dislocation in the area. The place-name Thingwall, which derives from a Scandinavian 'Thing' or moot, implies that he was free to organise the north-west corner of the Wirral peninsula in a fashion comparable with Man or Iceland.

Scandinavian place-names are not numerous among Cheshire's townships and most are concentrated on Wirral. There are only a handful of pure Scandinavian names of township or parochial status, several of which are topographical (such as Meols – 'Sandbank'). A minority are settlement-names with the suffix -**býr** (Raby, Frankby, Kirkby) of a type common to the Danelaw and Man. Gaelic also occurs in Arrow (**aerge**) and Noctorum and Irby reflect an Irish presence of some sort. More numerous are place-names which compound elements drawn from more than one language such as Pensby (Old Welsh **Pen** with -býr) or 'Grimston-hybrid'-style names (such as Thurstaston) which would be at home in Yorkshire.

That Scandinavian was still spoken in the region long after the Norman Conquest helps to explain this *mélange* of linguistic influences and the widespread minor- and field-names of Scandinavian origin in the area. Early attempts to treat the entire group as proof of Ingmund's settlement (Dodgson 1957) have been severely criticised and far more complex interpretations proposed, centring on migration from the Isle of Man (Fellows-Jensen 1983, 1985, 1992), but it seems likely that it was a combination of Ingmund's lordship and maritime contacts via Meols that began the process of Scandinavianisation.

Excepting only Helsby, near Frodsham, the Viking-type names occur in the north-western quarter of the Wirral peninsula. The place-names Raby and Hargrave at the south-eastern extremity of this grouping contain elements which refer to boundaries and it is possible that both mirror the nearby limits of Bromborough's minster parish, and so the core of what was then perhaps a royal estate based on Eastham. Ingmund's territory was therefore perhaps only about a quarter of the *Wilaveston* Hundred of Domesday Book (Fig. 4.2), focused on the extensive parishes of Woodchurch and West Kirby, where a church dedicated to St Bridget was in existence by 1081 (Thacker 1987, p. 256). This part of the peninsula had the greatest exposure to high winds and was poorly drained. It may well have been land of comparatively poor quality in the tenth century and it was probably over-shadowed by a major royal estate focused on a fortified court (at either Eastham or Bromborough) only a short distance away.

Ingmund was apparently dissatisfied with his subordinate position and limited territory which lacked a fortified centre. The 'Three Fragments' details his assembly of a force of Norse, Danes and Irish (his own following probably augmented from south-western Northumbria) and his attempt to storm Chester. It may have been in expectation of this confrontation that Ethelred refurbished the ruined city, which held out against the Vikings despite the sickness which delayed his arrival. Ethelred died in 911, according to the Irish annalist, of the same disease which already afflicted him in 907. Whither Ingmund's force retired

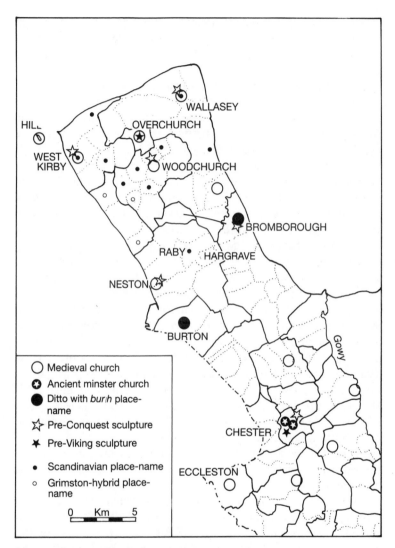

Fig. 4.2 The organisation of early Wirral

is unrecorded but the grouping of another Thingwall, several place-names indicative of Gaelic-inflenced Norse, and Danish **býr** names may imply that they were established under the oversight of the Danish kings of York in south-west Lancashire (Higham

1992c). The polyglot origins and cultural sympathies of this group of soldiers underline the difficulties of making deductions concerning the settlement of different groups on the basis of place-name evidence alone.

The Irish Norse are not known to have further troubled Mercia. It was the kings at York who would be the principal adversaries of Ethelred and his wife over the next few years. The river Mersey was the sole frontier between territories controlled by the English and the Northumbrian Danes. Fords on this river, therefore, probably saw the passage of a large English army in 909, which ravaged for five weeks in the territory of the 'Northern Army'. Two pieces of evidence imply that the eastern flank of this campaign was protected by a diplomatic accord between Ethelred and the Danish areas of northern Mercia: the 'C' version of the Anglo-Saxon Chronicle for the same year recorded the removal of the relics of St Oswald from Bardney (Lincolnshire) to English Mercia in terms which imply diplomacy rather than force, with Danish rulers conceding English objectives; additionally there is evidence of English land purchases in Derbyshire in 906–10. Ethelred had apparently also secured his western frontier with Wales. The English invasion of Northumbria was, therefore, part of a carefully developed expansion of Ethelred's interests. It resulted in the isolated Danish leadership at York recognising Ethelred as king (or 'overking') – which may well mirror his status in the Mercian Danelaw. Ethelred had, therefore, by Christmas 909, attained considerable success in restoring the Mercian kingship to its ancient greatness.

In the following summer, the York leadership responded to the *débacle* of 909 by launching an invasion of English Mercia, reaching the Avon and ravaging west of the Severn before retiring homeward. There can be little doubt that this force also crossed into Mercia via the Mersey (but cf. Hill 1981, p. 56) and raided Cheshire *en route*, but few regained the crossings; the Vikings were heavily defeated at Wednesfield (or Tettenhall) in Staffordshire early in August (Æthelweard, 909 (Campbell 1962); ASC(C), 910).

Ethelred did not, however, live long enough to build on this decisive victory. In default of a son, his core territories passed into the keeping of his wife, Æthelflæd, but shorn of Oxford and London which Edward the Elder (King of Wessex) reclaimed.

Ethelred's supremacy over his neighbours seems to have died with him. Æthelflæd proved to be a leader of considerable capabilities, who probably shared her husband's objectives although she proved readier to adopt West Saxon strategies. Among these was the use of the *burh* (fortified centre) as a weapon of offence and defence, which she deployed throughout the western Midlands. It was she who constructed the second phase of English defences along Mercia's frontier with Northumbria, building Eddisbury early in 914 and Runcorn late in 915.

There are two sites in Cheshire with traces of fortifications which bear the name Eddisbury, one in Rainow near Macclesfield and the other in Delamere (Fig. 4.3). Either could have been the tenth-century *burh* but it is generally identified, on the basis of rather inconclusive archaeological evidence (Varley 1950), with the prehistoric hillfort in central Cheshire (Plate 3). If so, Æthelflæd apparently had in mind the oversight of the Roman roads from the Mersey crossings at Warrington and Stretford, by which the Danes had perhaps invaded in 910. The Runcorn *burh* was probably on Castle Rock, a promontory jutting into the Mersey valley from the south side which was removed in 1862 to improve navigation. If so, it was primarily intended (like Bridgenorth, which she fortified in 912) to guard a major river crossing against Danish forces (see the discussion in Higham 1988a, pp. 201–4).

These defences were, therefore, designed to deter raids from Danish Northumbria such as had hitherto been responsible for extensive damage in Cheshire and further south. In so doing, they made Chester far more secure and insulated it from the front line of a volatile war zone. It may never have been the intention to hold Eddisbury on a permanent basis but efforts were apparently made at Runcorn to reorganise local land tenure and parochial authority, focusing both on the new *burh*. The dedication of what was almost certainly a new church there to St Bertelin suggests Æthelflæd's responsibility, given her recent acquaintance with this obscure Mercian cult at her new *burh* at Stafford (Thacker 1985; Higham 1988a; see p. 155). Such factors may imply that Æthelflæd intended that Runcorn should be a permanent fort.

With her northern frontiers guarded against attack, Æthelflæd was free to restore her husband's supremacy over eastern Wales

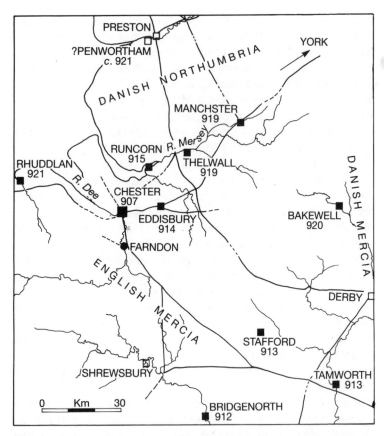

Fig. 4.3 The frontier zone between English Mercia and the Danish lordships in Northumbria and eastern Mercia

(ASC(C), 916) and then turn against the Mercian Danelaw. In 917, she and her brother attacked the Southumbrian Danes and her Mercian troops stormed Derby. In 918 the Danelaw collapsed. That the Danes at Leicester sought (and gained) Æthelflæd's protection suggests that most communities there preferred her supremacy to that of the West Saxon king, Edward the Elder. Once again, the Mercian kingship was close to restoration.

Even as the Danes at York negotiated for her protection, Æthelflæd died at Tamworth on June 12th (ASC(E), 918, ASC(A), 921). Her brother moved swiftly to occupy the palace and transfer Mercia's hegemony to himself. Æthelflæd's recent conquests and her Welsh and Danish protectorates were forcibly transferred to his oversight and Edward completed her work in the Midlands by taking Nottingham, the oldest Danish centre in the region (probably occupied since 867). The rump of English Mercia was left in the hands of Ethelred's daughter, Ælfwyn, but its independence was clearly curtailed by Edward's 'overkingship'.

Ælfwyn's administration proved short-lived. The seizure of York by Ragnald and the Irish Norse led to renewed confrontation between English and Viking leadership in Britain at the end of the decade. Edward removed Ælfwyn from Mercia to Wessex and took direct control of the region. His first task was to reinforce the Mersey frontier in case of a Norse attack. Æthelflæd's fortifications there predated her seizure of Derby and may have been out of touch with the threat posed in 919. Edward's *burh* at Thelwall has never been identified (Hill 1976; Thacker 1987, p. 291; Higham 1988a, pp. 207, 222) but the general vicinity suggests that it was constructed to control the important fords between Wilderspool/Latchford and Warrington. Thelwall's inclusion as a detached part of the medieval parish served from Runcorn may imply that Edward was keen to place his two *burhs* on the middle Mersey under single management (see p. 158) and his successors may have long retained a similar attitude to the residual function even after the defences became derelict. Edward despatched a further Mercian force to fortify and hold Manchester in Northumbria, so taking control of an important Roman road junction between the Mersey and York, and challenging the Viking kings to intervene. Such aggressive use of *burhs* was consistent with Edward's wars in the southern Danelaw in previous years. There can be no doubt that it was deliberately confrontational. With these built and garrisoned, Edward crossed the Pennines to strengthen his hold on the northern Danelaw.

To be a match for King Edward the Elder, Ragnald needed to unite the Scandinavian communities of the north with those same Mercian Danes and it may have been to excite their revolt against English rule that his cousin and ally, Sihtric, reputedly destroyed Davenport. If this was the site named as a Domesday manor near Congleton (Morgan 1978, 267a), then his forces presumably crossed the Mersey and harried that part of eastern Cheshire where their deeds would make the biggest impact on an audience in Danish Derbyshire. The Danes there did not rise against King Edward and Ragnald came to terms by which he and the other northern kings recognised Edward the Elder as 'father and lord' (ASC(F), 924).

The West Saxon supremacy c. 920 ended an era of at least thirty years during which the Mersey had been the only frontier common to English lordship and Danish Northumbria. From 907 to 919 this border zone witnessed the construction of more fortifications than any area of comparable size in England. It was also repeatedly devastated, by English forces in 893 and Scandinavian raids thereafter. Although no contemporary account exists, it was probably in consequence of Edward's triumph that southern Lancashire was detached from the Northumbrian kingship. Its incorporation in the diocese of Lichfield, its hides (as opposed to carucates), its hundreds and shires (as opposed to wapentakes), all bear witness to its transfer to the orbit of Mercia's rulers. That this occurred after the advent of carucates in Northumbria (in 867) is made clear in the Domesday Book (DB, 269d), in which the region is known by the clumsy and presumably bureaucratically conceived Latin name of *Inter Ripam æt Mersham*, 'Between Ribble and Mersey'. That name is first recorded in the will of Wulfric Spot, a prominent Mercian nobleman who also held an estate on Wirral c. 1000 (Sawyer 1979). He or his forebears may have bought these estates from Scandinavian lords unsettled by the conquests of the West Saxon kings.

If it was Edward who acquired control of southern Lancashire, it was presumably intended to act as a buffer for north-western Mercia and to carry his territorial lordship to the Ribble, which was probably the main artery for continuing co-operation between York and Dublin. Edward may have built a *burh* at Penwortham (Higham 1988a, pp. 213–14, 1992d). He certainly built a large fortification at *Cledemutha* (Rhuddlan) (ASC(C), 921; Wainwright 1950; Manley 1985), so once more, as ruler of Mercia, seizing control of much of Powys.

The shiring of Cheshire

Hitherto, north-western Mercia appears to have been organised in comparatively ancient territorial units and through old-established mechanisms. The province of the *Wrocen sæte* remained a meaningful term into the mid-ninth century and there seems little reason to think that it had become meaningless even half a century later. The lesser *Pencer sǣte* and *Tomsǣte* are only recorded in ninth-century documents, but the royal court at the centre of each was still active in the tenth century, so these territories probably also persisted in some sense as organs of government.

If Chester had long been a focus of ecclesiastical organisation, then it may also have played a role in secular government in the Mercian period. However, its revival and fortification in 907 signifies a resurgence of royal interest in this peripheral site. As long as Mercia's northern frontier remained volatile, Chester was important enough to be manned permanently with royal troops, but the gradual proliferation of *burhs* in the western Midlands and then along the Mersey placed an increasing strain on the Mercian field army.

With the collapse of the Northumbrian challenge *c.* 920, Edward the Elder emerged triumphant from a period characterised by crisis management and frenetic military activity, during which he is unlikely to have had energy to devote to reorganising his new kingship of Mercia. That kingdom had been on a permanent war footing since Ethelred had taken charge. With the war won, military activity could be scaled down and the defensive capacity which had been developed delegated to local authority.

This entailed shifting responsibility for the Mercian *burhs* to the regional community. It was this process that brought the shires into existence (Stenton 1971, pp. 292–3), probably between 920 and 923. A document known as the Burghal Hidage which dates from a decade or so earlier may provide the key to Edward's reorganisation; responsibility for manning each *burh* was calculated on the basis of four men for each pole of the circuit, with each hide responsible for one man (Hill 1969; Keynes and Lapidge 1986; Hill and Rumble, forthcoming). The region on which this responsibility lay was the shire attached to that *burh*.

That this has some local relevance finds support in the statement in the Domesday Book that the reeve responsible for Chester in 1066 used to 'call out one man to come from each hide of the county to repair the city wall and bridge' (Morgan 1978, 262d). Cheshire's twelve hundreds at Domesday and 1,200 hides in the eleventh-century document known as the County Hidage imply that it was initially expected to find 1,200 men for *burh* duty, suggesting a circuit in the order of 5,000–5,500 ft (1,520–1,672 m; see also Hill 1969; Alldridge 1981; Thacker, forthcoming). It was arguably the length of the wall which dictated the number of hides and therefore both the extent of the shire and the weight of its hidation.

The perimeter of Ethelred's refortification at Chester is a matter of debate. The Roman walls were still standing in the tenth century and must have provided the basis for the Viking defence of the site in 893. It seems most unlikely that he ignored the fortress but the Roman walls far exceed the length as computed from the Burghal Hidage formula. Before Edward the Elder's renewal of Towcester, in 917, English *burh* construction was probably always in timber. Excavations in Linenhall Street revealed a line of very substantial post holes capable of supporting a massive fence. It has been suggested that this represented the Mercian defences (Thompson 1969), but the feature is undated. An alternative is the view that the Mercian defences were 'L' shaped, using the north and east walls of the Roman fortress (*c.* 4,530 ft) but relying on a fortified bridge and the Dee itself for the remainder of the circuit. Such a layout has close parallels with Ethelred's Gloucester, is consistent with the detail of the Domesday customs (above) and would have encompassed the known tenth-century occupation levels in and around Lower Bridge Street within the defensive circuit (Dodgson 1968; Hill 1969; Thacker 1987, pp. 250–1). If the Dee was expected to complement the defences, the Mercians presumably had no fear of water-borne Viking attack. This (like Runcorn which made similar use of river defences) points to a degree of confidence in English ships in the region. Ethelred may have followed Alfred's example in developing (or hiring) a fleet which, although it would presumably have been based at Gloucester, could have been deployed at Chester. Alternatively, such dispositions may merely reflect the Mercian concern with attack by land-based, Scandinavian forces.

Those responsible for allocating hides to Chester, and so for shiring the area, had comparatively few options. Cheshire had to be the northernmost Mercian shire, and the pre-existing frontier of the kingdom on the Irish Sea and the Mersey was necessarily the shire boundary, irrespective of Edward's apparent seizure of southern Lancashire. North-eastern Mercia had been under

Danish control for half a century and this can only have sharpened existing awareness of a major frontier between two Mercian provinces with very different histories and origins along the western edge of the Pennines. If Edward's new dispositions encroached upon the territory hitherto dependent on Derby, it seems unlikely that *Legeceaster scir* (Cheshire) gained anything more than the Pennine edge and 'panhandle' of Longdendale. Its potential as an invasion route into, or out of, southern Yorkshire may have prompted Edward to attach this valley to a securely English shire. It may also have been royal policy to organise the eastern region of the county around a substantial royal estate at Macclesfield, which oversaw yet another gateway into Danish areas, either via the Scandinavian-named Kettleshulme, or through Buxton.

That the other *burhs* along the Mersey were seen by Edward as short-lived campaigning forts is made clear by the lack of interest in them at this stage. Even where oversight was arguably maintained, presumably no attempt was made to commit local resources to the maintenance of these defences as an alternative to Chester. All were probably judged obsolete by a king in control of the north bank of the river.

Cheshire's western boundaries depended on government decisions concerning north-east Wales. Edward's construction of a *burh* at Rhuddlan of comparable size and on a site similar to that of Chester implies that he proposed to restore Mercia's acquisition of northern Powys of a century before (Higham 1988a). Had he succeeded, Wales west of Wat's Dyke and east of the Conway would probably have been shired. It was presumably intended that Wat's Dyke, which had long been the western boundary of Mercia, should serve as the perimeter of Chester's shire.

The hidated area of *Atiscros* Hundred was dominated in 1066 by a large comital estate and parochial centre at Hawarden, with links to Chester emphasised (at least in 1086) by its control of two city residences (DB, 268d). In 920, Hawarden was probably a royal estate, controlling the coastal routes into northern Wales. Further south, the area between the Dee and Wat's Dyke was formed into *Exestan* Hundred, but only a handful of impoverished manors were recorded there in the Domesday Book (Fig. 4.4). Although this area had apparently been under Mercian control since the seventh century, it consistently displayed a strong sense

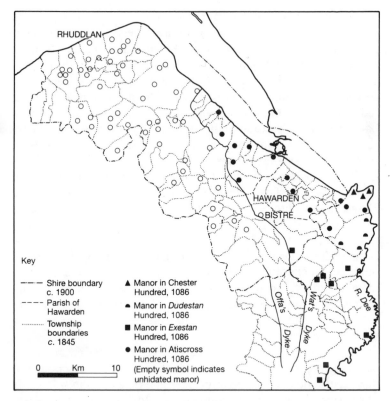

Fig. 4.4 Atiscross and *Exestan* hundreds and Domesday manors, set against the later shires of Flint and Denbigh

of its own Welsh identity and its retrieval long remained an aspiration of Welsh kings. Its place-names display a bewildering complex of spelling variations, duality and naturalisation which emphasise the bilingualism of an area where Welsh-speaking may never have died out (Owen 1987). The robustness of Welsh culture in the hundreds west of the Dee must be a significant factor in assessing the geopolitical structure of the region at an earlier period.

It was only in the south, therefore, that Edward's administrators had significant room for manoeuvre and Cheshire's somewhat confused southern boundary was the result. What was later

to be Maelor Saesneg (the detached portion of Flint) was incorporated in *Dudestan* Hundred but its organisation in just three
great comital estates in 1066 is markedly different from the structure of the remainder of the hundred, which has numerous much
smaller freeholdings grouped around the courts of the bishop
and earl (p. 139). Its different treatment implies that its earlier
territorial history diverged from that of Cheshire. As noted
above, Bangor Iscoed may have formed an eastern redoubt of the
kingdom of Powys, until it became detached through Mercian
rationalisation of the frontier (Fig. 3.3).

The southern boundary of Cheshire diverged from those of
local minster parishes and great estates to a greater extent than
its other borders. If this was already a feature in the tenth
century, it may have resulted in part from the difficulties of
disentangling rights of common shared by diverse communities
which had hitherto had access to a large belt of well-wooded
territory characterised by numerous names in **-leah** (Fig. 4.5).
This woodland formed the south-western extremity of the Lyme
and had probably divided the anonymous sub-group of the
Wrocen sæte in Cheshire from the core of this same people in
Shropshire and the *Pencer sæte* based on Penkridge in the valley
of the upper Trent (see pp. 88–90). Signs that communities in
Cheshire came badly out of this reorganisation may imply that
the entire exercise was undertaken at one of the royal palace sites
further south, perhaps at Tamworth which had been Æthelflæd's
regional headquarters, or Penkridge – that *locus famosus qui
dicitur Pencric* at which Edgar was later to make a substantial
grant of lands in Cheshire to St Werburgh's (Tait 1920, p. 9).

Edward's high-handed treatment of Mercia in general and
Ælfwyn in particular may have occasioned widespread indignation
within a kingdom with such a long and distinguished tradition of
autonomy, but active resistance to him was focused in Cheshire
and North Wales. The king died in July 924, at Farndon-on-Dee
(ASC(D)). According to the admittedly late account of William
of Malmesbury (Giles 1876), he was retiring south at the time
after suppressing a revolt of the Welsh and Mercians centred
at Chester, where he had found it necessary to leave a loyal
garrison. His foundation of a *burh* at Rhuddlan accounts for the
hostility of the northern Welsh who were probably successful in
frustrating his ambitious plans for Clwyd and pushing the frontier

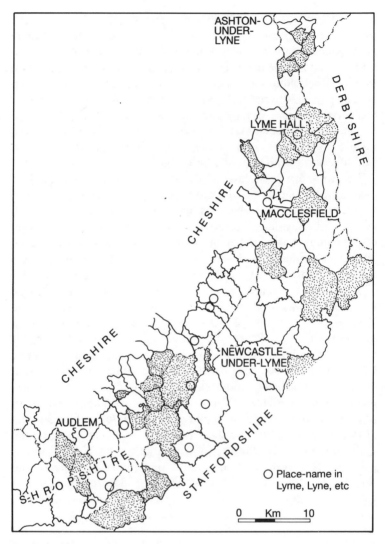

Fig. 4.5 Woodland type township-names and the Lyme on the borders of eastern and southern Cheshire

back to Wat's Dyke. In Cheshire, the presence of several hundreds (or parts thereof) carved out of Powys may have encouraged local sympathy for the Welsh cause but it was arguably onerous levels of hidation which brought local men out in revolt (Higham 1988a). The region was one which appears not to have been heavily taxed by the Mercian kings, although local men may have been expected to maintain and man the western dykes. It was an area with little market activity, poor farmland and low levels of agricultural output which had been repeatedly disrupted by raiding during the Viking Age. The imposition of a system of obligation based on 1,200 hides was probably viewed as tyrannous.

By Domesday, the hidation of Cheshire had been reduced to c. 512 hides. The discrepancy is so great that it cannot be accounted for by small-scale reductions in geld liability on behalf of individuals during the late Saxon period or William's reign. Within the estates granted by Edgar to St Werburgh's, the difference between the hidation in 958 (seventeen hides) and at Domesday (sixteen hides) is so small that the overall reduction from 1,200 to 512 must already have occurred by that date. Exactly when is undocumented but King Edward's intended heir, Ælfweard, died only sixteen days after his father (ASC(D), 924) and the Mercians may have played a prominent part in the elevation of another of Edward's sons, Athelstan. William of Malmesbury was later to claim that he had been raised at Æthelflæd's court, but it is unclear on what authority (Dumville 1992). Even without William's comments, Athelstan's sympathies are revealed in his adoption of Mercia among his royal titles and the choice of Kingston upon Thames for his investiture. It is tempting to identify him as the man responsible for reducing Cheshire's hidation to more acceptable levels.

An English shire

There are several indications of Chester's prosperity under the tenth-century English kings. One is the presence of a scatter of Viking Age metalwork, some of which has come from occupation deposits such as those excavated between Princess Street and Hunter's Walk. Another is the vigour of its mint. This was certainly in operation during the last years of Æthelflæd's rule and proved to be one of the most productive mints in England until its sudden decline in the late 970s. That a quarter of its moneyers had Scandinavian names and one Hiberno-Norse (Smart 1986, p. 179), emphasises the role of Chester at the interface between England and other communities around the Irish Sea. Opportunities existed here for foreigners to enter royal service and various aspects of Scandinavian culture were consistently popular among the urban community. St Bridget's could be a tenth-century foundation (Thacker, forthcoming) although St Olaf's cannot predate the death of this Norwegian king in 1030. Such churches were founded by groups of residents who wished to emphasise their own identification with the Viking world. There are other indications of Scandinavian influence on the organisation of this urban community and its pattern of street- and district-names (Dodgson 1966/67–, V). Marked concentrations of such evidence may imply the presence of Scandinavian merchants on the riverside and south of the fortress along Watling Street towards Handbridge.

As a port of southern Britain giving access to the Irish Sea north of Wales, Chester clearly had a role in any expansion of trade between England and Wales, Ireland or Man, perhaps via the ships of the Ostmen of Dublin. Its explosive rise was necessarily at the expense of Meols (although trading continued there as well) and probably owed much to its official status as a royal *burh*, with a market and a mint under direct governmental control. Yet the conditions in which Chester operated so successfully in the tenth century were little different from those which one might envisage in the pre-Viking period, the mint alone excepted. Why did its mint become the most prolific in England during the reign of Athelstan?

It is possible to distinguish changes in the circulation of coinage at this time and the inception of a money economy in the English land market, in trade, tax and judicial penalties. These factors may have helped but there is still no trace of a cash economy operating in the shire outside Chester. Where pre-Norman occupation has been postulated in the shire it is characterised by tiny quantities of artifacts which do not include coins. At Tatton, for example, extensive excavation identified occupation associated with a single sherd of 'Chester Ware' and a late Saxon clay loom weight (Higham, forthcoming (a)). If the urban community bought in produce from local farmers, they either bartered for it or persuaded the rural community to exchange their coins for services within the *burh*. Alternatively, local men may have brought to market little more than was necessary to pay their own taxes. The pattern of Roman coinage and artifacts in the region is not entirely dissimilar (p. 57). The pattern of plough-lands, mills and fisheries enshrined in the Domesday Book suggests that surplus production was largely in the hands of the social elite. Large quantities of farm produce arguably reached Chester in the form of renders paid to the bishops, the principal minsters and the crown or its agents – later the earls. The town houses of these groups probably constituted a significant and influential element within the city.

If Chester's immediate hinterland offered little scope for profitable commerce, was it able to participate in lucrative long-distance trade? It is clear that Chester was in contact with Dublin and various other sites around the North Sea. In 1066, marten skins were entering the city's port (*portus civitatis*), perhaps from Ireland or Wales, but it is difficult to establish what else was being traded. 'Chester Ware' was reaching Dublin from manufacturing sites in the north-west Midlands, probably via Chester (Wallace 1986), and small quantities of metalwork clearly crossed in both directions, but neither represents a particularly lucrative trade. Speculation concerning the export from Chester of salt, cloth and slaves (Thacker, forthcoming) offers one solution but there is very little evidence for this, and it seems improbable that trade in such goods was sufficient to generate a trade imbalance on the scale implied by the output of Chester's mint.

Alternatives to interpretations based on trade focus on political factors. Chester's mint began its rise to prominence within a year or two of Æthelflæd establishing supremacy over the kings of Powys and Gwynedd. With her death, her hegemony passed to her brother, King Edward, who took direct control of Mercia shortly after. Both may have required tribute payments from northern Wales to be paid at their principal northern *burh* and port. If Athelstan's much-trumpeted imperial status had any substance (Wood 1983), then he presumably also took tribute from lesser kingships in the Irish Sea Basin and particularly from those kings of Gwynedd who occasionally witnessed his charters as *subreguli* (subkings).

This relationship is more fully documented for King Edgar.

Following his coronation in 972, he visited Chester in company with the entire English fleet and there received the submission of the kings of the north and west, from Scotland to Wales. Their subservience was graphically illustrated by their rowing him along the Dee, from the palace at Farndon to Chester. As the Laud Chronicler recognised (ASC(E), 975), Edgar's control extended beyond the British coast:

> Throughout Many Nations,
> Kings honoured the son of Edmund
> Far and wide over the gannet's bath,
> And submitted to the sovereign,
> As was his birthright.

If his superiority was reflected in regular tribute payments, then the mint of the *burh* where these kings attended on him in 973 may have been that at which their bullion was normally transformed into coins. It is noticeable that the two sites chosen by Edgar for his imperial demonstration in this year – Bath and Chester – held the only two mints whose coins bore distinctive marks in the reign of Edward the Elder. The relationship between English 'overkings' and Welsh tributary kings may have occasioned both circumstances. It may also explain temporary oscillations in the mint's output, with a decline under Edmund (940–6) who had to reimpose his control of the Mercian Danelaw and Northumbria by force of arms. Edgar's death in 975 began a long-drawn-out crisis within England which led directly to the disasters of the reign of Ethelred II. If his Irish Sea tributaries interpreted his death and the succession of a minor to the English crown as an opportunity to cease tribute payment, this would satisfactorily explain the collapse of Chester's mint in the late 970s and the several coin hoards deposited in and around the *burh c.* 980.

The dominance of the English kings over Britain was sustained only by military superiority and there can be no doubt that Athelstan's seizure of Northumbria was bitterly resented both inside and outside that kingdom. There were successive attempts by Irish Norse kings to overturn the English supremacy and revive Scandinavian fortunes in Britain, and various Celtic kings either joined forces with the Vikings (as did Constantine of the Scots) or took advantage of their campaigns to rebel (as did Idwal of Gwynedd, *c.* 943).

Only one of these campaigns seems likely to have had direct repercussions in Cheshire. In 937, Olaf (or Anlaff) of Dublin and Constantine of Scotland raided deep into English territory but were caught by English forces while retreating and heavily defeated at *Brunanburh* (Campbell 1938). The late Professor John Dodgson strongly endorsed the identification of Brunanburh with Bromborough on the Wirral (Dodgson 1957). A more recent reappraisal of the battle and its context rejected this in favour of an unknown site east of the Pennines (Wood 1978–80), but this rests on evidence of the most circumstantial kind. If Olaf's campaign followed the pattern established early in the century then he led his men into English Mercia across the Mersey. That the battle was fought on its banks finds support in the *Annals of Clonmacnoise* (Campbell 1938, p. 159) which notes that the battle occurred 'on the plaines of othlynn'. The *Annals* are now only extant in a seventeen-century English translation, but this would seem to be a clumsy rendering of 'the plain *oð* (up to) the Lyme', a term which places the battle west of the Pennines. Cheshire was, therefore, hard hit once more by large Scandinavian forces deliberately wasting the lands of their enemies. This episode emphasises the peripheral location of the region and its political, rather than purely mercantile, role on the interface between English kings and their western neighbours.

1 *left* Farming on the Pennine edge: Sherrowbooth, Pott Shrigley. Snow lies in sheltered spots in May, helping to pick out the earthworks of old enclosures and fields, some of which are lyncheted

2 *below* The Bridestones chambered Neolithic long cairn

The Iron Age hillfort of
Castle Ditch, Eddisbury.

Kelsborrow Castle: a
univallate Iron Age pro-
montory fort, the rampart
of which is now severely
damaged by ploughing

5 Chester from the west. The Roodee, in the foreground, was the site of the Roman port. The road layout is still influenced by the

6 King Street Roman road at Rudheath. The road seems to be the earliest man-made feature in this enclosed landscape

7 Crop-marks at Somerford, which could signify an early enclosure system, although alternative explanations are at least as likely

8 The very early medieval 'longhouse' under excavation at Tatton in 1979

above Malpas: a church of *c*. 1400 stands beside the long-abandoned earthen motte of the Norman castle. The organisation of the settlement around them is reminiscent of a minor borough, and burghal tenure was recorded here in the later Middle Ages

right Halton Castle: a late medieval stone castle constructed by the Duchy of Lancaster has obscured an important regional centre of the late Saxon and Norman periods

11 Preston-on-the-Hill: a candidate for the pre-Æthelfædan church site of northern *Tunendune*, it is typical of the hamlet structure of settlement now to be found so widely in Cheshire

12 Rostherne church is perched above a substantial mere amid earthworks which may conceal evidence of early settlement. The modern village is largely an early nineteenth-century estate settlement

13 The crosses in Sandbach market place: these are by far the finest pre-Viking crosses in the north-west Midlands now surviving and were erected early in the ninth century, possibly under the patronage of the bishop of Lichfield

15 The Greenway Cross, Sutton. This is perhaps the crudest of the east Cheshire group of late Saxon crosses but is still probably in its original position.

14 Round cross-shafts of typical Mercian type, grouped in West Park, Macclesfield

16 The late twelfth-century oratory at Prestbury, largely reconstructed in the Victorian period

17 Chester Castle, now council offices. King William sited his castle between the south-west corner of the *burh* and the river, the principal crossing of which was via the bridge just downstream (behind the castle). The Roodee, in the foreground (now the racecourse), would then have been under water. Of the very extensive medieval structure, little more than Caesar's Tower now survives

18 Aldford: the Norman motte and bailey castle lies north (left) of the church, from which the village stretches out in what was probably a planned grid. The Dee and adjacent water-meadows are in the foreground

19 *above* Abandoned
crofts at Sutton, near
Macclesfield

20 *right* An abandoned
and partially reoccupied
croft with associated field
boundaries at Newton,
Tattenhall

5

The territorial organisation
of Cheshire

By the standards of much of lowland England, the early territorial development of north-west Mercia is obscure (see Hooke 1981; Brooks 1984). It was not until the late ninth century that the Wessex-derived Anglo-Saxon Chronicle developed an interest in Mercia's north-western frontier province. From 894, occasional but approximately contemporary references to Chester appear, in the guise of *Legeceaster*, *Legceaster* and *Legceastre*), continuing the nomenclature first enshrined in Bede's *Historia Ecclesiastica*. There follows a scatter of references to new fortifications and battles but the total recorded within Cheshire before 1086 is only six. This is barely supplemented by charters, despite the presence of the place-name *Bocland* (Dodgson 1966/67– , IV, p. 2) which at least confirms that land was locally held by charter or 'book'. None such survive which detail grants of extensive local estates before the Viking Age and the single tenth-century example exists only in a late copy (King Edgar's to St Werburgh's in 958; Tait 1920). Otherwise, references to lands on Wirral and to Newton 'by the wich' (probably Middlewich) in the will of Wulfric Spot are the only pre-Conquest written sources for the area (Sawyer 1979).

In consequence, pre-Conquest territories cannot be reconstructed with any degree of certainty. The suggestions which will be offered here rest upon a range of evidence which is suggestive but rarely prescriptive and they rely on models first developed on the basis of observations made in other parts of Britain (e.g. Jolliffe 1926; Jones 1976). There seems scope for some general conclusions concerning the organisation of Anglo-Saxon Cheshire (e.g. Thacker 1987), but the tentative nature of this reconstruction derives from our all-too-frequent dependence on evidence drawn from the eleventh to thirteenth centuries, at earliest.

The basic technique used here is to reconstruct early estates (or 'shires', to use the Northumbrian term) by combining evidence of parochial development with the pattern of land tenure in King Edward's reign as enshrined in Domesday Book. This must be done in the context of the physical environment within which these early systems operated. Certain basic assumptions are a precondition of this method and these must be clearly under-stood; perhaps the most fundamental is the assumption that the parochial responsibilities of early churches mirrored the areas of authority of their patrons and founders; the second is the assump-tion that the pre-Viking Age was characterised by comparatively few mother churches or minsters, with responsibility for large *parochiae* (minster parishes), which were later much reduced in size and authority through the establishment in the tenth, eleventh and twelfth centuries of large numbers of lesser churches (e.g. Sylvester 1967; Blair 1988; Bassett 1992). It is only by the identi-fication of these later parishes that the extent of pre-existing *parochiae* can be reconstructed and this process is often hazard-ous, necessitating value judgements on the basis of the physical attributes of later parishes, dedications and the accident of early documentation or physical remains. Even where minster *parochiae* can be reconstructed (e.g. Croom 1988), the resulting picture lacks clear chronological parameters. It is particularly difficult to distinguish between pre-Viking organisation and alterations to this in the tenth and eleventh centuries.

Some indication of the status of a church can be obtained from Domesday Book (Blair 1985, 1987): superior, mother or minster churches frequently had more than one priest, substantial lands that were separately noted and an element of tax exemption (Foot 1992). In Cheshire, however, the number of clergy attached even to superior churches in 1086 was small, perhaps owing to the general poverty of the region. Excepting the pair of wealthy minsters at Chester, only Halton (i.e. Runcorn), Farndon and Acton were credited with more than a single priest and few churches held lands so substantial that they were separately noted. With specific exceptions, therefore, the local church was not well-endowed in 1086 and this bodes ill for attempts to distinguish the more important churches from later manorial foundations.

Conversely, it was probably the low levels of return from their estates which discouraged many local thegns from investing heavily in manorial churches in the tenth and eleventh centuries. Throughout the Middle Ages, much of the shire was characterised by large parishes encompassing numerous manors. Most of these churches were certainly present by the end of the eleventh century and many were arguably already ancient then. On the basis of much later maps and parochial information spread over a long period, it can be shown that a significant number of these parishes reflect natural divisions of the landscape, as regards topography and soils. In this regard, many display a pattern characterised by a core of good agricultural land which is associated with place-names reflecting clearance, settlement and cultivation. More wooded landscapes, heavy clay soils, hill-country or mossland (and place-names appropriate to them) lie on the periphery.

At the core too it is sometimes possible to identify a major estate even as late as 1066–86, which may be a relic of an older land unit, once coterminus with the parish of the superior church. It is the combination of a geographical rationale and tenurial and parochial patterns which suggests that many parishes orginated as units of the 'shire' type. Those units provided the means by which the crown and regional aristocracy were maintained, largely by food rents or renders of the kind which were still in place in unhidated portions of Cheshire in 1086, as the Domesday entry for Bistre demonstrates (Morgan 1978, 269b). By 1066, those parts of the shire which had consistently been part of Mercia had long owed geld in coin to the crown but the obligation of every hide to send a labourer to work on Chester's bridge and walls survived, presumably from the early tenth century.

Western and southern Cheshire

Chester and western Cheshire
The pair of superior churches at Chester, St John's and St Werburgh's, have some claim to an early date (Thacker 1982, 1987, p. 268). Although little historicity need attach to later

medieval claims of a seventh-century foundation, St John's extra-mural location adjacent to the focal Roman fortress and cemeteries, its ancient association with the Mercian bishops, its status as a manorial landholder in 1066, the wealth of pre-Conquest and even pre-Viking sculpture and the number of its canons (seven, and a dean) all imply early foundation. If the Mercian kings were already Christian when they took direct control of this erstwhile British territory, they may well have transferred to their own bishops whatever British churches and ecclesiastical properties were present. If not, they arguably adopted Christianity soon afterwards. King Wulfhere's gifts of land to Wilfrid (666–9) imply that Mercian kings were keen to provide God and his clergy with a substantial share of royal renders, if only in order to further their own competition with the Northumbrian kings. Many land units were perhaps in consequence divided between king and clergy.

For over thirty years, most of Mercia's churchmen were trained in the Irish tradition, a circumstance which may have reduced potential tensions between them and any surviving British priests in the area. A *familia* (community) of diocesan clergy at the principal sub-Roman site of the northern *Wrocen sǽte* would certainly seem appropriate, and the legend of St John's foundation by King Æthelræd of Mercia in the 680s is at least consistent with this.

The *parochia* of St John's may initially have encompassed much of the lower Dee Valley, Wirral and whatever parts of north-east Wales were then subject to the Mercian king. In Domesday Book, however, excepting only eight houses in Chester and a small manor in 'Redcliff', it was the Bishop's or St Chad's holdings which were detailed. Since these were already held by the Bishop in 1066, this pattern of tenure seems unlikely to reflect the recent removal of the Lichfield diocese to St John's. The latter therefore had little independent wealth in the late Saxon period, when its fortunes seem to have been eclipsed by those of St Chad's at Lichfield and St Werburgh's, the minster inside the fortress at Chester which profited from rich patronage from English kings, queens and earls in the tenth and eleventh centuries.

St Werburgh was a royal Mercian saint reputed to date from the seventh century but her association with Chester was comparatively late. The thirteenth-century Chester monk, Ranulph Higden, claimed that her remains were removed from Hanbury (Staffordshire) and redeposited at a college of secular canons in Chester in the 870s (Taylor 1966; see the discussion in Tait 1920; Thacker 1982). In about 1500, Bradshaw claimed that the earliest minster at Chester had been dedicated to Saints Peter and Paul and erected 'soon after Lucius and afore Kynge Arthure'. This church, he claimed, had survived the Saxon Conquest to be refounded by Æthelflæd, 'Lady of the Mercians' (Hawkins 1848). Neither of these much later claims need be historical and both may have been motivated by political purposes, but Æthelflæd's sponsorship of Mercian saints is well-known and there seems little reason to doubt that St Werburgh's was at least refounded in the early tenth century. From that time (at latest) it was also presumably associated with St Oswald, whose remains she and her husband had had transported from Bardney in the Danelaw to their own palace site at Gloucester. Indeed, the proximity of Cheshire to Oswald's place of death (perhaps Wigan) may have encouraged his relatives among the late seventh-century Mercian royal family to initiate a cult of St Oswald in the region long before Æthelflæd revived interest in his remains (Fig. 3.5). Whether St Werburgh's was already ancient *c*. 900, albeit with a different dedication, must be in some doubt, but the tendency for paired mother churches to be founded at the principal foci of royal and episcopal patronage at an early date (as at Canterbury, York, Gloucester, Lichfield) is at least suggestive. Conversely, the claim in favour of Saints Peter and Paul might be regarded as a totally spurious plea for parity between St Werburgh's and St Augustine's foundation at Canterbury. Their joint monopoly of burial rights in Chester in the Central Middle Ages would suggest that the two Chester minsters long shared a *parochia*, but this need not predate the Viking Age.

How extensive that *parochia* was is now little more than guesswork. When it becomes possible to map parishes in the early modern period, there is a noticeably radial pattern around Chester, suggestive of subdivision of an older and simpler organisation in consequence of the creation of parishes for St Mary on the Hill, Holy Trinity and Plemstall (Fig. 4.2). The last of these was probably a tenth-century foundation, reflecting the local associations of St Plegmund, King Alfred's Mercian friend and

Archbishop. The others also belong to the Central Middle Ages. The extensive but unconsolidated parish of St Oswald's was clearly the result of a partial amalgamation of St Werburgh's territorial acquisitions of the tenth to twelfth centuries with the pre-existing interests of this minster, but it is rarely possible to distinguish the two. The dedication to St Oswald at Backford, for example, may suggest that St Werburgh's had interests here prior to the creation of St Mary's parish, and it may be relevant that neither Backford nor its parochial neighbour Stoke (dedicated to St Lawrence) were named as manors in Domesday Book. Pulford and Shotwick were properties of St Werburgh's in 1066, but the association need not predate the tenth century.

Outside this core, within which the interests of Chester's churches were dominant, medieval parishes such as Dodleston and Eccleston may have been pre-Conquest foundations (see p. 81). Both have curvilinear churchyards and dedications to St Mary, and Eccleston may have had a pre-Conquest cross (now lost; Thacker 1987, p. 288), but neither had churches acknowledged in Domesday Book and Dodleston at least then had strong links with the City and with the Earl, chief patron of St Werburgh's (DB, 268d). It seems unlikely that churches at either site were then of more than local significance. It should be noted that both these manors were important elements of large baronial holdings in the early Norman period and this may be the period when their churches were founded or refounded.

The small medieval parishes which radiate from Chester can be distinguished from the generally larger medieval parishes of central Wirral and the northern end of the Mid-Cheshire Ridge (see below, p. 146). Wirral is one of the most difficult areas in which to investigate early territories, owing to what seems to have been extensive reorganisation in consequence of Scandinavian land grants and temporary self-government to the west of Raby (Dodgson 1957). At Domesday, the Hundred of Willaston extended across the entire peninsula and south to the vicinity of Chester itself, including the western side of the Gowy valley, but much of this southern territory was later transferred to Broxton Hundred. The hundred presumably met at Willaston (Neston parish; perhaps at Hadlow: Dodgson 1966/67– , IV, p. 167) but the district name, Wirral, is older and even more extensive (e.g. ASC(A) 893: 'Chester, a deserted city in Wirral'). The district name means 'nook where bog-myrtle grows' (Dodgson 1966/67– , I, p. 8) and the first element may derive from translation from the Welsh, *Cilgwri* ('nook') with an Old Welsh personal name. It is, therefore, a name associated with an extensive area of considerable antiquity. It may have been the region directly dependent on Chester itself before the Viking Age, and so be equated with the *parochiae* of Chester's minsters.

Beyond the Chester-centric parishes of the southern end, there are vestiges of an older and far more extensive system of territorial organisation. At the core of the multi-township parish of Bromborough (with its dependent chapelry of Eastham) in 1066 was the Earl's twenty-two hide estate of Eastham, which dominated the eastern side of the peninsula. To it in 1086 was attached a priest who was presumably stationed at Bromborough, given the pre-Conquest stonework which has been found in and around the church of St Barnabas (Thacker 1987, p. 286). On the west side was the equally extensive parish of Neston, likewise centred on a church (dedicated to St Mary) where pre-Conquest sculpture has survived. A priest was present in 1086, and an unusual formula combined with a very low hidation may imply that the church was endowed with uncatalogued tax-exempt land ('two parts of two hides gelded' (DB, 266a)). Neston was then a core part of a large group of manors held by a thegn named Arni.

Their extensive medieval parishes, potentially early dedications and pre-Conquest sculpture imply that both Bromborough and Neston date back to the tenth century at latest, but there were other and perhaps earlier churches in this region. It may be significant that the only place-name in Cheshire to record a Welsh church, Landican (later Woodchurch), was credited with a priest in 1086. Its parish extended across ten townships in the later Middle Ages but its dedication to the Holy Cross (Gastrell 1845, p. 180) is unlikely to be early. The only site on the peninsula where pre-Viking stone working has so far been claimed is Overchurch (Bu'lock 1958), the medieval parish of which was confined to the single township of Upton.

The pre-Conquest organisation of Wirral is therefore unusually complex by local standards and its pre-Viking form seems beyond reconstruction. The high status of Eastham manor and the Bromborough mother-church is quite clear and Neston and Landican are not dissimilar. However, a possible early church at

Overchurch was later nothing more than a manorial church which eventually came into the hands of St Werburgh's. Its early dedication is obscure.

Nor is the role of the bishop's church at Burton easily understood (assuming the Domesday Book rubric here to be an error and the entry to refer to Burton in Wirral, not Burton by Tarvin; Sawyer 1987, p. 344, note 20). The place-name could refer to Chester once that was thought of as a *burh*, but it was never to be an element in Chester's name. It might, therefore, refer to Bromsborough, a place-name which is first documented in the tenth century. This may imply that the Eastham/Bromborough land unit had reached the Dee estuary, before grants to the bishop and to secular tenants severed the initial unity of the southern half of the peninsula and encouraged the proliferation of tenth- and eleventh-century churches. The *parochia* of *Brunanburh* may, therefore, have encompassed all central Willaston Hundred before the Viking Age. However, an alternative interpretation would derive this *burh* -tūn name from the undated promontory fortification on the shoreline of Burton itself (Dodgson 1966/67– , IV, pp. 211–12).

That the Bishop's five estates in Domesday Cheshire were scattered across four of Cheshire's hundreds (plus further claims on land in Maelor Saesneg and *Exestan*) may reflect an early attempt by the Mercian kings to endow clergy who were expected to preach throughout a large region with a network of bases (cf. HE, III, 5, but for words of caution, Higham 1988a, p. 216, note 53). That two of these manorial names – Burton and Wybunbury – contain reference to fortifications may be significant. They may, therefore, reflect ancient grants to the Church of royal renders and the enclosed courts to which they were paid. Such grants may have established *parochiae* of considerable size in what may still have been a very Welsh countryside.

By 1086, Farndon had two or three priests, Wybunbury one and Burton one. This is a high proportion of priests to estates in comparison with the landholdings of the secular aristocracy and implies that, as one might expect, the bishops had been exceptionally active in church foundation. Wybunbury, Tarvin and Farndon were all large medieval parishes and the Bishop's interests here are unlikely to have been accidental, particularly since they imply access to rich tithes. Farndon contained six,

133

Tarvin eleven and Wybunbury (with the parishes of Audlem, Coppenhall and Wistaston which derived from it during the Middle Ages) about twenty-six medieval townships. Farndon also retained interests in *Exestan* in the later Middle Ages which probably derive from the bishop's pre-Conquest property in that hundred.

There are clear signs that the *parochia* of Farndon had suffered fission, if rather earlier than Wybunbury; a second estate named Farndon in Domesday Book is generally equated with Aldford, but the date of fission of the parish is variously suggested as tenth-century (Higham 1988a) or twelfth-century (Dodgson 1966/67– , IV, p. 68). The attenuated geography of the medieval parish of Farndon suggests that it is a remnant of a much earlier *parochia* (Fig. 5.1). The pattern of interlocking territories which it shares with Tilston, Coddington and Shocklach parishes may imply that these had become detached during the late Saxon–Norman period. The place-names of Shocklach parish suggest use of this riverside wetland as summer shielings – hence Caldecott ('cheerless shelters') and Shocklach ('boggy stream haunted by an evil spirit'). The tenure of Caldecott in 1066 by Wulfgar the priest and three thegns may imply a continuing dependence on the ecclesiastical *familia* at Farndon. The area may have been one in which the farmers of a much larger district formerly enjoyed rights of summer pasturage.

It is possible, therefore, to postulate an early minster parish based on Farndon which encompassed the medieval parishes of Farndon, Aldford, Tilston and Coddington, including everything between the Dee and the southern end of the Mid-Cheshire Ridge. This was separated from the vicinity of Chester and Tarvin by a broad area of poorly drained land between Tattenhall and the Dee. This terrain is characterised by place-names reminiscent of a well-wooded landscape (Lea Newbold, Handley, Chowley, Huxley), hunting (Huntington) or wetland (the two Golbournes, literally, 'Marigold stream'). Small parishes, which were probably of late formation, are also dominant here, the place-names within which reflect the marginal quality of the land for agriculture (e.g. Waverton parish including Hatton ('Farm at a heath') and Huxley).

This territory marches to the south-east with the parish of Malpas and this parochial boundary is clearly older than the

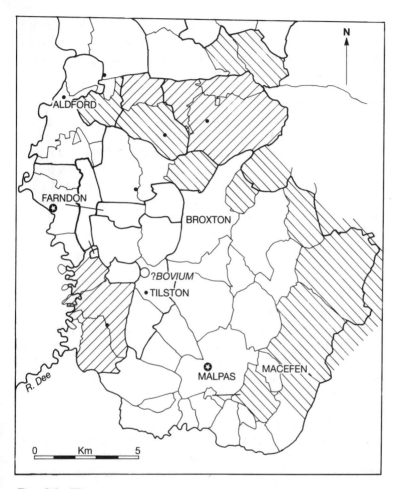

Fig. 5.1 The organisation of south-west Cheshire: woodland type township-names are hatched

boundaries of the townships on either side. In 1086, Malpas was still known by its Old English name (not Celtic; Higham 1992a, p. 139), *Depenbech*, a topographical name which refers not to the township but, apparently, to the steep valley of the Wych Brook on the southern edge of the parish. At its core in 1066 was a large estate of the earls of Mercia and the several holdings of a thegn also named Edwin. Alongside the principal topographical name were several others (such as Edge and Chidlow ('Cidda's mound')) but a preponderance of settlement names. Most of these use the suffix **-tūn**, 'farm' or 'enclosure'. Since Agden contains an Old Danish personal name some were clearly of late origin. The evolution of township names necessarily occurred over a very long time-scale. Around the eastern periphery lies a continuous belt of woodland place-names which reflects wetlands in the basin around the Bickley Brook, Bar Mere and the Quoisley Meres, through which the Shropshire Union Canal now runs. Between the core place-names and these peripheral, well-wooded townships lies Macefen, Old Welsh **Maes y ffin** ('open land near a boundary'). Supposing that the boundary referred to is that of the land unit and *parochia*, rather than some hypothetical political boundary between Welsh and English territory (as suggested by Dodgson 1967–), this place-name reflects with some precision the balance of land use and landscape, with cleared and cultivated land at the core of the estate and woodland on its periphery (Fig. 5.1). It also implies that both estate and landscape have origins which precede the spread of English place-names, so pushing this unit back to the seventh century at latest. The non-appearance of a contiguous group of township names in Domesday Book coupled with the numerous (fourteen) plough-lands allotted to *Depenbech* (Malpas) demonstrate that the Domesday manor stretched far beyond the later township of the same name.

Given the clarity of the case for a mother-church here, it is perhaps surprising that no mention of church or priest occurs in Domesday, but the church was active by the late thirteenth century and its dedication to St Oswald (and a chapel to St Chad) may imply a pre-Conquest origin (Plate 9). The barony was in moieties by the late twelfth century and that was manifested in the division of the rectory (Gastrell 1845, pp. 190–2).

If Malpas parish was an early land unit, the renders paid by local farmers to its lords (arguably the Mercian kings) may be enshrined in the place-names; the numerous **-tūn** names presumably provided bread or other farm produce, but Bickerton ('Bee-keeper's farm') and Bickley ('Glade of the bees'-nests/ beehives') imply that responsibility for renders of honey lay with a specific group within the estate. Honey was an important element in renders and tribute payment in early medieval Wales. The numerous **-lēah** place-names probably reflect a predomi-

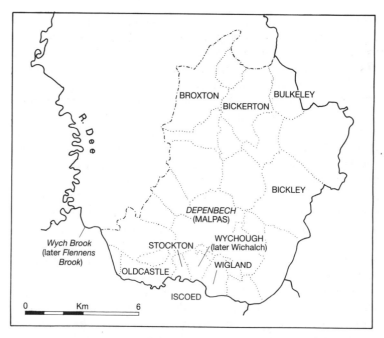

Fig. 5.2 Township-names reminiscent of estate renders in Malpas parish

nance of woodland grazing and the exploitation of other forest resources, but Bulkeley ('Bullock's **lēah**') implies a specialist beef-fattening establishment and Stockton ('enclosure at a dairy hamlet') suggests a farm specialising in milk products (Fig. 5.2). Salt may have been produced at Wychough ('Valley at a **wic**'). It was certainly produced in the Middle Ages at Higher and Lower Wych (Iscoed and Wigland, respectively) and at *Burwardestone* in 1086 – probably Lower Wych on the opposite side of the significantly named Wych Brook (Tait 1916, p. 121). If production occurred during the Anglo-Saxon period then woodland may have been managed to provide a regular supply of fuel, which may already have been in short supply, given the marked absence of **-lēah** place-names on the south side of the parish.

One township place-name on the Wych Brook – Oldcastle – implies that the southern boundary of the parish was at some stage defended from potential enemies in Maelor Saesneg. The township name almost certainly derives from the rather amorphous earthworks on Castle Hill (Dodgson 1966/67–   , IV, p. 44) which were subjected to small scale, trial excavation by Hugh Thompson in 1957 (Thompson 1967). Although he found no datable artifacts, and the earthworks do not at first sight seem to demand interpretation as a medieval castle, Thompson's conclusion that this was a small frontier work of the Norman period (perhaps the later twelfth century when Maelor was lost to English control) is probably sound. The name is not recorded before the late thirteenth century and is a Middle English construction. Other instances of 'Castle' in Cheshire's place-names are almost always associated with post-Conquest castles. The obvious exception is Kelsborrow Castle, but this is an Old English -*burh* compound to which 'castle' has been added at a later date. It seems unlikely, therefore, that Oldcastle has anything significant to tell us about the pre-Conquest territory of *Depenbech*.

Its later territorial integrity, the sensitivity of its boundary to the landscape, its high status in 1086 and the internal pattern of place-names all imply that the parish of Malpas derived from an early land unit of the type known in Northumbria as a shire. There are, however, indications that this may have been only part of an even larger and earlier unit. The boundary between Malpas and the Farndon group of parishes runs through a landscape which, on place-name evidence, was consistently cleared and farmed on both sides. On this count, it does not look like an early boundary. The belt of woodland names on the eastern and northern edges of Malpas parish proceeds westwards to become the northern limit of the Farndon group of parishes (see above), so seeming to enclose the larger group.

That this may reflect a very early (necessarily pre-Anglo-Saxon) estate finds some support in the location and name of Broxton – Burzæsn, ('Burial place') – a township on the periphery of Malpas parish but which shares borders with five medieval parishes (Bunbury, Coddington, Farndon, Tattenhall, Tilston). Indeed, the pattern of boundaries in this area suggests that a desire to remain in touch with Broxton was an influential factor in the formation of parish boundaries during the subdivision of Farndon's *parochia*. This may imply that the entirety of southwest Cheshire had once formed a single estate, one focus of which was a cemetery at Broxton, on or close to the southern end of the Mid-Cheshire Ridge.

The boundary of the later township touches Maiden Castle, an

Iron Age hillfort which might have been viewed in the sub-Roman period as a suitable location for burial (e.g. James 1992). Given the frequency with which Romano-Celtic temples occur in hill-forts, this site may earlier have had some ritual significance. Alternatively, this reference to a cemetery may originate from Roman burials on the southern bounds of the township, associated with the ill-defined evidence for a settlement (possibly *Bovium*) near the Roman road in Carden and Tilston.

When this putative early land unit fractured, the southern part (Malpas) was retained in royal hands. The dedication of its church to St Oswald mirrored the sentiments of the leaders of Christian Mercia at latest in the early tenth century. The northern half was presumably granted to the bishop. It focused on the clearest example of a circular churchyard in Cheshire, at Farndon, which may have been the earliest and most influential Christian centre in this region. Parallels with early medieval Welsh and Irish sites abound. It retained a dedication to St Chad, but the land unit eventually split between ecclesiastical and secular landholders, perhaps in the late Saxon period, with new estate centres and new churches planted predominately along the Roman roads. That King Edward the Elder died here in 924 does not prove it was then in royal hands since he may easily have taken refuge at an episcopal centre. It was, however, necessarily then a place of focal importance.

The removal of King's Marsh (formerly Overmarsh) from Farndon's authority eventually left the rump of this minster *parochia* in two detached portions. The hand of secular agents can be seen at least in this final disruption of the early territory.

Without archaeological confirmation, suggestions concerning Broxton must remain little more than speculation but they may find some support in the adoption of Broxton as the hundred name by *c.* 1260. The name-change may imply, but does not prove, that the lost name of the Domesday Hundred, *Dudestan* ('Dudd's stone') applied to a site in this township. A notion of its central role may, therefore, have lasted into the later Middle Ages and then triumphed, despite the low status of this manor, its inconvenience to travellers and peripheral location within the secular and parochial organisation of the region.

Taking all the evidence into account, therefore, the bulk of the *Dudestan* Hundred of Domesday may have originated as a single land unit focused on one royal court (Farndon) and one possibly pre-English cemetery (Broxton), embracing a territory defined both by topographical features and a consistent pattern of place-names. To it had earlier been added several townships within Wirral. The origins of this early unit are obscure but it may be relevant that a single Roman settlement lay at its core, on the Roman road near Tilston (perhaps *Bovium*) and that Farndon lay on the Roman crossings to Holt, a site of very special interest to Roman authorities for many years. Subdivision of this early territory between king and bishop began its progressive fragmentation but it was the latter's holdings which were more vulnerable. The estate retained in royal, then comital, hands proved comparatively robust.

Southern Cheshire

Despite the pretensions to fortified status which may be implicit in its name, its episcopal tenure and the wide authority and auspicious dedication (to St Chad) of its church, Wybunbury manor was not exceptional in the late eleventh century, paying geld at half a hide and with only two ploughlands (DB, 263a). It was, however, credited with extensive woodland and two enclosures (*haiae*: hedged enclosures or parks associated with deer management) which may have lain in neighbouring Lea (**leah**) township, since neither that nor Hough was separately listed. They may alternatively have lain at a greater distance, in the well-wooded periphery of the shire. These woodland resources may imply that the court of this manor had once been of high status and accustomed to visitors who expected to be fed on venison, but such hedged enclosures were comparatively common in Domesday Cheshire.

The neighbouring townships of Shavington cum Gresty and Rope were not named in Domesday Book and it is noticeable that Walgherton and Stapeley both appear only as diminutive manors, averaging one ploughland each. These small and poor estates may represent a process of estate fission or leasing in the late Saxon period, particularly given that Wybunbury was itself eventually lost by the same process to the Malbank barony (Ormerod 1882, III, p. 482). At the core of the parish is a small, tight group of townships – Wybunbury, Hough, Lea and Walgherton – which interlock spatially and differ in size and

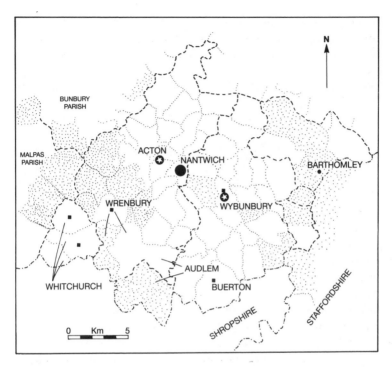

Fig. 5.3 The early organisation of *Warmundestrou* hundred in southern Cheshire: woodland type township-names are shaded

shape from their neighbours (Fig. 5.3). These may well represent a medial stage in the gradual process of fragmentation of an early land unit, when a much larger core territory remained in the hands of the bishops.

The parish lies along the shire boundary with Staffordshire and Shropshire. Indeed, Checkley township extends into Staffordshire. It may have been the presence of extensive woodland that determined decisions concerning the shiring of the region in the tenth century. This woodland formed the southern end of the Lyme, the name of which is enshrined in Audlem. It was eventually shared between the parishes of Malpas, Acton and Wybunbury (Cheshire) and neighbouring communities in Shropshire and Staffordshire in a fashion which implies that it had been used as common grazing by communities resident on all sides. If so, the eventual subdivision suggests that access to woodland grazing for the inhabitants of each parish/land unit, rather than each shire, was taken into account when shiring occurred; Wybunbury's parishioners were compensated for loss of access to nearby woodland which was incorporated in Domesday Staffordshire, by allocation of Dodcott cum Wilkesley and a share of Newhall, both of which were more naturally parcels of Acton parish. Acton was separated thereby from the shire boundary, with access primarily to woodland to the south-west of its main farmlands. The equivocal position of Checkley and Wrinehill, and the division of Newhall township between the parishes of Acton, Audlem and Wrenbury both imply that the allocation of woodland resources was secondary to the fundamental ordering of the region into large territories.

There are signs that territorial boundaries may have been forced to accommodate the formation of the shire. Although Aston ('Eastern farm') does lie on the eastern edge of Acton, Weston occupies the extreme north-east corner of Wybunbury parish and is more likely to have been named from either Barthomley parish or a focal site now in Staffordshire, from which it became tenurially detached at latest when the shiring occurred. Stoneley (later Shropshire), Marbury, Norbury and Wirswall all appear in Domesday Cheshire but were berewicks (outlying parcels of demesne) of Earl Harold's manor of Whitchurch, suggesting that an ancient land unit and *parochia* focused there had retained rights to well-wooded land even across the tenth-century shire boundaries. Similarly, Malpas parish extended via Whitwell chapelry into Iscoyd, in what would later become the detached portion of Flintshire.

Barthomley parish exhibits similar traits, consisting of five townships and a fraction of a sixth (Hassall, otherwise in Sandbach parish), of which one (Balterley) lies entirely in Staffordshire. Alsager apart ('Ælle's arable land'), the township names are redolent of a woodland landscape and include one Old Welsh monosyllabic name – Crewe ('Fishtrap' or 'Weir'). A priest was included in the Domesday description of Barthomley, implying that it was then already a separate parish. The Siward who held demense lands at the church settlement in 1066 was probably the same individual who held Buerton, the name of which may imply some earlier association with Wybunbury. The presence of a church and of extensive woodland suggests a landholder of high status.

A wealthier thegn in 1066 was Osmer at Crewe, supposing him to be the same man as held some at least of Audlem, Davenham and Shipbrook and tenanted lands in five further Cheshire townships, plus Claverton in Wales. The dedication of Barthomley church to St Bertelin almost certainly means that it existed in the early tenth century. It could already have been dedicated to the patron saint of Stafford minster before the Viking Age, but this is more likely to have been a parish which has been carved out by a prominent thegn in the tenth century. It lies in a heavily wooded area – hitherto part of the Lyme – where the wide spacing of ecclesiastical and seigneurial foci might have made it possible for free men with political influence to acquire extensive lands, presumably by charter, which had hitherto been exploited from more distant centres within a wider estate system.

An examination of the parish boundaries implies that this area had been an integral part of the land unit based on Wybunbury and it may have been the decay of effective lordship there during the early Viking Age which enabled Barthomley to be detached from the mother-church of St Chad. The founder might even have been an associate of Ethelred or Æthelflæd, whose interest in St Bertelin is a matter of record and whose influence may well have sufficed to enable an important thegn to transfer the tithes of his own tenants from the bishop's minster to a new foundation.

In 1066, Acton manor, on the west of Wybunbury, was both large and wealthy. It was then held by Earl Morcar, a secular tenant of the highest status (Higham 1988b). It may, before Æthelflæd, have been a royal estate. In 1086 it had a hall large enough to accommodate the manorial court, and the highest number of ploughlands of any Cheshire manor (thirty). This estate clearly extended far beyond the boundaries of the later township. Once more, secular lordship had proved more effective than the bishop in maintaining the territorial integrity of an early estate, but there may here have been an additional factor: Nantwich lay in Acton parish and manor and a tax-exempt salthouse was attached to the manor. That the earl also enjoyed a one-third share in the revenues from a further eight salt-houses

143

implies that the estate was responsible for the general management and exploitation of this, the most profitable of Cheshire's
late Saxon *wiches* (DB, 268b).

The salt industry at Nantwich required large quantities of wood
for fuel and this may well have come in part from managed
woodland within Acton manor or parish. Since much of this was
on the periphery of the parish, retention of it for the use of the
wich meant that the integrity of the estate had to be conserved.
Morcar's woodland at Domesday was estimated as six leagues
long and one wide, and much of this may have lain at a distance
from the townships at the core of the estate.

Even so, parts of this peripheral and well-wooded terrain had
already passed into the hands of lesser men; four townships
which would eventually emerge as Wrenbury chapelry comprised
five manors in 1066, sharing six and a half ploughlands and
responsibility for taxes on only three hides. Baddiley was, in
1066, the demesne tenement of one Ælfric, a local freeman or
thegn of some importance who was probably closely associated
with Earl Morcar, and who also probably held tenanted lands
in Chorley, Stapeley and Worleston. Ælfric may have been
the earl's reeve. This demesne manor eventually gained its own
church but the several detached portions of its parish emphasise
the late date at which this is likely to have occurred.

The remainder of the northern end of Acton parish in 1066 was
similarly either in independent manors or sub-tenancies (Church
Minshall, Cholmondeston, Aston, Poole). This, however, left a
large block of townships in between, most of which apparently
formed part of the Acton estate. That this central manor and the
remainder of the parish derived from a single land unit is implicit
in their respective hidations; Acton manor clearly enjoyed the
benefit of much lower taxation in proportion to its resources than
other holdings in the parish and these in turn had advantages
over the remainder of the hundred (Thacker 1987, p. 265;
Higham 1988b). The inverse relationship between taxation and
resources implies strong links between core and periphery, to the
advantage of the former.

The revenues of the Hundred of *Wa(e)rmundestrou*
('Warmund's tree') were apparently paid in 1066 to the hall
at Acton. The meeting-place is unlocated but John Dodgson
suggested that it may have lain in Rope, a place-name which he

likened to the Rapes of Sussex (1966/67– , III, pp. 1, 68). This lies in Wybunbury parish. If he was right there seems some cause to suggest that the parishes of Acton and Wybunbury had derived from an earlier single territory which had been divided on the line of the river Weaver and Birchall Brook, excepting only a controlling interest by the lords of Acton in the *wich* on the eastern banks of the Weaver (Fig. 5.3). The subsequent history of this early unity may have been similar to that of *Dudestan* Hundred to the west; an early division between secular and episcopal lordship was reflected in the emergence of a pair of *parochiae* (as at Chester itself). That of the bishop (dedicated at some point to St Chad) retained extensive tithes but it had only vestiges of abnormal secular status by 1066, having lost the bulk of its renders to secular tenants. In contrast, Acton church (dedicated to St Mary) retained its early importance and its two Domesday priests had a plough, and so probably a ploughland. The manor to which it was attached at Domesday still evidenced numerous traces of its central role in its control of the *wich* and the hundredal court. Acton's court was clearly the principal focus of secular patronage in south-east Cheshire.

As at Malpas, a scatter of place-names (Dodgson, 1968–9, III, pp. 113–59) may reflect the ancient pattern of renders; Acton was 'Oak farm', its tenants perhaps obliged to produce lengths of timber for fuel for the *wich* and maintenance of the lord's hall (as in southern Lancashire; DB, 269d). An interest in woodland products may also have given rise to Brindley ('Burnt clearing') and Hurleston ('enclosure/farm associated with hurdles'). The community at Henhill may have paid renders in eggs and fowl and those of Cool Pilate in dairy produce and oats ('cow hill', 'pill oats'). The place-name Worleston probably recalls the presence of pasture used for draught cattle, perhaps associated with the neighbouring *wich*, salt from which was transported by ox-cart (DB, 268b). Stoke is a place-name normally used of a settlement dependent on a superior site elsewhere (Gelling 1990, pp. 281–4). Most other township names derive from 'personal name **-tūn/lēah**, denoting a proprietorial or tenurial interest. These forms are even commoner in Wybunbury parish, where only Buerton ('farm/enclosure belonging to a *burh*') and Stapeley ('wood/clearing where posts are obtained') are suggestive of ancient links between Wybunbury and other communities in the parish. It may well be that the township-names of Wybunbury are generally somewhat younger than those of Acton.

If these two contiguous *parochiae* derive from the fission of an earlier land unit around the upper reaches of the Weaver, then *Warmundestrou* Hundred, like *Dudestan*, may have originated as an early English (or even British) unit of territorial organisation. At its centre lay the only Roman site known in the region, at Nantwich, but if links existed between the Roman settlement and the Early Medieval estate they are at present obscure.

Central and eastern Cheshire

Rushton Hundred

On, and east of, the Mid-Cheshire Ridge, the numerous small parishes concentrated around Chester give way to fewer, much larger parishes. The Domesday hundred of Rushton (*Riseton*) consisted of just four medieval parishes, Tarvin, Tarporley, Bunbury and Over (Fig. 5.4). To these should probably be added part of the parish of Delamere, which derives ultimately from Earl Hugh's afforestation of much of the northern end of the Mid-Cheshire Ridge. The parish was not created until 1812. In 1066, the hundred moot was presumably held at Rushton in Tarporley parish, and that name is here used for the hundred, but the parish displays no sign of being an early focus. The situation is confused by what is probably a mistake in the Domesday rubrication which places Rushton in *Dudestan* Hundred (see the discussion in Sawyer 1987, p. 295). Tarporley parish consists of four townships, Eaton ('Farm at a dry place'), Rushton ('Rush farm'), Tarporley (a lēah compound) and Utkinton ('farm named after Uttoc'). Local place-names emphasise the importance of drainage in this low-lying and clayey terrain on the watershed between the Wettenhall and Waterless Brooks, tributaries of the Weaver and Dee respectively. The area was well-wooded in 1086 but there was no mention of church or priest and the dedication of Tarporley's church to St Helen (mother of the Emperor Constantine I) should not be taken as indicative of pre-Conquest foundation.

Over parish was reorganised in consequence of the foundation of a Cistercian house at Vale Royal in the late thirteenth century. It eventually formed Over and Whitegate parishes and Little

Fig. 5.4 The early organisation of Rushton and Ruloe Hundreds in central Cheshire: woodland township-names as in Fig. 5.3

Budworth chapelry. By 1066, it had already been subdivided, with four manors independently bearing the parish name, but the dedication to St Chad and the remnants of a curvilinear churchyard might (but need not) imply that the church had formerly been attached to the diocese. In 1066, the entire parish was in the hands of secular tenants among whom the most influential may have been Dunning, holder of its most substantial manor at Oulton, whose name appears against a further five manors in the shire. That these included the important church at Sandbach implies that he may have been a thegn of some consequence.

Bunbury parish has characteristics which suggest that it was in many respects the focus of the Domesday hundred; the reference to a *burh* recalls other ancient church sites of high status, the church dedication to St Boniface (martyred in Germany in 754) could be consistent with a pre-Viking origin, and the estate was credited with a priest in Domesday Book. The parish exhibits the same sort of linkages between ecclesiastical jurisdiction and secular authority as have already been noted elsewhere. The place-names particularly support this interpretation; place-name etymology implies that calves were an important part of renders paid by communities at Calveley and red lead by those at Tiverton, some township names suggest farming (Peckforton, Haughton) or exploitation of woodland (Ridley) but several others imply that this parish served as a focus for a wider area. Beeston, with its hillfort and Romano-British settlement, is 'The rock where a market is held' and this long predates its refortification by the Norman earls. Wardle is 'watch-hill', perhaps a beacon site. Spurstow is a compound place-name, the prefix of which is obscure (Dodgson 1966/67– , III, p. 315) but which uses a well-known suffix, **stōw**, which was used to denote meeting-places of various kinds (Gelling 1990, p. 285). At the core of the parish are, therefore, four townships each of which suggests a focal activity; Beeston's market, Wardle's civil defence, Bunbury's mother-church and Spurstow's meeting-place.

Within the medieval parish of Bunbury but included in *Dudestan* Hundred in Domesday Book (DB, 264c) is Burwardsley, 'the **lēah** of the *burh*-guardian'. Its peripheral location, subdivision between three manors and subordination to the interests of the Earls in 1066 may explain its inclusion in the same hundred as Edwin's greatest estate in the region at *Depenbech* (Malpas) but the place-name may reflect some earlier responsibility of its holder for the central *burh* of this land unit at Bunbury. It may alternatively contain nothing more signifiant than an Old English personal name – '*Burh*-ward'.

Of the township names of Bunbury parish which occur as Domesday manors (including Burwardsley), ten (spread over seven names) were held in 1086 by Robert fitzHugh, lord of Malpas. A certain Dedol had held Bunbury in 1066, with tenanted land also at Tiverton, but by far the most important local landholder was Earl Edwin. He held the manor of Alpraham at a geld of two hides, with four ploughlands and extensive woodland, much of which may have lain in neighbouring Calveley or even more distant Ridley, since neither appears otherwise. Robert's holdings in these two adjacent parishes as Earl Edwin's successor may imply that the other named landholders in both parishes in 1066 were tenants or dependants of the Earl. Dedol could have been his reeve. The centralisation of these landholdings may, therefore, have been far greater *T.R.E.* than is immediately apparent from Domesday Book.

The presence of a comital estate with vestigial but still extensive woodland interests, the several meeting-places, 'watch-hill' and references to a *burh* in combination imply that Bunbury parish originated as the core of a secular lordship within an exensive land unit. That unit may initially have been as extensive as the hundred. In a fashion which is by now becoming routine, it seems to have been divided into two, and one part – the northern half – granted away, perhaps to the bishops, while the southern part was retained by the Mercian kings, then parcelled up and leased or granted away, with the vestigial seigneurial interest eventually passing to the earls.

In the northern part, control shrank into a core centred on the parish and manor of Tarvin which was convenient for oversight from the bishops' local administration based at St John's, Chester. The dedication to St Andrew is consistent with an early date for a church under Roman control. It was a dedication favoured by St Wilfrid (e.g. Hexham; see also Gregory's monastery at Rome and Rochester Cathedral), although it could of course have been given much later. If this was an episcopal manor from the late seventh century onwards then the retention of a pre-English river-name for the estate is the more explicable.

In 1086, the manor of Tarvin had the exceptional complement of twenty-two ploughlands, implying over 2,000 acres of cultivable land (Higham 1990), some of which was in demesne. The north-west quarter of the parish comprised the manor of Barrow ('the wood') which was also of exceptional size and, in 1066, in the hands of Thored (or Thorth), a close associate of the bishop in Cheshire. Barrow ultimately became a separate parish but it was described until the sixteenth century as a free chapel in the Tarvin prebend (Gastrell 1845, p. 124), and so it was presumably a parcel of the parish of Tarvin before the Conquest. It had been part of King Edgar's grant to St Werburgh's in 958 (Tait 1920, pp. xviii, 9) and this may date its separation from the episcopal manor. St Werburgh's tenure had clearly lapsed by 1086.

Of the other township names within the parish, four are compounds of **-tūn** while six are topographical, three of which refer to hills of various sorts. The **-tūn** names include Burton ('the farm/enclosure of/at the *burh*'), which may reflect the churchyard at Tarvin itself, despite the lack of a *burh* place-name in this instance (cf. Bromborough, Bunbury, Wybunbury).

In 1086, excluding Barrow, only two of the townships in the parish were noted as manors but both were large. Ashton (five ploughlands) had been held by Thored and Clotton (six ploughlands) by Stenulf, who also had a small landholding at Weaver but whose demesne seems to have been at Tilstone in Bunbury parish. These were both apparently influential men and were probably the sort of thegns to whom reference was made in Domesday Book concerning the holdings of 'the bishop and all his men' west of the Dee (DB, 263a). Again, Domesday Book refers to those responsible for the geld in late Saxon England but omits to note the patterns of dependency and commendation which must have linked many of the lesser landholders with the regional leadership (e.g. Sawyer 1985). The remainder of the parish was probably included in the bishop's manor, sub-tenancies within which are implied by the presence of 'radmen' (literally 'those who owed riding services') among the tenants.

Further east, what may have been the bishop's share of the earlier land unit comprised a belt of poor claylands of less value for agriculture. Landholders here may have begun as episcopal tenants or holders by *boc* but they eventually gained sufficient independence to establish two further parishes. The afforestation of much of the Ridge which intruded between these two areas between 1071 and 1086 can only have exacerbated this process, causing several manors to become deserted and perhaps also removing common grazing.

Whether or not the earlier territory should be linked with the focal sites of an earlier era is unclear. It could be argued that the territories of a group of pre-Roman defended sites at Peckforton, Beeston, Oakmere and Kelsborough had influenced this configuration. The adoption of Rushton as the hundredal centre seems an anomaly in the context of the central functions recalled by the various township names in Bunbury parish. It could have been influenced by the proximity of the Roman villa at Eaton-by-Tarporley, which was probably an important focus *c*. 400. Further villa sites may one day be identified in this vicinity, for example at Kelsall, which might also have some relevance. There seems some reason to think that Rushton Hundred originated as a single land unit which was successively divided and subdivided, or subinfeudated, during the Anglo-Saxon period. Its eventual choice of meeting-place more probably reflects a compromise between bishop and earl than any earlier influence but the total land unit may have very early origins.

Ruloe Hundred

At Domesday, the northern end of the Mid-Cheshire ridge and its adjacent lowlands, between the rivers Gowy and Weaver, constituted the Hundred of Ruloe (Fig. 5.4). By far the least hospitable land lay along the Gowy, where extensive mosses were still being dyked and drained in the late Middle Ages. That this process was already under way in the eleventh century seems clear from the extent of the agricultural lands attached to the manors of Dunham and Elton (nine and seven ploughlands, respectively), although neither Thornton nor Bridge Trafford were of comparable size. In 1066 Æscwulf held Dunham *in paragio* ('in common'). His partners were not named but one must suspect either the Earl (it was in Earl Hugh's hands in 1086) or St Werburgh's, who held nearby Bridge Trafford as demesne. Thornton-le-Moors was already the parochial centre, with a church and priest in 1086, but there is some debate concerning the early dedication, with both St Helen and St Mary being cited (Gastrell 1845, p. 146; Ormerod 1882, II, 21). Activity on the site *c*. 1000 is attested by the survival of a cross fragment (Thacker 1987, p. 291). The tenure of the manor in 1066 by the otherwise unknown Stenketel looks suspiciously like a sub-tenancy. The township names are a mixture of topographical compounds (Dunham, Hapsford, Trafford) and compounds with **-tūn** (Thornton and the aptly named Elton ('Eel-farm/enclosure')), which relate closely to the widespread wetlands of this estuarine region. Woodland names are conspicuous by their absence. Ince ('The island') was probably separated from Thornton parish in consequence of its acquisition by St Werburgh's, before 1086.

Thornton parish enjoys little of the topographical diversity to be found in most ancient *parochiae*, being excluded from the Mid-Cheshire Ridge by its eastern boundary on the Hornsmill and Peckmill Brooks. Beyond lies the much larger parish of Frodsham, which (assuming it once included parts of Delamere parish) encompasses the entirety of the north of Ruloe Hundred as far as the lower reaches of the Weaver. Excepting Frodsham itself ('Frod's settlement') and the Scandinavian settlement-type name Helsby, all the townships bear names compounded with **-lēah** ('wood' or 'clearing'; Dodgson 1966/67– , III, pp. 219–35).

The focus of this parish was the manor of Frodsham which was a central place of considerable importance throughout the Middle Ages. In 1066 it was held by Earl Edwin who had demesne lands there as well as a priest and church, a 'winter mill', extensive woodland, fisheries and half a salthouse in *Wich* (? Northwich). The hundredal court was overseen, to the Earl's considerable profit, via Frodsham's court. A borough existed by the early thirteenth century under the earl's protection (Beresford and Finberg 1973, p. 74). The church was dedicated to St Laurence, a continental martyr familiar to English churchmen by the 680s (HE, III, 29) and there is every reason to think this an ancient mother-church. A carved grave-cover of pre-Conquest date implies that it was a burial place of high status (Thacker 1987, p. 289). That this land unit was at some stage centred on a royal estate finds support in the place-name Kingsley ('King's wood/clearing'), which was already in use in 1066.

By local standards, Frodsham parish seems overly endowed with well-wooded land, while neighbouring Thornton entirely lacks this. There is no comparison between the status of Frodsham and any manor in Thornton parish; the wealthiest secular land-holder in the latter in 1066 was probably in partnership either with the Earl or with his minster, St Werburgh's. It seems likely that subdivision of an earlier land unit embracing everything between the Gowy and Weaver had occurred at some stage before *c.* 1000, but not necessarily very long before. In the aftermath, the more wooded territory on the Ridge was retained by the superior manor, while settlements of lesser status along the lower reaches of the notoriously badly drained Gowy valley achieved sufficient independence to transfer their tithes from the mother-church to a new church at Thornton.

Kingsley was held in both 1066 and 1086 by one Dunning. His unusual ability to survive the Conquest with this landholding undiminished implies that he was able to offer some exceptional service. Since the manor had extensive woodland (which the Earl had by 1086 afforested), fisheries and four *haiae*, Dunning was most probably the Earl's forester even before the Conquest, and the steward for his court at Frodsham. If so, then the extensive woodlands on the northern end of the Ridge were already a comital chase. Kingsley's name implies that this pattern of land use predated the formation of the earldom, so going back to the tenth century at latest (Higham 1988a), and perhaps before. The location of Norley ('northern clearing/wood'), on the southern marches of the parishes of Frodsham and Weaverham implies that the bulk of this woodland already in the late Saxon period lay in what later became Delamere parish at the core of the Earl's forest, but the name is unattested before the thirteenth century. Ruloe Hundred incorporated Eddisbury, *Aldredelie* and Done in 1086 (DB, 263d; Sawyer 1987, p. 346, Footnotes 43, 44) and these presumably paid tithes to Frodsham.

Frodsham township remained of exceptional size throughout the Middle Ages, with several farming hamlets. A pattern of dispersed foci developed reminiscent of Bunbury but here within a single township; the church stands at Overton but the Norman castle or manor house was adjacent to Netherton, at the western end of a borough which was founded on the presumed line of the Roman road. Frodsham also became a minor port in the later Middle Ages, Earl Edwin's court is unlocated but should be sought in the vicinity of the parish church.

Like Frodsham, Weaverham parish may have lost some territory to Delamere but it was probably always a more compact unit. At its core was an estate of the Anglo-Saxon earls which had the distinction of being named first of Earl Hugh's many Cheshire manors in Domesday Book. It had eighteen plough-lands, demesne land, a mill and hall, a church and priest, extensive woodland interests (which Earl Hugh afforested) and burgages in Chester. The manor dominated the salt industry at Northwich, with seven salthouses attached in 1066, and it was arguably its lucrative supervisory function here which had ensured that the manor had remained virtually intact up to the eleventh century. The church (dedicated to St Mary) long remained in the patronage of the Norman earls.

Of the other townships in the parish, only two were named as manors in Domesday; Cuddington ('Farm/enclosure called after Cuda') was a small and probably sub-tenanted manor of Wulfwy, Hartford ('Hart's ford') was held as two manors by Doda. That the numerous references to this name in 1066 refer to a single individual is sustained by the exceptional characteristics of Hartford, which, though only having two ploughlands, had a smith and one and a half salthouses in 1086. This was, therefore, a component part of a much wider estate system, through which Doda had access to the *wich*. Place-names within the parish reflect the importance of the salt industry (Dodgson 1966/67– , III, pp. 193–210); Acton ('Oak farm') may have owed renders in timber (as suggested at Acton by Nantwich); Wallerscote is 'Salt boiler's cottage'; Norley and *Conersley* were typical woodland names suggestive of fuel and wood pasture and Earnslow (Grange), in Weaverham-cum-Milton is 'Eagle's wood'. Crew Wood in Crowton suggests a place where material was obtained to make baskets (Dodgson 1966/67– , III, pp. 195–6), which might well have been used in some quantity in the salt-works. The survival of a pre-English name may indicate a long but otherwise undocumented history of exploitation of the local salt industry. Milton takes its name from the mill attached to the Earl's manor. Like Frodsham and Alpraham, the focal court, and hence the estate and parish, was endowed with a **-ham** place-name, the prefix deriving from the river Weaver.

The Hundred therefore focused on two sites; Frodsham was the court from which public jurisdiction was overseen. It was the centre of the larger land unit and may have been favoured as an occasional residence by the Mercian kings, then earls, when they wished to escape the pressures of state business and Chester in favour of the hunt. From Weaverham the principal industry and market of the region was supervised and tolls levied. This too may have been a royal centre at an early date. Both had mother-churches with extensive *parochiae*, either of which could easily date back to the seventh or eighth centuries. Given the very different functions of these sites, neither may have been considered sufficiently expendable *in toto* to alienate from the crown, even to the bishops of Lichfield, so neither church became episcopal property or gained an extensive endowment in land. Ecclesiastical lordship did make an appearance but probably not until the tenth century and after, by which time the *parochia* of the Frodsham minster had already been fractured by the foundation of a church (possibly in origin a chapel) at Thornton-le-Moors. This church then established its claim to tithes from several peripheral estates in an area where St Werburgh's would eventually develop both territorial and parochial interests.

Tunendune *Hundred*

This Domesday hundred was almost entirely coterminus with two medieval parishes, those of Runcorn and Great Budworth, with the addition of the small post-Conquest parish of Grappenhall and the exception of Wincham (in Great Budworth parish but in Bucklow Hundred; Figs. 5.5, 5.6).

Runcorn parish is probably the best-known example of an early land unit in Cheshire, owing in part to the exceptional number of directionally named townships within it; Weston, Aston, Norton and Sutton (Thacker 1987, p. 272; Higham 1982, 1988a; Greene 1989). In 1066 the capital manor was at Halton, where a castle was later built (Plate 10; cf. Malpas), but there are signs that the construction of a *burh* on the Mercian frontier at Runcorn had inaugurated major reorganisation of its immediate hinterland (ASC(C), 915; Higham 1988a, pp. 204–6). It was probably only at this stage that the mother-church was removed to Runcorn, a bleak and inhospitable site in the far north-west corner of the *parochia*. Its dedication to St Bertelin may well have been deliberate policy on Æthelflæd's part (Thacker 1985, p. 19), in which case the earlier dedication is lost. Place-name evidence implies that the earlier church site was at Preston-on-the-hill ('Priests' farm/enclosure'; compare Prestbury and Prestatyn, Plate 11). The possibility that this was a mother-church is strengthened by the plural implicit in several forms of the place-name (Dodgson 1966/67– , II, p. 156). The directional place-names (and other **-tūn** names such as Clifton) may have derived from the renaming of dependent settlements consequent on tenth-century reorganisation but they do not relate to the township of Runcorn.

Otherwise these township names are unexceptional, comprising a mix of **-tūn** compounds with several names indicative of woodland exploitation (Eanley, Stockham ('at the tree stocks'), Acton ('Oak farm')). Apart from the directional prefixes above, there are some indications of dependent settlements; both Stockham

---

155

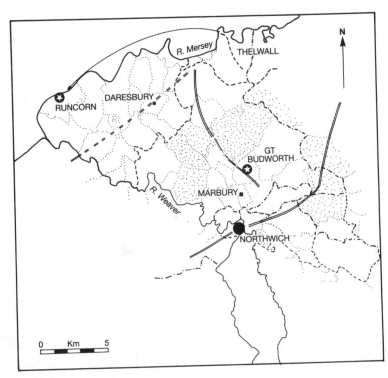

Fig. 5.5 The early organisation of *Tunendune* hundred: woodland township-names as in Fig. 5.3

and Stockton imply the existence of a settlement of higher status nearby, and the two Waltons may refer either to Britons, or more probably at this date to slaves. The **-wīc** suffix of Keckwick could refer to a market but its combination with an Old Scandinavian personal name and its hard last syllable (contrast Northwich, etc.) suggests that this is a late formation relating to a settlement which might better be interpreted as a dairy farm. The only place-name of exceptional status is Daresbury. Given the frequency with which *burh* place-names occur at early medieval foci in the shire, this may have been the secular centre of this land unit before 915. Its position on the probable line of the Roman road, propinquity to church land at Preston and its later status as a dependent chapelry within the parish all support, but do not prove, this suggestion. It might alternatively have been the earlier

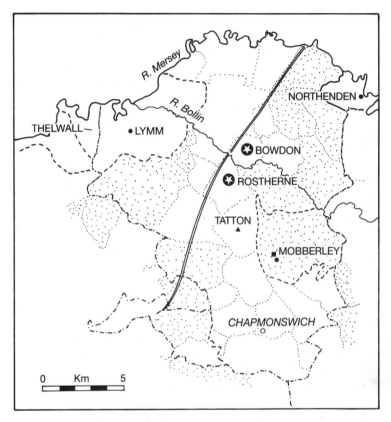

Fig. 5.6 The early organisation of Bucklow hundred: woodland township-names as in Fig. 5.3

church site (Greene 1989, p. 30), with church land at Preston, nearby.

Several **-tūn** township names (Appleton, Dutton, Bartington) lie between the southern boundary of the medieval parish and a consistent line of woodland place-names (Fig. 5.5). The latter occurs across a belt of exceptionally flat, clayey and poorly-drained land. These woodland place-names might have been expected to have separated the early *parochiae* to north and south. If the mother-church of the northern parish was removed in 915 from Preston or Daresbury to Runcorn, this may have occasioned a redrawing of the boundary and the transfer of several communities from the ecclesiastical authority of Runcorn to Great Budworth. It seems otherwise difficult to explain the boundary adopted.

In 1066, Halton was the chief tenement of Orm, a thegn who was apparently responsible for policing the fords over the middle Mersey. The court of his very extensive (twenty ploughlands) estate had a salt-house and extensive woodland attached to it. Other landholders in the parish were probably his undertenants or associates and shared his responsibilities; Uhtred and Toki (at Norton) probably had estates on both sides of the lower Mersey (Lewis 1991a); Gruffydd (five ploughlands at Weston) is unlikely to have been a local man and may have had connections with Earl Edwin (see below); Leofric (at Aston) had a mill and fisherman attached to his two and a half ploughland estate, both of which suggest high status.

Although it was later to become a separate manor, Grappenhall probably originated as part of Runcorn parish. Its tenure in 1066 and 1086 by thegns of the highest status implies that there may already have been a tension between the lords of this outlying manor and a mother-church which had apparently been removed to the furthest corner of the *parochia*. That it was perhaps held by a family who patronised the churches at Lymm and Great Budworth can only have exacerbated the situation. There is no mention of either church or priest at Domesday, but the dedication to St Wilfrid may imply that a manorial church or chapel already existed then.

With twenty-one townships and two dependent chapelries, Great Budworth was by far the larger of the two *parochiae*, extending via its chapelries into the Domesday hundreds of Ruloe and Middlewich. In discussing the pre-Conquest situation, these chapelries are best ignored since they would seem to be post-Conquest accretions. Nether Peover chapel was largely the responsibility of the Grosvenor family in the thirteenth century and its dependence on Great Budworth arguably derives primarily from the close links then existing between Richard Grosvenor and Norton Priory, the rector of Great Budworth.

Great Budworth manor centred in 1066 on the hall of a certain Edward, who had a priest and a mill. Compounds with the suffix **-worð** ('an enclosure') were, however, uncommon as ancient foci (in Cheshire, only Gawsworth also became a parochial centre, and that only in the later Middle Ages). The manor was small (gelded at one hide and with two ploughlands), probably entirely within the township and only valued at six shillings in 1086. The church dedication is to God and All Saints, which is unlikely to be much earlier than 1066, although this could represent a replacement of an existing dedication, perhaps after it came into the hands of Norton Priory. Great Budworth therefore has few of the hallmarks of an ancient centre or mother-church, despite the large parish and Domesday priest.

Edward also held one of the two small manors at Dutton and (Little) Leigh, within the parish, one of two manors at Clutton and one of four called Peover, but his principal interests probably lay at Lymm, where an Edward (probably the same man) retained land in 1086. The status of neighbouring Thelwall as a detached portion of Runcorn parish should probably be associated with the construction of a *burh* there in 919 (Thacker 1985; Higham 1988a). Links between the manors at Lymm, Great Budworth and Grappenhall may imply a later governmental interest in oversight of the Mersey crossings at Warrington, comparable to that of the holders of Halton over the fords at Runcorn.

If Great Budworth was not the earliest church site in this *parochia*, its predecessor is a mystery. Marbury ('Mere-*burh*') is one candidate as a centre but was not even named as a manor in Domesday Book. Another is Wincham ('Wigmund's hām'), but at present these are no more than guesses based on far-from-conclusive but recurring patterns of place-names.

The parish was characterised by numerous small estates in 1066, many with names which refer to a well-wooded landscape. There are some which may reflect dependence: Aston ('East settlement/enclosure', which is directly east of Great Budworth, and so may be a name post-dating that church site); Appleton (which may have paid renders in apples, albeit originally perhaps to a more northerly centre); Plumley ('Plum-lēah'); and Lostock (Gralam), the name of which reflects pig-farming. Woodland was clearly very widespread in the region but the parochial core around Great Budworth is characterised by a group of settlement-type place-names. Woodland names are only dominant in the north-west and south-east sectors of the parish. Single place-names often served to describe more than one Domesday manor, although Peover (the river-name) was exceptional in its application to four manors. Numerous place-names were also used to describe landholdings on both sides of the parish boundary; hence Peover, Hartford, Lostock and Tabley. In many respects, therefore, the parochial geography of Great Budworth implies a region which had, by 1066, long lacked the authority of a landholder of high status in control of a core estate.

It was a poor area which lacks any trace of markets, other than Northwich. Although the latter lay in the medieval chapelry of Witton ('wīc-settlement'), it was clearly administered from Weaverham at Domesday, albeit that several thegns had salt-houses attached to their manors in Great Budworth parish. Great Budworth's extensive parish does, however, imply that the standard pair of land units and *parochiae* underlay *Tunendune* Hundred.

If the border between these two *parochiae* was the subject of a major realignment early in the tenth century, it was presumably achieved under royal authority, This implies that the crown then had a controlling interest in both halves of the hundred. In 958, St Werburgh's received an estate at *Eston* (Middleton in Runcorn parish), by gift of King Edgar (Tait 1920). The Runcorn/Halton land unit was at that stage, therefore, probably still under royal control. Runcorn had briefly been an important part of Æthelflæd's military strategy, and Thelwall of her brother's. Their interests were arguably still active by proxy (through Orm) in 1066. Royal interest in Great Budworth had, by contrast, ebbed away, It was an area of weak manorialisation without central authority – hence its unfocused structure by 1066, when its various Saxon landholders just might have been dependants of Orm at Halton (see below, p. 209).

Eastern Cheshire

Bucklow Hundred

This northern hundred had four churches and/or priests in 1086, to which a fifth – Mobberley – had been added by the twelfth century at latest. This last was probably in origin a part of Rostherne parish, but it displays several signs of unusual status even before its emergence as a single township parish; the township name refers to 'a clearing at the *burh* where meetings are held', implying that it had at some stage been a central place of some significance. Although it is only known in late sources, Grims Ditch Farm, on the south side of the brook in the middle of Mobberley (Dodgson 1966/67– , II, p. 66) may denote the location of this defensive site. Dot had this manor in 1066 and he appears to have been a man of considerable influence in the shire. The tenure of an unnamed thegn here in 1086 implies the survival of an English tenant of relatively high status and his four ploughlands suggests that it was a substantial manor by local standards. The church's dedication to St Wilfrid and its conversion to an admittedly struggling and short-lived Augustinian Priory in the twelfth century may imply early foundation and minster status, but it is never likely to have been anything more than a manorial church unless the minster church of Rostherne parish was at some stage located here.

St Wilfrid was also the dedication at Northenden ('Northern enclosure'), where a church was noted in Domesday Book. This parish barely extended beyond the township and has no claim to great antiquity or unusual status. It could have been founded at any stage during the later Anglo-Saxon period by a landholder of the necessary political stature. The manor was held in 1066 by Wulfgeat. If one individual should be identified as the holder of the majority (even all) of the manors against this name in 1066 then he was a man of exceptional status, who held other local manors with churches (at Lymm and Rostherne) or manors where churches would soon emerge (Tarporley). His family probably wielded sufficient local influence to divert tithes at Northenden to their own manorial church, but when this occurred is unclear. An examination of this parish's later bounds suggests that it had been part of Bowdon parish, and it was quite specifically in Bucklow Hundred in 1086 (DB, 268a), despite its later incorporation in Macclesfield Hundred. Its peripheral location in Bowdon parish beyond a consistent line of woodland place-names may have encouraged the construction of a manorial church here (Fig. 5.6).

At Lymm, the churchyard is curvilinear and the dedication to St Mary (Thacker 1987, p. 290). In 1066 two manors utilised the name (an Old English topographical name derived from the stream in the centre of the township), with half the church in each. Both moieties were held by men of high status – Edward and Wulfgeat. The church then held tax-exempt land (albeit only a virgate divided between the two manors), with a priest apparently appointed alternately by the joint rectors. It is, however, difficult to make a case for its *parochia* having ever extended outside the medieval parish and it seems likely that this peripheral holding was detached from Rostherne parish during the later Anglo-Saxon period. The spectacular gorge (albeit now dammed and flooded) beside which stands Lymm church is a unique phenomenon in this region of generally flat terrain and sluggish waterways, and its physical characteristics may long have attracted ritual activities. It may, therefore, have originated as an early parochial chapel or manorial church.

Rostherne church is also dedicated to St Mary, but this church is poorly evidenced in the Anglo-Saxon period. Neither fabric nor clergy are named in this manor in 1086, although both were referred to as attached to the two manors at (High) Legh, held by Wulfgeat and Dot in 1066. Rostherne was waste in 1086 but had also been held in 1066 by Wulfgeat, and all three manors were held in 1086 by Gilbert of Venables; so the mention of church and priest at High Legh may be no more than an administrative convenience (Higham, forthcoming (a)). The extraordinarily low hidation of Rostherne (one virgate) could derive from the presence of unrecorded geld-free church land. The church was certainly there in the late twelfth century (Plate 12). The place-name is unlikely to predate the Viking Age and is of a type which is unusual in minster sites. It therefore seems likely either that the church settlement had previously been known by another name or that the church had lain elsewhere.

The medieval parish was extensive, including all or parts of about seventeen townships, running from High Legh in the north-west as far as Over Peover. It eventually included two chapelries (Over Peover and Knutsford) which catered for the more distant south-east end, but neither are likely to predate the foundation of a borough at Knutsford in the late thirteenth century, It shared parts of its western boundary with the hundred, along a belt of extremely poorly drained boulder clay which was in part in Great Budworth parish, where woodland was still extensive in the central Middle Ages (hence Arley,· Crowley, Northwood, Bentleyhurst, Tabley). The core of the parish is the well-drained, if slight, ridge of fluvioglacial sands and gravels and Keuper marl along which the Roman road from Mere to Hatton once ran and which carried the medieval road linking Knutsford and Warrington (now the A 50). The township name (High) Legh reflects the tapering of this ridge at its northern end, where land suitable for agriculture is surrounded by heavy clayland and the now extensively drained Sink Moss. These form a natural barrier of less hospitable terrain separating this land unit from its northern neighbours, across which woodland place-names are commonplace (Bradley, Swinyard or Swindhead, Agden ('Oak-tūn') and numerous woodland farm names).

The parish contained no single estate of any size at Domesday but there were two concentrations of landholdings at its core; Knutsford and one of the two Tatton manors comprised the total landholdings of Egbrands, while three manors were held by Wulfgeat (Sawyer 1987, p. 324). It contained the meeting-place of the hundred at Bucklow Hill on Watling Street. The site was convenient both for those travelling via that street from north-east of the Bollin and via the ridge from Rostherne parish. It lies only *c.* 1200 m from Rostherne church, probably on the point of intersection of the townships and manors of Millington, Rostherne and Mere. The first of these refers to a mill (probably in the vicinity of Booth Bank), but this is unlikely to have been in use as late as 1066 when the manor had little arable land. The strong links between mill ownership and large estates held by men of high status (see p. 196) imply that this place-name is a relic of the earlier existence of a substantial landholding with manorial appurtenances, which had suffered dissolution by 1066.

The parish contained one further place-name of focal significance in *Chapmonswiche* ('Trader's market'), now lost but in Ollerton, near Knutsford. There are, therefore, vestiges of a commercial centre and a focus of high status to set beside the church site at Rostherne, which collectively suggest the presence of a grouping of focal functions in the Knutsford–Rostherne area, at the core of this *parochia*. The presence of an extremely large and arguably sub-Roman building at Tatton (p. 66 and Higham, forthcoming, (a)), central to this core, may be relevant to this focus. Even so, Mobberley must have some claim as an earlier focus, because of its church, its *burh* place-name and its 'moot'.

The remainder of the hundred lay in Bowdon parish which, until the loss of Ashton on Mersey, comprised thirteen townships. Warburton may additionally have become detached from it in consequence of the establishment there of a convent of Premonstratensian canons in the next century (Dodgson 1966/67– , II, p. 34). Given the role of the middle reaches of the Bollin as a parochial boundary, its location east of the lower course of this river suggests that it had become detached from Bowdon rather than Lymm. Excluding the two manors of Warburton, nine manors were named in Domesday Book, all of which were held by, or closely associated with, one Alweard (or Alfweard) in 1066. His principal demesne lay at Dunham but his mill was at Bowdon, and the later construction of a motte and bailey on the banks of the Bollin in that township emphasises the seigneural interest there. The church (dedicated to St Mary) held half the hide on which this manor paid tax. The hilltop site and the topographical place-name ('Hill shaped like a bow') are entirely consistent with this being an early mother-church. The reference in both Dunham and Bowdon to **dūn** emphasises their common origin as a single estate focus. The absence of other manorial lords of any consequence in 1066 suggests that a land unit coterminous with the *parochia* was still almost intact in 1066. The bulk of it passed to Hamo de Mascy and became the core of the barony of Dunham Mascy, wherein a group of focal sites – the borough at Altrincham, the seigneurial centre at Dunham and church at Bowdon – continued the earlier organisation of central functions into the later Middle Ages.

The place-name evidence implies that much of this parish was well-wooded in the early Middle Ages (hence Ashton, Ashley, Sale ('At the willow'), Baguley ('**lēah** of the badger'), Timperley ('Timber-glade')), and there is an unusual group of names in **-ing** – Carrington, Partington and Altrincham – none of which were named in Domesday Book, and which may have been tenurially subordinate but heritable settlements. Carrington derives from an anglicised form of a Scandinavian personal name (Dodgson 1966/67– , II, p. 17), so that at least is of late origin. The balance between settlement and woodland names reflects the topography, with **-tūn** and **-hām** names clustering around Bowdon Hill itself, while a consistent line of woodland place-names separate the core of the parish from Rostherne (Ashley, Ringway

('Ring hedge'), probably referring to a deer park, Mobberley) and from Northenden.

Bochelau hundred was therefore unexceptional in containing two mother-churches and their *parochiae*. Both these church sites and Lymm may have offered particular attractions as ritual centres. The land unit represented by Bowdon's *parochia* was still very much in evidence in 1066, through the holdings of Alweard, although it was a poor and backward corner of a peripheral and economically underdeveloped province of Mercia, which had no recorded commercial focus. Rostherne displays traces of a grouping of early foci but lack of central authority here appears to have allowed an early land unit to fragment before 1066. Manorial lords had successfully detached peripheral parts of both these *parochiae* by 1066. Both instances illustrate the comparative ease with which small patches of well-drained terrain isolated from the core of an estate by lēah place-names and heavy clayland could be removed from the integrated and centralised social, economic and religious system of the early land unit (Fig. 5.6).

Middlewich Hundred

This, the south-eastern hundred of the shire, stretched from the heavily faulted uplands of Mow Cop and the Cloud, north-westwards to the poorly-drained Peover valley. Much of it is comparatively flat boulder clay, with all the problems of drainage which that implies. Substantial areas of fluvioglacial deposits were overly dry and had only severly pauperised soils, hence the numerous heathlands of this region in the Middle Ages (Rudheath, Brereton Heath, Wheelock Heath, Ettiley Heath, etc.). The hundred took its name from the saltwich, and the hundred court presumably met there but there were neither comital lands nor lords' salthouses. In 1066 the *wich* brought in a farm of only eight pounds, with the hundred court contributing another two pounds (DB, 268b). Management of the hundred was, therefore, not directly associated with a manorial court of the earldom in the late Saxon period. The parochial structure reflects this absence of close supervision (Fig. 5.7).

Excepting only the parochial chapelries of Great Budworth in the extreme north, the hundred comprised two groups of medieval parishes. The more southern and westerly group en-

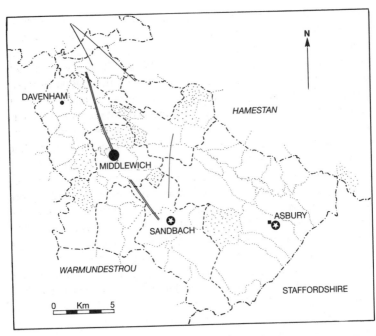

Fig. 5.7 The early organisation of Middlewich hundred: woodland township-names as in Fig. 5.3

compassed Davenham, Middlewich, Warmingham and Sandbach, Davenham eventually included ten townships and had a priest and church in 1086. Its dedication to St Wilfrid might suggest that it could have belonged to a similar phase of Anglo-Saxon church foundation as Northenden, but any date from the late seventh to the early eleventh centuries is feasible. The tenure in 1066 of four manors (including Davenham itself) by an important thegn called Osmer suggests that a focal estate still then underpinned the structure of the parish, which was dominated by this landholder; the only township names outside his tenure being the small manors of Shurlach (cum Bradford, two manors), Wharton (two tenants) and Moulton (Leofnoth).

Despite its considerable size, there seems no reason to think that the medieval parish of Middlewich originated before Domesday, and the dedication to St Michael and All Saints certainly counts against this. Middlewich was not even an estate in the

Survey. The church probably began as a manorial foundation built at Newton-by-Middlewich, a holding which formed part of the estates of Burton Abbey in the very late tenth century (Sawyer 1979). Its association with Wulfric Spot and Burton Abbey may well account for its having a priest in 1086. This association and the place-name of characteristically late form both imply that it was a product of the late tenth to early eleventh centuries.

Despite its circular churchyard (Thacker 1987, p. 292), there is no good reason to date Warmingham church to the eleventh century or before. This place-name is not mentioned in Domesday Book, when the entire parish was probably represented by the manor of Tetton. The dedication is to St Leonard, a saint popular in Norman England but not before, and the church seems unlikely to predate the Conquest.

The parochial geography suggests that the entire area of these four parishes was initially the *parochia* of a single mother-church at Sandbach, from which by 1066 a large but subordinate *parochia* had become detached at its northern extremity. Domesday Book records a church and priest here (the dedication is to St Mary) but this church appears to have suffered a severe decline in its fortunes since *c.* 900.

Sandbach's minster church is associated with a unique group (in Cheshire at least) of pre-Viking stone sculptures, the best-known of which are the two great relief-decorated crosses in the market place (Plate 13). The remains represent at least three crosses in all (the smaller is topped by what is probably part of a third) and there are the remains of three much smaller examples and a coped grave-cover in the churchyard (Thacker 1987, 291). The entire group shares a consistent style of decoration, although the largest cross was arguably the first to be produced. Collectively, these monuments reflect the presence of an active sculptural workshop centred on Sandbach early in the ninth century, which was in contact with current developments in Continental Europe and interested in complex but canonical theological concerns (pers. comm., Dr Jane Hawkes, on whose work the following two paragraphs are based).

There can be identified on the east face of the larger cross scenes representing the Adoration of the Magi, Crucifixion, Nativity, Transfiguration of Christ (on Mount Tabor) and a

Traditio Legis cum Clavis (Christ's presenting of the keys to heaven and the new law to Saints Peter and Paul, respectively). The choice of scenes, their relationship to one another and specific details express repeatedly the themes of witnessing the universality of Christ's salvation (particularly to the Gentiles), the role of the Church established in Christ, and the important place of the Gospels and Eucharist within that Church. Further scenes can be identified on the west face and on the smaller cross which offer similar 'messages'.

The iconography of these monuments is not relevant only (or even primarily) to a monastic audience but was more likely to have been produced for a 'secular' Christian context. The 'messages' are those applicable to all Christians, and there is a strong emphasis on the power and authority of the Church which contrasts with the more normally monastic context of so much pre-Viking sculpture in both Northumbria and Mercia.

These exceptional aspects of the Sandbach monuments may imply that this was a non-monastic church, but one in contact with the highest ecclesiastical authorities in the region. That bishop Hygebeorht of Lichfield had been promoted to the rank of archbishop in 787 provides the most obvious link with contemporary Gaul and Italy. The see was downgraded in 803, but Hygebeorht's successor, Ealdwulf, and his circle, may well have been in unusually close touch with the Continent, in part as a legacy of the previous incumbent and in part in the hope that his archdiocese might be renewed. If the bishop or his lieutenants made regular visits to Chester or its vicinity, they may well have needed a substantial estate in south-east Cheshire to break the journey. If Sandbach was the capital of such an episcopal estate before the Viking Age, then control of it was entirely lost thereafter, but the exceptional group of pre-Viking monuments must at least encourage speculation on this point. Even so, by the middle of the thirteenth century the parish had been reduced to a core around the church and a detached chapelry, eventually two chapelries, Holmes Chapel (or Church Hulme) and Goostry.

The small size of the manor, the absence of comital estates and the dispersed landholdings within its *parochia* at Domesday all bear witness to the collapse of whatever powerful patronage had, two centuries or more before, given such rich commissions to a school of sculptors. In 1086, Sandbach and Kinderton had the largest hidations (three each) and Sandbach had four ploughlands. This rather high ratio of hides to ploughlands could reflect the income to the manorial church from its extensive tithes. It clearly did not enjoy the benefit of tax exemption, or even beneficial hidation. Place-name evidence may reflect an older pattern of renders to an ecclesiastical estate: Moulton may contain **mūl** ('mule'), so 'farm supplying mules'; Shipbrook refers unequivocally to sheep, and Whatcroft is 'Wheat field'; Elton derives from eels and Stublach from 'tree-stumps'; Eardswick Hall (Minshull Vernon) alludes to a herdsman's sheds (Dodgson 1966/67– , II, *passim*). Most township names are either personal name and **-tūn**, or descriptive, topographical place-names, as at Sandbach, 'Sandy valley-stream'. Some of the latter may be comparatively early formations but the entire area is undocumented before Domesday Book.

The remainder of the hundred consisted of the single medieval parish of Astbury, with its four parochial chapelries (Brereton, Congleton, Lawton and Swettenham), all of which were probably post-Conquest in origin. The church (dedicated to St Mary) was granted to St Werburgh's in the process of its refoundation in 1093 but the presence of several late Saxon fragments of a cross and other sculptured pieces suggest that it was a mother-church of some consequence in the pre-Conquest period. If some of these fragments of masonry were architectural (Thacker 1987, p. 286) then this was perhaps an Anglo-Saxon stone church. In 1066 it was held by Wulfgeat, probably the same individual as has been noted elsewhere as the proprietor of churches in eastern Cheshire (see above) and who held four ploughlands at neighbouring Brereton.

If the 'East *burh*' of the parochial place-name is meaningful, it may reflect the more easterly situation of this church, as opposed to Sandbach. The nearest *burh* place-name to the west is Wybunbury, also an important church site. The parish consists of the valley of the Dane and this, the principal topographical feature, lies at its centre. The place-name Davenport implies a commercial centre named after the river and this may have been of some consequence, perhaps in trade between Cheshire and the Danelaw to the east, when Sihtric and the Irish Norse sacked it *c.* 920 (see the discussion in Dodgson 1966/67– , II, p. 301; Higham 1988a, p. 211). It should perhaps be seen as a pre-Conquest precursor of Congleton. Scandinavian influence is present in the place-name Congleton, but otherwise Old English dominates in major place-names, many of which contain topographical elements (hence Moreton, Hulme Walfield, Lawton, Church Hulme).

There has been some doubt concerning the relationship between several of the manors of this parish and the hundredal organisation at Domesday. Cranage and Kermincham were both listed in Domesday Book under *Hamestan* Hundred, but in both instances the problem is probably one of rubrication. Middlewich regularly follows *Hamestan* in the listing of the landholdings of Earl Hugh's tenants in 1086. The hundredal rubrication had been inserted in the margin immediately below the entry for Hugh fitzOsbern's berewick of Kermincham (DB, 266c) and this correction may well have been misplaced, perhaps because the berewick was in 1066 an appurtenance of Godric's lands in *Hamestan* at Bosley or Marton. Cranage is likely to have been a simple case of omission of the rubric. It was Robert fitzHugh's sole manor in the hundred (DB, 264d). Somerford Booths was likewise probably the subject of an error (Thacker 1987, p. 296). In general, difficulties here are more likely to have arisen from the defects of Domesday Book than real irregularities in the boundaries.

Middlewich Hundred does, therefore, betray the same bipartite organisation as so many of Cheshire's hundreds, consisting very largely of the early *parochiae* of two mother-churches at Sandbach and Astbury. The first of these had enjoyed by far the larger territory in the pre-Viking period when it had centred on the most important church in eastern Cheshire. The religious community here may have been directly dependent on the diocese and a favoured residence for the bishops, at least in the late pre-Viking period, when the site was chosen as an appropriate one to be endowed with an exceptional group of religious monuments. It had, however, lost much of its authority by the eleventh century, by which date the church had sunk to manorial status and its *parochia* begun to fragment, with a large number of communities already by this date paying their tithes to Davenham. Even so, the dedication of that church to St Wilfrid may betray a continuing tradition, spurious or not, of his role in the foundation of Sandbach.

From less auspicious beginnings, Astbury church retained extensive interests in a large parish and, under the oversight of St Werburgh's the process of later subdivision was more tightly controlled. Astbury may well have been under more immediate secular patronage and control than Sandbach during the Viking Age and it was probably the principal seat of Gilbert, Wulfgeat's Norman successor, until it passed to St Werburgh's. Kinderton then became the baronial centre. That it was named Newbold in 1086 implies the presence of a substantial new residence on the site at that date.

That the Domesday hundred took its name from the **wīc** at its core is a reminder that *Salinae* was the sole Roman site of any size known in the region. This may be a coincidence. Alternatively, it is possible that the Anglo-Saxon hundred represents the survival of an administrative district which had originated in the Roman period.

Hamestan *Hundred*

For nine manors in this hundred (using eight place-names), the Domesday Survey departs from its standardised account of Cheshire's manors in favour of a list of estates and tax liabilities (DB, 264a). To this was attached a summary noting the number of landholders in 1066 (eight), the total of ploughlands (sixteen), and a shorter list of manorial woodlands. This unusual presentation is not unlike that used in parts of Lancashire and may have stemmed from similar problems of obtaining, then checking, information beyond that available from late Saxon geld lists. This circumstance underlines the exceptional problems confronting an analysis of pre-Conquest organisation in *Hamestan* Hundred, the poorest and least hospitable of any part of the region, which took the first brunt of Norman wasting in 1070. To give just two indications of the unusual difficulties of farming in this region, it has the most references to extensive woodland in any part of the Domesday shire (Terrett 1948). It also has an unusually generous ratio of geld to ploughlands; the sixteen manors for which figures are available were assessed at only sixteen hides and one virgate yet were attributed eighty-two ploughlands, so at a ratio of one to five. The ratio elsewhere in Cheshire rarely deviates far from one to two.

At Domesday, the hundred focused on two estates of Earl

171

Edwin (then Earl Hugh) at Macclesfield and Adlington. Their combined ploughlands (twenty plus twenty) were close to a quarter of the whole and their geld liability (two and four hides respectively) over a third of the total. They did not, therefore, enjoy beneficial hidation of the kind recognisable at the earls' estates of Acton, Malpas or Frodsham, but rather the reverse. The absence of demesne and presence of radmen suggests that the Adlington estate consisted of a group of manorial tenancies intermingled with extensive comital woodlands, described as eleven leagues by two, in which seven *haiae* and four eyries emphasise the earl's interest in hunting. Macclesfield had demesne land and a mill serving the court, suggesting that it was the earl's principal residence in eastern Cheshire and his share of the profits of the hundred were attached to it. Macclesfield also had extensive woodland and seven *haiae* and the directional place-name Sutton presumably derives from its local superiority.

Strong similarities between the accounts of Macclesfield and Adlington (twenty ploughlands and seven *haiae* each, each worth eight pounds in 1066 and 20s in 1086) imply that the management from which these figures derive was unitary and the division between two tax – paying estates a cosmetic one. Wulfric's retention of Butley (the only manor named between Adlington and Macclesfield) from 1066 to 1086 may imply that he was, throughout, the earl's steward and in effective control of *Hamestan* Hundred (Fig. 5.8). It may be significant that Wulfric's name is also recorded at Bredbury in Longdendale, implying that his responsibilities extended to the oversight of Cheshire's remote 'panhandle' in the extreme north-east of the shire.

There are neither churches nor priests recorded in Domesday in this hundred but there are indications that such existed in the late Saxon period. Round-shafted crosses have been located here and in neighbouring parts of Staffordshire, in particular, in some numbers. Most were probably ninth- or tenth-century products and there are parallels between these monuments and several found in the far north-west, as at Beckermet St Bridget (Bailey and Cramp 1988, pp. 54–6) and with the Pillar of Eliseg, in Powys. Although many of the Cheshire examples have been moved from their original positions (e.g. Marshall 1975; Thacker 1987, pp. 286–92), they still reflect the general vicinity in which they were erected. Almost all have come from the medieval

Fig. 5.8 The early organisation of *Hamestan* hundred: woodland township-names as in Fig. 5.3

parish of Prestbury, which encompassed the thirty-three town-ships in the centre and south of the hundred in the central Middle Ages (Plates 14, 15). Their presence enhances the exceptional status of Prestbury's church in the tenth and eleventh centuries, and that of its patrons. The church was the only ecclesiastical foundation named in the parish in the Papal *Inquisitio* of 1291 and had then been held by St Werburgh's since some time between 1175 and 1184. It was probably the monks who were responsible for the earliest surviving masonry on the site, now substantially rebuilt, but recognisably a late twelfth-century oratory (Plate 16).

The combination in this place-name of 'Priests' and *-burh* is consistent with a pre-Conquest origin. The plural form implies a mother-church with several clerics, so perhaps with an extensive *parochia*. A group of sculptured stones survives on the site. It may be significant that the church is only yards from the boundary of Wulfric's manor of Butley, implying that its location was of greater convenience to the earls' lieutenants in this region than to the earls themselves.

A central group of settlements can therefore be identified as the several foci of the hundred in 1066: the earl's court at Macclesfield oversaw the administration of the hundred and acted as the centre of patronage in the region; he had also a second large estate at Adlington overseeing the northern half of this vast territory, and a mother-church at Prestbury. The whole was overseen by a steward or *prepositus* who may be identifiable in 1066 as Wulfric, the holder of one of the two manors named Butley at the centre of this system. A candidate for the hundredal court is Mutlow ('Moot-mound') in Marton (Dodgson 1966/67– , I, p. 81) but its peripheral location and tenure by a minor thegn in 1066 must imply that it was not then the meeting-place. Macclesfield, to which the hundred penny was attached, seems the more likely option at Domesday.

There does, however, seem to have been major reorganisation in the later Anglo-Saxon period. Prestbury parish divides on a near-continuous line of woodland place-names into two unequal parts (Fig. 5.8). That Prestbury church was sited in this woodland belt implies that its parish had been augmented with a large part of what may earlier have been a separate northern *parochia* and land unit. That this northern part of the parish was organised independently in 1066 through a court at Adlington emphasises the diverse origins of the two areas. Its acquisition may, therefore, have occurred at some stage after *c.* 900 but before the reign of Ethelred II, when the Macclesfield estate may have been intentionally enlarged. Its strategic location *vis-à-vis* the Danelaw may well have recommended such changes to any of Ethelred, Æthelflæd or Edward the Elder.

While Macclesfield may well have been an ancient centre, the *parochia* with which it had been identified in the pre-Viking period is likely to have been significantly smaller than the medieval parish of Prestbury and centred on a church site further south. The presence of two *burh* place-names inside a single ancient territory is unusual and it may be that the place-name Prestbury was formed only in consequence of reorganisation. Henbury is a possible candidate for the site of an earlier mother-church.

At the north end of the hundred there may have been a second minster church, perhaps at Cheadle. Pre-Conquest cross fragments are preserved at the town hall. Although their origin is unknown the church is at least a possibility and the dedication is to St Mary. The interlocking parochial geography of the medieval parishes of Cheadle and St Mary's at Stockport indicate a single origin, from which Stockport was separated under the patronage of its barons, perhaps when the borough was created in the thirteenth century. The place-name Stockport ('The market-place at a dependent settlement') implies the existence of a superior settlement in the vicinity. In 1086 Cheadle was in the hands of Gamel, an important thegn, to whom it had descended from his father, and it was then the most significant centre on the upper Mersey. A manorial church of pre-Conquest origin is at least a possibility. By contrast, Wilmslow church is unlikely to predate the creation of the Bollin Fee for the Fitton family by the Norman earls. St Michael's at Mottram-in-Longdendale may predate the Conquest but its *parochia* is unlikely to have extended beyond the valley, and the early parochial organisation of this region is as likely to belong with Glossop as any Cheshire centre. There are two *burh* place-names in the region, Bredbury and Norbury. If early *parochiae* here had been much altered by the expansion of that linked to Macclesfield, both might be candidates for pre-Viking minsters, Bredbury for Longdendale and Norbury for the Stockport region, but there is no supporting evidence in either case.

The attenuated geography of *Hamestan* hundred and the extensive woodlands recorded there suggest that its organisation owes something to recognition of the frontier qualities already present in the Lyme. The hundred name is repeated in western Derbyshire, where *Hamenstan* seems to have been equivalent to the two medieval hundreds of Wirksworth and High Peak (Roffe 1986). Combined, the Cheshire and Derbyshire *Hamestans* form a large territory which stretches from Tintwistle in Longdendale south to Ashbourne (Fig. 5.9). If areas of the Pennines inside Staffordshire be added (i.e. the Domesday hundred of Totmonslow), the result is a discrete unit containing all the pagan period graves of the *Pecsaete* and this may, in fact, be an effective way to reconstruct that early medieval territory. The construction of a *burh* by Edward the Elder at Bakewell could be interpreted as recognition as late as the tenth century of a distinct 'Peak' community on the borders of English and Danish Mercia. If so, then the division of *Hamestan* between the shires of Chester and Derby should be interpreted as the deliberate division of an ancient Mercian province, occurring either during the Danish land-grab of the late ninth, or the English reconquest and reorganisation of the tenth century.

Territorial organisation: some tentative conclusions

The tenurial and parochial structure of several parts of the shire was so altered during the late Saxon period that there is little opportunity to assess earlier organisation; this most affected the Wirral peninsula and the immediate vicinity of Chester but other hundreds also experienced major reorganisation. Even so, it is possible to identify a common pattern of early territorial organisation. Seven or eight of the ten Domesday hundreds which lie inside medieval Cheshire were based on pairs of minster *parochiæ*, and so probably on paired ancient land units or 'shires'. In many cases one of the pair was arguably the product of a royal grant of land to the church, resulting in the fission of pre-existing and larger territories.

The regularity of this organisation on Cheshire is at odds with the disorder which is a characteristic of minster *parochiæ* nationally (e.g. Morris 1989). The exceptionally disciplined pattern which can be detected may result in part from the very late date at which most manorial churches came into existence. Cheshire was distant from the competitive church-building of the tenth and eleventh centuries which characterised parts of East

Fig. 5.9 The two hundreds of *Hamestan* (Cheshire and Derbyshire) and the hundred of Totmonslow (Staffordshire): a possible reconstruction of the *Pecsæte* of the Tribal Hidage

Anglia and the south of England, and had resources too meagre to encourage excessive investment in this area. The late Saxon period arguably saw a shift in the balance between local Church and secular revenues in favour of the latter, with what had apparently been a major ecclesiastical establishment at Sandbach, for example, reduced to a parochial church, and the earls as ready to reclaim and redeploy church estates as they were to augment them. Few late Anglo-Saxon thegns built new churches.

There are some indications that these land units existed when the Mercian kings established direct control of the region. It is even possible that the fundamental division between royal and episcopal tenure may in some instances predate the English take-over. Specific instances have been discussed where relevant, above. There is also the possibility that this territorial organisation owed something to the Roman period. Many units contain the ruins of a single substantial Roman settlement: Wirral – Chester; *Dudestan* – *Bovium*; Middlewich – *Salinæ*; *Warmundestrou* – Roman Nantwich. Where Roman nucleated settlements are scarce, the Domesday hundreds adopt a radial pattern around those which there are – as do Ruloe, *Tunendune*, Middlewich and Bucklow around Northwich. Of the rural hundreds, only Rushton and *Hamestan* fall outside these patterns. Coincidence, perhaps, but a degree of continuity in territorial organisation is an alternative explanation.

These early territories can sometimes be identified through the examination of place-names. Settlement and topographical place-names are concentrated at and around the core of such units and the periphery defined by names indicative of woodland, marshland or upland. It is this type of evidence which implies that major reorganisation occurred in *Tunendune* and *Hamestan* hundreds in the late Saxon period, where later parochial boundaries deviate markedly from consistent belts of woodland-type township-names.

Many such territories have single examples of names in *-burh*. Their distribution appears significant. Many *-burh* place-names were attached to ancient church sites and they were present sufficiently early to influence the naming of dependent settlements (e.g. Buerton, Burton). The English expected British church sites in this region to bear names in *-burh* at least as early as the eighth century, when Bede claimed that the monastery of Bangor

(Iscoed) was known in English as *Bancornaburg* (HE, II, 2). It should be noted in passing that this English word was pejorative, meaning 'The *burh* associated with the murderer of the seeds' – the latter a term with Biblical connotations. It is likely to have originated as a clever, bilingual, but vicious, pun current among English clerics, like Bede himself, who were virulently hostile to the British clergy, despite the fact that it eventually entered common parlance (Bede's term was certainly in use in the later Middle Ages). *Burh* is apparently here used as an approximate translation which emphasises the enclosed (and probably em-banked) nature of the monastery, the Welsh name of which means 'Fence', hence 'Fenced enclosure' and so 'Monastery'. This has important implications in Cheshire where so many -*burh* place-names are associated with early church sites. Some may be pre-English foundations.

Many other place-names of high status are topographical in origin (e.g. *Depenbech*, Farndon, Sandbach, Bowdon). That these are early finds support in the frequency with which such names occur in early English sources (Cox 1975–77). Some may be translations of pre-English district names, many of which were probably topographical in origin, of which a few survive (e.g. Werneth, and see comments above concerning Wirral). Others again use the suffix -**hām** (e.g. Frodsham, Weaverham, Eastham, Davenham), meaning 'settlement'. A higher proportion of -**hām** names were attached to early parishes or comital estates than is the case with the far more numerous names in -**tūn**, but names in -**inga-hām** are not distinguished in 1066 by their high status (e.g. Kermincham, Tushingham – both in Domesday Book – and several others which were not named as manors). There are clearly difficulties in distinguishing names in -**hām** from those in -**hamm** ('a water meadow'), particularly given the late date at which local place-names are documented (Kenyon 1986b) and the riverside locations of many examples. Names in -**tūn** and -**inga-tūn** are numerous but very rarely associated with sites which had an early focal role, despite what would seem to be a tenth- or eleventh-century adoption of Halton as an important secular centre. Although there is a certain risk of circularity in arguments of this type, it does seem clear that -**tūn** and related name el-ements were used locally for settlements or estates of middling to low status.

179

Place-naming may also reflect the pattern of ancient renders within an estate system. Patterns are certainly not entirely random, although naming occurred and recurred over such a long time-scale that it is often impossible to distinguish names of the eighth and ninth centuries from later accretions.

The recurring pattern of core and periphery within these early land units can be specific to the hundred (e.g. *Dudestan*) but more often relate to the paired *parochiae* within each hundred. These generally incorporated a balance of different types of terrain, so providing access to as wide as possible a range of resources. The periphery of such territories was apparently characterised by extensive land use. In consequence, most were bounded by uplands or extensive wetlands. It seems to be at this level that the rural economy was normally organised in the pre-Viking period and specific types of terrain allocated to particular uses. There are widespread references in place-names across Cheshire to the use of summer pasture (e.g. names in **-heord** **-bōth**, or **-erg**). Given the general accessibility of low-lying wetlands, there was less need than in other parts of Britain (e.g. Kent, Sussex, Arden) to organise transhumance over long distances. Many *parochiae* had access to extensive areas charac-terised by place-names in **-lēah**, which may have provided com-munal grazing at an early date, but most grazing was probably even more localised than this. Most individual townships or manors included in their bounds woodland and/or moss or heath-land which could have been used for such purposes. Indeed, a concern to obtain a diversity of resource apparently influenced the pattern of township boundaries in many parts, as around Astbury and in low-lying areas such as the Dee valley, where the elongated Eaton township retained access to woodland at Belgrave ('Fire-wood'). It was not until the later Middle Ages that improvement and draining of these common lands led to a marked decline in the availability of pasture and timber. Some settlements may, however, earlier have been specialist establishments, providing a central household or ecclesiastical *familia* with a particular resource (as at Bulkeley and Moulton).

Those early territories proved most resilient where large parts were retained in the hands of the kings, then the earls. It is noticeable that it was these comital estates which tended to monopolise the management of royal justice and the principal industrial and market centres. There are indications that the kings were careful to retain such assets when the division of early land units occurred. Where important assets were associated with both sections of a primary land unit (as at Frodsham and Weaverham), then both were retained.

The long-drawn-out military crisis of the later ninth and tenth centuries required that the leaders of English Mercia reward the military service of large numbers of thegns. It was probably this which led to the partial dismemberment of earlier land units and the proliferation of numerous but much smaller estates based on the individual township or a fraction thereof. This process brought to an end whatever elements of a unit-wide economy that had previously existed and provided considerable opportunities for new proprietors to rename whatever territory they had obtained.

These conclusions would suggest that the hundreds of Domesday Cheshire were based on a territorial organisation that was already old when the shire was created. This impression is confirmed by the obscurity of many of the hundredal names. The precise location of *Tunendune*, *Hamestan*, *Exestan*, *Warmundestrou* and *Dudestan* are all lost and the hundreds were reorganised soon after the Domesday Survey, perhaps so as to bring them closer into line with the geopolitics of the period. The whole shire is, therefore, younger than its parts, being based on a pre-existing political, social and religious organisation based on land units, many of which can be identified.

Whether or not there was a Mercian equivalent of the shire is unclear, but the possibility that the northern territory of the *Wrocen sǣte* had some political structure of its own in the age of King Offa should not be overlooked, particularly given the existence of *-sǣte* names attached to communities far less extensive than the *Wrocen sǣte* in Staffordshire. Our inability to confer one or more titles on the peoples of Mercian Cheshire may be due to nothing more significant than a dearth of written sources. The hundreds of late Anglo-Saxon Cheshire ultimately derive from subdivisions of the *Wrocen sǣte*. These were probably taken over as a going concern by the Mercian kings when they suppressed the client kingship of this region (for parallels, see Bassett 1992), but their marked regularity throughout much of the shire and the limited suite of dedications must owe something to the Mercian rulers themselves.

181

6

Saxon Cheshire and the Normans

Late Saxon Cheshire

When, in 958, King Edgar granted seventeen hides to St Werburgh's (Birch 1885–87, No. 1041; Tait 1920; Fig. 6.1), he chose to donate not one estate but lands 'in diverse scattered places'. This suggests the donation of parcels of land attached to several royal estates. There was probably, therefore, still extensive royal land within the shire. His patronage of reformed monasteries and reform of the coinage are two of several indications that Edgar was concerned to reinforce royal control throughout his large kingdom. That Chester was one of the few provincial mints where die-cutting did not revert to the old regional centre in the late tenth century may imply a special royal concern to retain control over this important window on the Irish Sea.

Cheshire was ravaged so severely by Viking forces in 980 that the fact gained mention in the Abingdon Chronicles (ASC(C)), which noted that 'a pirate host from the north' was responsible. This suggests a fleet from Scandinavia or the Isles, rather than the Irish Norse. Chester was later used as a base by Ethelred's fleet when it was commissioned in 999 to support his campaign against Strathclyde, but actually attacked the Isle of Man (ASC(E)). The port's role was, therefore, little changed from earlier in the century, but Ethelred was unable to dominate his northern and western neighbours as his father had done.

Royal control of the region had been delegated to powerful ealdormen during the mid-century, with men such as Ælfhere

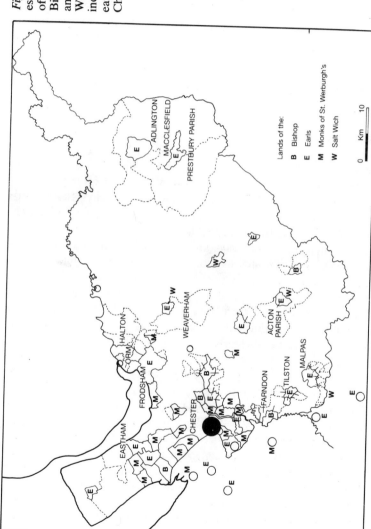

Fig. 6.1 Domesday estates of the Earls of Mercia, the Bishops of Lichfield and the monks of St Werburgh's, as indicators of possible early royal estates in Cheshire

(956–83) exercising extensive power throughout Mercia even to the point of opposing King Edgar's dispositions in favour of St Oswald, Bishop of Worcester. The freedom of action of such men was much enhanced by the power struggle which succeeded Edgar's death and the accession of successive minors to the throne. Regional rivalries and Viking attacks fatally weakened the regime of Ethelred II (978–1016). Eadric Streona, the senior Mercian ealdorman (1007–17) increasingly played the role of king-maker, and it may have been the unreliability of his local lieutenants which led Ethelred's son, Edmund Ironside, with his brother-in-law, Earl Uhtred of Northumbria, to ravage Cheshire, Shropshire and Staffordshire in 1016 (ASC(D,E)).

These three shires seem to have been united in a single ealdormanry in the late Saxon period and can occasionally be identified acting in concert. The estates of Earl Leofric's family were concentrated within this region in 1066 (Fig. 6.2) and it was the focus of the Mercian rebellion against King William in 1069–70, and was consequently wasted by Norman armies (Chibnall 1969, II, pp. 234–6). The recurring association of Mercia's three north-western shires is unlikely to be coincidental (cf. Roffe 1986, commenting on the Mercian Danelaw). They had anciently approximated to a single kingdom, then a Mercian province. That they continued to act in concert implies an ongoing regional identity which transcended the tenth-century shires. It was this identity that was recognised by Anglo-Saxon governments when they treated these three counties as a unit. It may already have constituted an ealdormanry under English kings in the mid-tenth century. It was more clearly a unit of government under Ethelred, when it was apparently associated with the ealdormanry of Leofwine, Earl Leofric's father, a nobleman from the Lincoln-shire area who was appointed ealdorman of the Hwicce in 994 (Sawyer 1979; Williams 1986; Thacker, forthcoming).

The exceptionally productive mint at Chester implies that it was this *burh* which became the principal administrative focus of the entire region during the tenth and eleventh centuries. That there were no royal estates in Domesday Cheshire, in contrast to the extensive and focal estates of the king in Shropshire and Staffordshire, suggests that the delegation of royal authority in the north-west Midlands to an ealdorman (then earl) was re-sourced by the allocation of all royal lands associated with

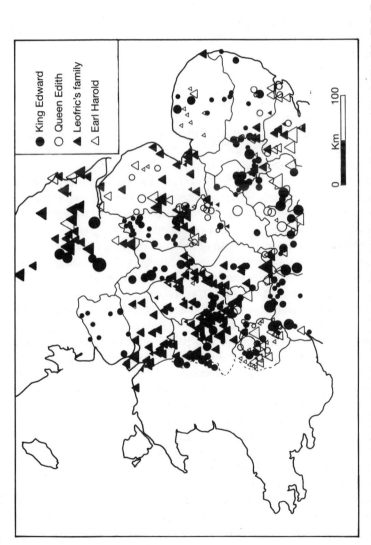

Fig. 6.2 Manors held by Earl Leofric's family, King Edward, Queen Edith and Earl Harold, *T.R.E.* The relative size of the symbol used reflects the number of hides for which each manor was liable for the geld (based on Hill 1981)

Chester, but only a share of those associated with Shrewsbury or Stafford. The focal role of the Earl's estates in Cheshire in 1066 certainly invites the interpretation that they had been royal estates at some stage in the past and these can be very tentatively reconstructed (Fig. 6.1).

The superior status of Chester in the region suggests that Earl Edwin's officers and affinity were centred there in the 1060s, as is indicated by the attempts by the *Cestrenses* ('Chester-men') to evict William's supporters from Shrewsbury (Chibnall 1969). It may also have been influential in the short-lived removal of the diocese thither from Lichfield in 1075. The cathedral was being resited to the administrative capital of the region of which it was the ecclesiastical focus. Florence of Worcester's list of the religious houses which Earl Leofric enriched is dominated by churches in and around the territory of the Hwicce – his father's ealdormanry. St Werburgh's and St John's at Chester both appear but no other north-western site is mentioned. Chester was, therefore, of exceptional importance to Earl Leofric and was probably the regional 'capital' of the more northerly of his two principal areas of responsibility. It had perhaps been of similar status under his father, Ealdorman Leofwine.

Despite Cnut's displacement of the English royal family in 1016, Leofwine retained the west Mercian ealdormanry and it passed from him to his son Leofric, Earl of Mercia (*c.* 1030–57), who was succeeded in turn by his son Ælfgar and grandson Edwin. This dynasty was one of the most influential, and one of the most robust, in late Saxon England, acting as virtual king-makers on behalf of Harold I in 1035, but it lost ground steadily in the reign of Edward the Confessor, once his court came to be dominated by Godwin's family. By 1066 the sepulchre of Leofric and his wife, Godiva, at Coventry was peripheral to the dynasty's influence and estates. Excepting Morcar's earldom of Northumbria (autumn 1065–66) and what were probably old family interests on the marches of Leicestershire and Lincolnshire, their lands were tightly focused between the Severn and the Mersey, where only Earl Harold's isolated estate at Whitchurch posed any threat to their supremacy (Fig. 6.2).

The descent of this earldom (like Godwin's Wessex) highlights the tendency in late Anglo-Saxon England for royal offices to become heritable. In many respects the earldom of Leofric approximated to the heritable and dynastically oriented counties of contemporary France. Its rulers could on occasion defy the king with comparative impunity, as Ælfgar did in 1055 and 1058, on both occasions resisting outlawry with Welsh and Norse support. Relations between Leofric and the Welsh had not always been cordial. King Gruffydd killed Leofric's brother in battle in 1039 but their differences were eventually reconciled through a marriage alliance between the Welsh king and Ælfgar's daughter, Ealdgyth (Maund 1989). Gruffydd probably benefited from the connection in his successful war to make himself supreme throughout Wales.

A controversial entry in Domesday Book (DB, 263a) implies that the peace between Gruffydd and King Edward negotiated by Earls Leofric and Harold in 1055–56 granted Gruffydd all Cheshire west of the Dee, and so the hundreds of *Exestan* and Atiscross. This grant may have bowed to long-standing Welsh grievances which originated with Mercian seizure of parts of Powys, but Gruffydd's alliance with Earl Leofric's family probably eased the transfer since the area could be construed as remaining within the family.

That Ælfgar's Hiberno-Norse shipmen came to Chester in 1055 to be paid highlights the role of the *burh* as the capital and treasury of rulers capable of pursuing a foreign policy on their own account, quite separate from that of King Edward. This impression is reinforced by the Norwegian backing which restored Ælfgar a second time from outlawry (ASC(D), 1057). Their support may imply that his family was then sympathetic to the claims of Harold Hardrada of Norway to the English succession, in opposition to Edward's Norman preferences and any ambitions which Harold Godwinson might already have been entertaining. Leofric's family had long looked and acted more like *subreguli* than officers of the crown.

It was probably only after Ælfgar's death, *c.* 1062 (it is nowhere recorded), that King Edward and Earl Harold felt able to destroy Gruffydd. He was surprised at his palace of Rhuddlan in that year, and attacked again in 1063, when Wales was extensively wasted, after which he was slain by his own followers. Gruffydd was replaced by Welsh leaders more amenable to Edward's 'overkingship' and Cheshire beyond the Dee and adjacent areas brought under direct English control. The young Earl Edwin was required to share control with the Bishop of Lichfield, who apparently granted most of his share to secular tenants such as Thored. The role of the bishop suggests that Earl Harold intended that he should shoulder much of the responsibility for the defence of *Exestan* Hundred and the crossings at Farndon, much as his own appointee as bishop had done at Hereford (ASC(D), 1056). If so, both he and the king may have sought to exploit Earl Edwin's minority to encroach on his earldom and establish central control via the only important royal appointee in the region. Although the bishop was probably Earl Edwin's man (see below) Earl Harold may have anticipated his eventual replacement with a nominee of his own, so enabling him to displace Earl Edwin on this crucial frontier.

Earl Edwin was left with the key manors of Hawarden, Bistre and Rhuddlan in 1066 and oversight of the north coast route to Wales. It was presumably he who had to contend with the waste condition of many of the estates which had been held by Gruffydd until 1063, when they seem to have been ravaged by his English and Welsh opponents. The hostility of Gruffydd's family to Earl Harold's new dispositions (e.g. ASC(C), 1065) may account for the bulk of the further devastation noted by Domesday Book along the western borders of Shropshire and Chesire.

In the summer of 1065, Harold and his brothers dominated England through their near total control of the Confessor's court and patronage and their near monopoly of the earldoms, with the inexperienced Edwin in the north-west Midlands an isolated and powerless exception. In the autumn, the situation changed radically. The Northumbrians revolted against Harold's brother, Earl Tostig, and chose Morcar, Ælfgar's younger son as earl (Kapelle 1979). They were joined in their march south by his brother, Earl Edwin, with an army made up of men from his earldom and Welshmen. The combined forces of Northumbria and the earl were sufficient to pressurise the king and Earl Harold into accepting their demands, and Tostig was exiled. When King Edward died, therefore, in January 1066, the position of Earl Harold was less favourable than it had been only a few months before. His usurpation now required support from a dynasty with which he had been locked in rivalry for two decades and which may have preferred the Norwegian candidate for the English succession as recently as 1058.

Harold apparently provided whatever assurances were necessary, left both earls in post and took their sister, the widowed Ealdgyth, to wife. Earl Edwin was only protecting his family interests when he drove off Tostig from Lindsey and the Humber (ASC(C), 1066), but he then marched north to assist his brother when the Norwegians entered the Humber. His attempt to hold York for Morcar and King Harold Godwinson ended in defeat at Gate Fulford on 20 September, but both brothers escaped from the battle with the remnants of their forces. It has been suggested that Mercian losses at Fulford were small, implying minimal participation (Lewis 1985), but such views assume that the English landholders *T.R.E.* given by Domesday Book necessarily relate to 1066. That the deceased Earls Godwin and Ælfgar were still well represented as landholders should remind us that such information derived from sources which could be anachronistic, perhaps in part from geld lists which had been little used, and so not updated, between 1052 and 1066. It is difficult to imagine where else Edwin could have raised a credible army other than from his own household and 'affinity' (to use a term of late medieval currency) in the north-west Midlands.

His decision to fight at Fulford against the most famous warrior of the age demonstrates that Edwin had little expectation that Hardrada would respect his family's interests should he displace Harold Godwinson. If Earl Ælfgar had flirted with the Norwegian cause in the 1950s, his sons' collective reconciliation with Godwinson in 1066 (or even slightly before) can only have created ill will towards them in Norway. Earl Edwin had little option, therefore, but to fight. His defeat in a hard-fought contest was the first of several blows to the military capability of his Chester-centric earldom. Neither he nor his adherents had reached Sussex when King Harold fell at Hastings on 14 October. Subsequent attempts to establish a government under Edgar the Ætheling foundered, probably primarily through the inadequacy of its military resources. Edwin and Morcar participated in the general submission to William at Berkhamsted, probably attended his coronation at Christmas, then were taken by the king to Normandy in the spring of 1067.

A chasm existed a priori between their interests and those of a Norman king whose cause they had contrived to join only after all alternatives were exhausted, and who was dependent on cash-

and land-hungry foreign warriors. Various alternative candidates for the crown had considerable support in England and native distrust of William's intentions concerning the tenure of estates and local patronage probably fuelled regional opposition to him.

Outside Northumbria, this was nowhere more strident than in Cheshire and the Welsh marches. Eadric 'the Wild' led a Welsh and Mercian attack on Hereford in 1067 (ASC(D)). His tenure of at least one estate in the extreme north of Herefordshire (Burrington; DB, 183c) may imply some link with Queen Edith, who held dower estates in the same area, or Earl Morcar, who held the very large estate and private hundred of nearby Lene. Eadric was also a major estate-holder in Shropshire, where the influence of Earl Edwin overlapped with that of King Edward. Eadric's revolt was, therefore, a response by sections of the local establishment rather than an attack from without.

As Earl Edwin's position *vis-à-vis* the king worsened, so the core members of his circle felt obliged to take the field against William. Orderic Vitalis, quoting William of Poitiers who was an eye-witness of these events, referred to 'many lawless acts' perpetrated by the *Cestrenses* ('Chester-men') and Welsh even before their siege of the king's supporters inside Shrewsbury. That it was Chester and its establishment which were central to this Mercian rising confirms the special relationship between that *burh* and the earldom. The rebels were the 'Chester-men', and the earl's Welsh allies, and it was to Chester that William directed his march late in the winter of 1069–70, followed by an unenthusiastic army which 'feared the wildness of the region, the severity of the winter, the scarcity of food, and the terrible ferocity of the enemy'. If this was not mere rhetoric on the part of the well-informed Orderic (Chibnall 1969, pp. 234–6, 261), it may imply that the 'Chester-men' already had a military reputation in the late eleventh century as great as that of the late Middle Ages. Additionally it was reputedly at Chester that King Harold's Widow, Earl Edwin's sister, had taken refuge.

William marched his unhappy forces over the Pennines in midwinter and suppressed the Chester-centric Mercian rebellion. Orderic's comment that the 'population was reduced to great wretchedness by the disturbances' (Chibnall 1969, p. 228) is probably an oblique reference to systematic wasting of Cheshire of the kind which had already occurred in Yorkshire. This finds ample confirmation in the waste condition of most of Cheshire and neighbouring parts of Staffordshire and Shropshire when granted to the holder current in 1086, and so at a sliding date between 1070–86 (Terrett 1962). William completed his conquest by building a castle at Chester (Plate 17), then another at Stafford, where he destroyed the last significant resistance from Earl Edwin's 'affinity' in battle before retiring south (Chibnall 1969, II, p. 228), probably early in the spring of 1070. He now controlled Shrewsbury, Chester and Stafford, via garrisons.

With the rebellion over, Earl Edwin had become an embarrassment. He and his brother fled from court too late to take over the Mercian rising. Morcar became embroiled in the revolt of Hereward the Wake and was taken when that collapsed in 1071 (ASC(E)), by which date Edwin had already been slain by his own men.

It was probably before he left Chester that William appointed the Fleming, Gerbod, as landholder-in-chief, though whether initially of Cheshire alone or the entire region of three shires is unclear. Orderic noted that his brief tenure was resisted by both English and Welsh, but personal affairs led him to return to Flanders, where he was taken by his enemies. By February 1071, William had granted all Cheshire barring only the bishop's lands to Hugh of Avranches. The final suppression of English and Welsh resistance was his work.

This grant mirrors William's determination to destroy the regional power-base of Edwin's earldom. Whereas Edwin had held important estates in both Staffordshire and Shropshire, Hugh was granted lands-in-chief in neither, despite his vast holdings elsewhere in England. Edwin's role in Shropshire was enhanced and subinfeudated to Roger of Montgomery, who also held lands in Staffordshire, but royal holdings in the latter were augmented with many of those hitherto held by Edwin's kin. The north-western Mercian earldom was at an end and with it Chester's claims to the political leadership of a wider and semi-autonomous region.

Earl Edwin's Cheshire

Just how little direct influence was wielded in the shire by Edward the Confessor becomes apparent through Domesday Book.

Cheshire was one of only three counties without royal estates (the others being Essex and Lincolnshire). The shire community paid the crown only the standard geld (which Edward rarely levied), tolls on Chester's port and the salt *wiches*, and the profits of coining and justice. Both tolls and judicial profits were divided on the basis of two to one between King and Earl (DB, 262c, 268a, b). The city was at farm for £45 and three *timbres* of marten skins, of which the King's share was two thirds. At some stage before 1086, a certain Mundret (an English name, so perhaps an Englishman) farmed Chester and the shire's courts on behalf of Earl Hugh. The same name occurs as an under-tenant of Earl Roger in 1086 on an estate previously held by Earl Edwin in Shropshire (Ellesmere), once in Suffolk and four times in Cheshire, as an under-tenant of Earl Hugh. In Cheshire, these holdings lay in what had been Earl Edwin's estates of Eastham and Upton, Chowley (Wulfeva's in 1066) and Bartington (Dunning's in 1066). The distinct tenures of Wulfeva, a rare female landholder, suggest that she was a lady (probably a widow) of the highest status, perhaps even of Edwin's kin. Dunning may have been his forester (p. 153). Although Mundret was not named among Cheshire's landholders in 1066 (the name occurs nowhere else, either), there is an implicit link with Earl Edwin across the decades which may suggest, but certainly does not prove, that he had been one of Edwin's immediate servants and associates – perhaps even his reeve or the otherwise unnamed farmer of Chester, *T.R.E.*

Domesday Book refers to the peace of a royal *legatus* but only in terms implicit of an occasional royal representative in, or messenger to, the shire *burh* (262c). The most senior royal representative normally present was a *iussus* – literally 'an orderer' – who was equated with a comparable officer representing the earl. Both were probably identical with the *praepositi* ('reeves') to whom reference was made elsewhere. The king's reeve had duties which included the receipt of entry fines from residents of the *burh*, oversight of the port and collection of fines for infringements of borough laws governing commerce. Given his low status and apparent lack of resources, the efficiency of this royal officer probably depended heavily on the goodwill of the earl. Indeed, it is by no means clear that he was an individual distinct from the earl's own reeve.

The only landowner in the Confessor's Cheshire who was in any sense the earl's equal was the Bishop of Lichfield. The bishopric had interests in justice, as well as fifty-six gelded houses in the 'bishop's borough' at Chester. These assets far exceeded episcopal rights at either Stafford or Shrewsbury (DB, 247a, b, 252a, 253a), despite the more extensive and valuable estates held by St Chad's in each of the latter shires. This factor points once more to the exceptional status of Chester as a regional centre for an earldom encompassing the three shires during the late Saxon period. It also suggests that episcopal interest in the *burh* dates back to the tenth century, when Chester was first redeveloped.

The bishop's landed wealth was not considerable. Apart from the substantial estate of Tarvin (six hides, twenty-two plough-lands), which seems to have been the subject of beneficial hidation, the diocese held only eight manors barely exceeding twelve hides, but this underestimates the bishop's influence. He was accounted various 'men' in Domesday Book, including a share (probably a third) of the city's twelve justices, a *minister* – probably a 'thegn' or 'reeve' – and other 'men' unspecified in Chester, all of whom were presumably tenants in his borough. In addition, the somewhat ambiguous comment concerning King Gruffydd and 'the Bishop and his men' (263a) suggests that he also had several tenants on rural holdings. One of these men has long been recognised in Thored (or Thorth), whose lands were intermingled with St Chad's at Allington, Gresford, Ashton and Barrow, but it is possible that other landholders, particularly in *Exestan*, were also episcopal tenants. Hope was held by one Edwin, whose name occurs in association with seven manors inside the parish dependent on the earl's manor of *Depenbech* (Malpas), as well as Poulton, Eccleston and Golbourne – all in the extreme west of the shire. Eccleston was later to be a key manor in the barony of Gilbert de Venables so may also have been the principal seat of this Edwin. He was described as a 'thegn' in the entry relating to Bickerton. That he was an important member of the late Saxon elite of western Cheshire seems clear.

It was probably in the interests of the bishop to lease lands in the Dee valley to men of influence whose own household troops and whose links with the earl could better ensure their protection from Welsh attack. With his substantial interests around Malpas, Edwin may even have been the earl's steward for his south-western estates and his role may have been not so very dissimilar to that of Robert FitzHugh, first Norman baron of Malpas.

At Erbistock, one Rhys held a small manor which had passed, with Thored's Gresford, to Reginald by 1086. Probably a Welsh-man, he was perhaps also an episcopal tenant. So too the priest of thegnly rank, Wulgar, and three other unnamed thegns at Caldecott near Farndon, and Eli, another rare Welsh name, at Crewe Hall.

The bishopric had clearly lost land since Cnut's reign, since the shire court supported the bishop's claims to three and a half hides in Bettisfield and Iscoyd, although not to a further half hide in Tilston. In 1066 all these were in the hands of the earl. The last Saxon bishop was Leofwine, former Abbot of Coventry, who was elected in 1053 (ASC(C)), when Earl Leofric was still at the height of his influence. His name and previous post mean that he must have been the earl's nominee for the diocese. His surrender of several episcopal estates to the earl was presumably part of a complex but mutually supportive political alliance. Bishop Leofwine was, therefore, an important and integral part of the political establishment headed by Earl Edwin in 1066, at which date he was probably one of the more senior of the earl's advisors.

If Earl Edwin was only the tenant of these episcopal holdings, it is very possible that Domesday Book listed other tenants as landholders in 1066 (see also Sawyer 1985; Sawyer 1987, pp. 316–17), so giving modern scholars a very incomplete picture of land tenure at that date. This problem can be explored to a very limited extent, by concentrating on those exceptional features of local estates which are closely associated with landholders of high status. The principal indicators are mills, salthouses, fisheries and churches and/or priests (Sawyer 1987, p. 300), the tenure of which is laid out in Table 1. The dominant position of Earl Edwin is immediately apparent, with seven mills, three manors with salthouses, four with fisheries and five churches and both the manors which had all four assets attached. The appearance of Earl Morcar, Alweard, Arni, Edward, Orm and Wulfgeat con-firm the status implicit in the comparatively high levels of geld for which they were responsible.

The problem of identifying individuals among numerous hold-ings associated with a specific name *T.R.E.* is a very real one. Only in the cases of the earls and the bishop can we be totally confident in ascribing manors to a specific individual. Several factors may assist in establishing the individuality of landholders along the Welsh borders: the rarity of a particular name (Sawyer 1987); the contiguity of estates; the passage of estates to a specific Norman successor and the Latin word-ending -us associated with the names of important men (Lewis 1985), have all been suggested.

In Cheshire, the last indicator is highly erratic and is best ignored. Instead, the presence of manorial assets indicative of high status offers an alternative approach which can help to confirm identity. For example, the contiguous group of six manors at the core of Bowdon parish attributed to Alweard all passed to Hamo (de Mascey) by 1086. The presence of a church and mill at Bowdon suggests that he was a man of high status, who could easily have held further land elsewhere. On that count, his tenure of Worleston and Shurlach should not be discounted out of hand, despite the distances involved and very different passage to Norman successors. That Shurlach was held by an individual of high status, but not normally resident, is implicit in the presence of a single fishery despite its tenure *T.R.E.* as two manors held by Alweard and Bersi. The latter name occurs nowhere else in the Cheshire Domesday Book. He may, therefore, have been the local steward of Alweard for this detached part of his estates, on which he also held a parcel of land by lease or grant, which was accounted a separate manor in 1066 but reunited with the remainder in 1086.

Similarly paired or grouped manors sharing a name are particularly common in Cheshire, occurring in three distinct patterns: there are those which were held by more than one (usually) named individual in 1066 then by a similar number of named Normans (e.g. Lymm, High Legh); others were several manors held by different individuals in 1066 but united into a single manor by 1086 (e.g. Shurlach); others again were noted as being two manors in 1066 but were then already in the hands of a single individual (e.g. Hartford), implying the presence of an unnamed tenant on at least one of them. Where a named tenant was associated *T.R.E.* with several unnamed tenants in 1066 (e.g. Caldicott), it seems reasonable to impute a gradient of status to the individuals concerned.

The obvious example of the latter is Somerford, held in 1066 as

Table 1 Cheshire under Earl Edwin: exception manorial assets and land tenure

Manor with: Landholder	Mill	Salthouse	Fishery	Church and/or priest
Æscwulf				Landican (Woodchurch)
Alfweard	Bowdon			Bowdon
Alfweard/Bersi			Shurlach	
Arni				Neston
Bishop				Burton
				Farndon
				Wybunbury
				Bunbury
Dedol				
Doda		Hartford		
Dot				
Dunning	Witton		Kingsley	Sandbach
	Gt Budworth			Gt Budworth
				Bettisfield
Edward	Christleton			Eastham
	Eastham			
Earl Edwin	Farndon	Frodsham	Eaton	Frodsham
	Frodsham		Farndon	Hawarden
		Iscoed	Frodsham	
	Macclesfield			
	Tilston			
	Weaverham	Weaverham	Weaverham	Weaverham
			Crewe Hall	
Eli				
Ernwy/Ansgot/Dot	Coddington			Poulton
Gamel				Newton
Gruffudd				

		Domus in *Wich*		
Leofing Leofnoth			Saughall Gayton Leighton	Acton Halton (Runcorn) Davenham
Leofric Leofwin	Aston			
Lothen	Golbourne			
Earl Morcar	Acton	Acton		
Orm				
Osmer				
Ragenald			Stanney	Barthomley Thornton-le-Moor
Siward				
Steinketel				
Thored	Allington Barrow		Allington	
	Gresford		Blacon	Gresford
Wulfgar the Priest + 3 thegns			Caldecott	
Wulfgeat	Brereton			Newbold (Astbury) Northenden High Legh (? Rostherne) Lymm
Wulfgeat/Dot				
Wulfgeat/Edward				
Wulfgeat/Edric/Luvede	Prenton			
Wulfsi	Stapleford			
Totals	20	5	14	26

three manors by Ravenswart, Ketel and Morfar, of whom Morfar was specifically unable to withdraw from his lord (DB, 267d), but which had become the sole manor of Tezelin by 1086. Tezelin's tenure may imply that a unified structure was not so very distant from the organisation of these small estates even in 1066. Neither Morfar nor Ketel occur elsewhere in Cheshire but the name Ravenswart recurs in association with Godric at nearby Odd Rode and, again with the unique Leofgeat at Barnston, in distant Willaston Hundred. This would suggest that Ravenswart, the first-named at Somerford, was the superior landholder, but all three may well have been ministerial tenants of Godric, whose name is associated with fourteen manors focused on the borders of the hundreds of *Hamestan* and Middlewich, and who may well have been a thegn of considerable local influence. If Barnston should also be linked with him, then his estates were reminiscent of several Norman baronies in having a core of territory at a distance from Chester but at least one more local manor from which a town residence could be supplied.

The Domesday commissioners responsible for Cheshire appear to have taken a very liberal view of what comprised a manor, one result being the multiplication of small manorial estates. The large landholdings of Earl Hugh and his principal barons in 1086 give the impression that a revolution had by then occurred in manorial tenancy (e.g. Fleming 1987), but this may well be an illusion created by peculiarities within the database. Manors had once more proliferated by the end of the twelfth century and large numbers of small manors, sub-manorial free tenements and quasi-manors were to be a continuing characteristic of the region (Sylvester 1960).

Cases where manors with exceptional assets were held by men devoid of substantial holdings invite interpretation as incidents of tenancies by agents of more powerful individuals. The name of neither Ernwy nor Arnsgot (Table 1) was associated with more than one further manor (Wepre and Lea respectively) but their co-holder of Coddington – Dot – was probably one (or more) thegn(s) with widespread assets. Leofing had no estates beyond Saughall, yet if the fishery there was the equal of that at Eaton it would have yielded a render of 1,000 salmon. Lothen appears only at Golbourne, Wulfgar the priest only at Caldecot and Luvede only at Prenton. In each case these were probably the tenants and/or reeves of more powerful individuals or institutions.

It has already been suggested that Wulfric may have been the Earl's reeve or steward in *Hamestan* Hundred (p. 172). That the earls did employ such men on a regular basis is demonstrated by the Domesday reference to Burwardsley, where the 'reeves of earls Edwin and Morcar' had 'sold one hide taken away from the church of St Werburgh to a certain Ravechil' (264c). This name occurs elsewhere only at Aston, near Earl Morcar's great manor of Acton, and it may well be that he was a member of Morcar's Cheshire following, certain members of which do seem to be identifiable (Higham 1988b). The unique reference to land sales may indicate that such were not uncommon in the region, particularly given that Earl Ælfgar was associated with similar sales in East Anglia. This entry also implies that the relationship between Earl Edwin and St Werburgh's was far from equal, with the senior earl treating the best endowed religious community in the shire much as he had done the bishop's lands – as an extension of his own property. There can be little doubt that he was the sole patron of this minster and in control of appointments within it, and it has every appearance of being his *eigenkirche* (family monastery), *T.R.E.*

Leofwin may have been another of the earl's officers. The 'house (*domus*) in the *Wich*' attached to his Tatton manor in 1086 is unlikely to be just another salt-house (*salina*). While the salt industries at Nantwich and Northwich were overseen directly by the estate managers of Earl Morcar (at Acton) and Earl Edwin (at Weaverham) respectively, that at Middlewich (DB, 268b) was without seigneurial salthouses and distant from comital estates. Yet an officer of the king and/or the earl seems to have been normally present and responsible for tolls and commercial offences. The name Leofwin occurs against seven manors responsible for only two hides *in toto*, scattered across four hundreds but including Wisterson, adjacent to Earl Morcar's Acton estate, and lands at Handbridge and Overleigh, adjacent to Earl Edwin's capital at Chester itself. Such holdings would be consistent with a career administrator in the service of Leofric's grandsons who had assembled a series of small grants and tenancies through comital favour (Higham, forthcoming (a)). He may have been one of the officers responsible for the *Wich* and hundred court of Middlewich. If so, Gruffydd was probably the other. He held two estates in 1066; the single-hide estate of Newton by Middlewich was unusual in an estate of this size in having a church, so some superior interest seems likely. Burton Abbey does not appear to have retained control of this manor but links between this house and Earl Leofric's family have already been mooted (Sawyer 1979); additionally the name Gruffydd is associated with Weston, a two-hide estate which was probably an integral part of Orm's interests, focused on Halton but encompassing both sides of the middle Mersey valley.

That the armies which Earls Ælfgar and Edwin led to war included Welshmen is a matter of record. The identification of various Welsh forenames in the Cheshire Domesday implies that some of these men were rewarded with holdings or office in the shire by the earls or their political associates. The frequency with which Leofric and his heirs are known to have raised substantial forces implies that their following, in Cheshire and elsewhere, was both large and organised for war. Although documentary proof is unavailable, it seems likely that many, if not all, Cheshire's landholders late in Edward's reign were beholden to the earl or attached to his cause. Conversely, few if any were likely to be the king's thegns in an area where royal interests had been so extensively delegated. No single landholder *T.R.E.* was said 'to hold of the king'.

If the earl's influence was so extensive, it may be that it was tangible even in those east-central hundreds which were without comital estates. His holdings certainly dominated the eastern hundred of *Hamestan* and Edwin's central role here serves to distinguish the Chester-centric political system within the Cheshire Lyme from that operating in Derbyshire. In the latter county, Edwin held a mere six carucates in 1066, although other members of his dynasty accounted for more.

Others of Cheshire's landholders probably had interests which transcended the shire boundary. The name Gamel was recorded in Cheshire in 1066 only at Cheadle and Mottram. Both were either already church sites or would soon become so, implying that these were holdings of high status and central to the organisation of local society. As has long been recognised, this Gamel should probably be identified with the important and privileged thegn holding Rochdale and some at least of the extensive holdings under this name in Yorkshire. The same individual may also have held extensive estates in Staffordshire, where a Gamel was a royal thegn, and Derbyshire (Lewis 1991a). It may be, therefore, that the Cheshire Gamel was an aristocrat with widespread interests in northern Mercia and southern Northumbria. Such a man cannot have been impervious to the influence of the Mercian earls in precisely the same areas. The responsibilities of Leofric and his descendants as earl in the east Midlands ensured that they tied sections of the local aristocracy there to their own interests. Earl Morcar had presumably begun to do the same in Northumbria by September 1066. Gamel's interests in Cheshire, which he had inherited from his father, may have been a direct consequence of such imperatives over the last few generations. So too may be that of Orm, Uhtred and Toki along the Mersey.

Exploration of Gamel's position opens other possibilities. That the name Wulfgeat appears in association with him in three Derbyshire manors, for example, may imply that the Wulfgeat who held extensive estates of high status in central Cheshire (including the churches at Northenden, Astbury and Lymm) also had interests outside the shire. The name Leofing – already identified as a potential reeve or steward in Cheshire – recurs on several estates in Derbyshire, including Burnaston and Bearwardcote, where one Gamel was the major holder. The name Godric also occurs widely in Derbyshire, but only in the eastern hundreds of Cheshire. In no instance is it possible to prove that a single individual was involved but it may be opportune to warn against the too-easy assumption that no such landholders had interests which transcended the comparatively artificial shire boundaries.

The Norman earls fulfilled a strategic function on England's frontiers, to perform which they had been granted vast estates elsewhere in England (Lewis 1991b). The Cheshire capital of the earldom was a comparatively minor part of his territories as regards hidation, ploughlands or valuation, but it was the focus and the centre from which he was expected to wage war against the Welsh. Earl Edwin's holdings outside Cheshire were less widely scattered but similarly wealthier than those within. He too held an office which arose from royal response to a strategic need. Like the Norman earls, Leofric's family had good cause to focus resources deriving from other parts of their earldom on Chester and its shire.

Just as Earl Hugh's principal barons held lands outside

Cheshire, so too may Earl Edwin's more prominent associates have done so. It may be no accident that Staffordshire's land-holders in 1066 include names such as Ælfric, Ælmer, Alfward, Alfwold, Arkell, Arni and Auti (just to focus on one part of the alphabet), all of whom recur in Cheshire. Shropshire's landholders also share numerous personal names. Much of this could well be due to the widespread use of a common stock of names, but the rarity of a few may indicate individuals. The Gruffydd at Biddulph, on Staffordshire's much wasted northern periphery, should surely be identified with the holder of Newton-by-Middlewich and Weston, whose association with the administration of Earl Edwin and Orm has already been mooted. Cross-shire landholdings may well have been far more common than has generally been assumed, but they remain extremely difficult to explore.

Settlement and land use: 1086 and after

In the absence of significant archaeological evidence, Domesday Book provides the only database by which to investigate the late Saxon countryside. Numerous references to small manors with only one or two ploughlands and the frequent repetition of manorial names implies that many Domesday estates were little more than a demesne farm or a handful of tenancies, perhaps organised around a radman or some other superior tenant. Such manors seldom much exceeded 1,500 acres. Few nucleated settle-ments (if any) can have been present, outside Chester itself and the *Wiches* – if they should be accorded urban status at this early date (Oxley 1982). Where larger manors exist in the Cheshire folios of Domesday Book, with significant numbers of manorial tenants, most if not all represent multi-township, so multi-settlement estates, within which dispersed settlement was prob-ably characteristic. In settlement terms, large manors (such as Malpas or Acton) were little more than groups of the same type of communities as constituted the more characteristic small manors. The numerous subinfeudations present at Halton, for example, or Malpas in 1086, reflect the ease with which these sub-units of the larger manors could be detached. In several instances, the number of subinfeudations approximates to the number of townships apparently incorporated in the manor, indicating that the township was the standard unit of lordship and of sub-tenancies.

In 1086 very few manors had sufficient manpower for the type of open fields which are generally found in association with medieval villages to be operative. Although figures were not given in Domesday Book for population levels in 1066, low hidations and estimates of ploughland imply that the conditions were not much different then (Higham 1988c). Cheshire's poverty in 1086 was not, therefore, merely a consequence of the 'wasting' of the early Norman period. On most counts, Cheshire would seem to have been the poorest of the Marcher Shires of England, with only Derbyshire, with its extensive uplands, competing for bottom place in the league table of shires in the region (Table 2).

A general shortage of labour was still apparent early in the thirteenth century. Perhaps in consequence, Norman lords were constrained from imposing heavy labour services on their manorial tenants, and the area remained free of 'week-work' throughout the Middle Ages, with manorial lords drawing their characteristically low levels of income per acre primarily from demesne exploitation, court-profits, rents and various monopolies such as corn mills.

Across most of Cheshire nucleation did not occur in the countryside and the late Saxon pattern of church hamlet, manorial holding and scattered farms prevailed. Convincing examples of deserted medieval villages are extremely rare in eastern and central Cheshire, where most modern villages (such as Great Budworth, Wybunbury or Rostherne (Plate 12)) or hamlets (such as Preston-on-the-Hill (Plate 11)) are either communities of estate labourers grouped around a vicarage, one or two gentry houses and a bare handful of farms, or a consequence of increasing craft specialisation in the seventeenth to nineteenth centuries. Large groups of farms such as characterise villages in, for example, parts of Yorkshire or Nottinghamshire, do not occur in these settlements, which are dominated numerically by non-agricultural holdings, most of which are of comparatively recent origin.

Exceptions are concentrated around Chester and more particularly on the estates of the earls and the bishops. Burton-in-Wirral clearly developed as a nucleated village on to which its episcopal landlords made some efforts to graft urban character-

Table 2 The counties of Western Mercia at Domesday: a summary of the assets of each shire listed in order of population size

	Population	Villeins	Bordars	Cottars	Serfs	No. place-names	Hides	Ploughlands	Ploughs
Gloucestershire	8,083	3,732	1,878	7	2,065	363	2,403	–	3,812
Warwickshire	6,656	3,764	1,843	6	880	279	1,480	–	2,238
Shropshire	4,907	1,987	1,196	16	922	440	1,255	3,078	1,809
Herefordshire	4,453	1,730	1,271	19	739	312	1,141[a]	–	2,421
Worcestershire	4,341	1,604	1,717	57	704	264	1,302	–	1,986
Staffordshire	2,866	1,693	886	–	231	341	446[a]	1,299	976
Derbyshire	2,746	1,776	734	–	20	335	681[b]	734	908
Cheshire (excluding areas later in Wales)	1,524	555	461	–	141	264	491[c]	936	457
Rank of Cheshire 1–8	8	8	8	equal last	7	7 equal 7th	7	–	8

[a] There are carucates in addition to hidation, but not in numbers sufficient to upset ranking.

[b] Carucates only.

[c] Inclusive of 3 carucates, 19 bovates and 16 acres.

Source: Darby and Terrett, 1954 and Darby and Maxwell, 1962.

istics. The earls' manor at Aldford focused on a motte and bailey castle, sited so as to control the 'old ford', beside which a manorial church perhaps developed from the castle chapel. Running south from the castle, the modern village shows distinct signs of a phase of planning post-dating the construction of the castle (Williams 1984/85) and this was presumably a later medieval initiative (Plate 18). Further south, Churton was probably a two-row village and its equal subdivision between the parishes of Farndon and Aldford indicates that it was already laid out when the parish of Aldford was created – perhaps as late as the twelfth or thirteenth centuries.

Open fields did develop locally and, except where destroyed by modern agriculture, cover much of the landscape of western and southern Cheshire. They were probably at their most regular in the same areas, where broad ridge and furrow is to be found not just on the better-drained lands of Aldford and Farndon, for example, but also across the landscape of townships with woodland place-names. Chester's large and comparatively affluent population presumably provided a consistently lucrative market for farm produce, as well as fish, from the immediate vicinity, but much produce probably left the farm gate not for profit but as rent or render to manorial lords.

Elsewhere, open fields were generally small but numerous and characterised by their unsystematic organisation. Many communities utilised not just two or three fields but ten or more. Even where centralised management of high status retained control, as at Frodsham, individual farming hamlets operated their own field systems (Booth and Dodd 1979). Most manors constituted a mishmash of open fields, crofts farmed in strips, crofts held in severalty, enclosed woodland or grazing and unenclosed common land. It was a landscape which offered widespread opportunities to those prepared to enclose from the waste and improve. Numerous manorial families produced younger sons for whom large farms and tenanted hamlets were carved out. Many new but sub-manorial settlements developed from such activities – as did Swineside (or Swinyard (Hall)), on the edge of Sink Moss, High Legh. Such assarting encouraged the dispersed character of local settlement (Plates 19, 20).

Although woodland was probably seriously under-recorded in Domesday Book for some parts of Cheshire (Higham 1982), it was widely reported. In the hundreds of Ruloe and *Hamestan*, concentrations existed in areas which Earl Hugh (or in *Hamestan*, perhaps his successors) afforested, but other comital forests had little woodland. This was particularly true of Wirral, which was afforested several generations later, reportedly for penal reasons. Widespread woodland existed in southern Cheshire, where there was a positive correlation with woodland place-names, for example around Malpas parish. Earl Hugh's massive subinfeudations here deprived him of the opportunity to create further chases had he so wished.

Examination of specific status groups in Domesday Book may provide insights into the late Saxon and Norman landscape. *Bordarii* ('bordars') are widespread in Cheshire, though less common than *villani* ('villeins'). The word may imply a role on the border or edge, so perhaps men active in assarting and the exploitation of woodland and waste (Harvey 1976; Postles 1986). The balance between bordars and woodland in Cheshire varies from west to east (Table 3). West of the Mid-Cheshire Ridge (but including Ruloe Hundred), there are 210 bordars listed of whom only 20 per cent occur on manors with woodland. In central Cheshire, 214 occur, but 79 per cent on manors with woodland. In *Hamestan* Hundred, by contrast, only sixteen bordars occur on seven manors, all of which have woodland and of the fifty-eight manors with woodland but without bordars, sixteen (28 per cent) occur here.

This relationship mirrors the very variable development of Cheshire's farmland. In the west, where royal and episcopal control had long been focused and the shire *burh* established, woodland was barely documented in Domesday Book. It was here that Cheshire's rural population, geld liability, ploughlands and ploughs were at their modest heights in 1086. Bordars are barely distinguishable from other sectors of this manorial community, although they tended to be less well-equipped and probably had less productive and smaller holdings of later origin than the *villani*. Woodland occurred more widely in central Cheshire, where it often characterised marginal areas along the borders of hundreds and parishes, particularly on heavy and poorly-drained claylands. Bordars here were particularly active in woodland areas, where assarting was apparently in progress. Further east, it had barely begun.

Table 3 Bordars and woodland in those parts of Domesday Cheshire which remained in England

Hundred	Bordars	Manors with bordars	Manors with bordars and woodland		Other manors with bordars but no recorded woodland		Other manors with woodland but no recorded bordars
			Manors	Bordars	Manors	Bordars	
Atiscross	2	1	1	2 (100%)	–	– (0%)	–
Bucklow	22	9	7	17 (77%)	2	5 (23%)	8
Chester	8	4	0	0 (0%)	4	8 (100%)	0
Dudestan	74	30	9	35 (47%)	21	39 (53%)	11
Hamestan	16	7	7	16 (100%)	–	– (0%)	16
Middlewich	45	21	13	36 (80%)	8	9 (20%)	9
Ruloe	23	11	6	13 (43%)	5	10 (57%)	1
Rushton	43	12	9	30 (70%)	3	13 (30%)	4
Tunendune	24	12	8	18 (75%)	4	6 (25%)	4
Warmundestrou	80	28	23	68 (85%)	5	12 (15%)	5
Total excluding Willaston	337	135	83	235 (70%)	52	102 (30%)	58
Willaston	126	42	2	5 (4%)	40	121 (96%)	–
Total	463	177	85	240 (52%)	92	223 (48%)	58

A. Atiscross
    Chester
    Dudestan
    Ruloe ?
    Willaston

    Total bordars 210
    % in manors with woodland: 20%
    % in manors without woodland: 80%
    Statistics exclude Chester and Ruloe

B. Groups
    Bucklow
    Middlewich
    Ruloe ?
    Rushton
    Tunendune
    Warmundestrou

    Total bordars 214
    % in manors with woodland: 79%
    % in manors without woodland: 21%
    Statistics exclude Ruloe

C. *Hamestan*

Focus and continuity

The basic fabric of Earl Edwin's Cheshire seems to have survived the convulsions caused by the Norman Conquest. Chester retained its primacy despite a decline in the number of houses from 495 in 1066 to 290, both *c.* 1070 and 1086 (DB, 262d). Rhuddlan apart, it was the only borough and would remain so for a century or so thereafter. It was by far the most important port and market in the region, the capital of the Norman earldom and the meeting-place of the medieval shire court. St Werburgh's retained its unique status and extensive endowments and was refounded as the first monastery of Norman type in the shire. The status and focal role of St John's was enhanced by the removal of the diocese from Lichfield. Even after the departure of the bishop to the wealthy monastery of Coventry (once Earl Leofric's favourite house), St John's presided over an extensive archdeaconry which embraced both Cheshire and southern Lancashire and the bishops long retained Chester in their title.

Even the territorial dispositions of the Norman earls took some account of the organisation and system of land tenure which they replaced. The Norman earls initially retained such focal comital estates as Frodsham, Weaverham, Aldford (comital Farndon), Macclesfield and Eastham. Others were subinfeudated but the larger examples invariably became the capital manor of a barony; Malpas (*Depenbech*) to Robert FitzHugh, for example, and Earl Morcar's great manor of Acton to William Malbank. In both instances, the Norman baronies extended throughout the parishes served from these centres in a fashion that implies that seigneurial interests could have been as extensive in 1066. If the baronial court of Acton presided over a consolidated honour encompassing the bulk of a hundred in 1086, it did so also under Earl Morcar's control. FitzHugh's role at Malpas need have been little more than a formalisation of the stewardship of Earl Edwin's interests operated by the thegn Edwin in 1066. Orm's influence in *Tunendune* Hundred, *T.R.E.* need have been little different from that of William FitzNigel in 1086.

One difference between the Norman and Saxon landholdings would seem to lie in the smaller number, and so larger, groupings of holdings in the former and its tighter dependence on barely a dozen men. To take a single example, William fitzNigel held twenty-nine manors in Cheshire, including all eight in Runcorn parish and a block of six at the core of Great Budworth parish, where his subinfeudations to men like Payne (or Pagen) may mirror Orm's relationship with Edward and other tenants *T.R.E.* Additionally he held a block of six manors at the centre of Rostherne parish, where pre-existing authority seems to have been weak, and a block of six estates in Chester and Willaston Hundreds, all of which came to him from Arni, once holder of Neston. Closely integrated with these holdings were sub-tenancies of St Werburgh's at Great Neston and Raby, which may indicate that links had earlier existed between Arni and the same minster. William was a tenant of the bishop at Wybunbury and also held Barrow, Thored's erstwhile manor adjacent to the bishop's great manor of Tarvin, from which it had presumably been detached. Clutton, in Farndon parish, perhaps reached William with other of Edward's estates, since all but the three which Osbern fitzTezzo received (on which Edward himself survived) had been granted to him. William was, therefore, expected to fulfil roles previously performed by Orm, Edward (perhaps Orm's subordinate), Arni and one or two other Saxon landholders, as a key member of the new comital establishment in Cheshire. His barony did not consist of a discrete block of Saxon estates, but it was far from being a random collection of tenancies, granted solely on locational criteria.

There is no more impressive indicator of continuity than the emergence of Norman castles or baronial courts on sites which were already closely identified with the leaders of English Cheshire. The castles at Chester itself, Malpas, Halton, Bowdon and Aldford are classic examples. Elsewhere the new Norman lords may have forgone formal castles, but prominent halls were presumably in use, as at Frodsham (where the 'castle' is a later medieval moated manor-house), Acton, Weaverham and Macclesfield. The last site was one where an important court and hall already existed in 1066, which served as the principal focus of the hundred. The precise location of Earl Edwin's hall is lost beneath the later town but it presumably lay on the hilltop, between the later parish church and the aptly-named Castle Street, which recalls the presence of the manorial court in the high Middle Ages. Trial excavation at Halton Castle failed to identify the pre-Conquest settlement (McNeil 1987) but, if the earliest medieval timber-framed buildings at Tatton were of comparable construction this need surprise no one. The Tatton examples were characterised by the simplest of post-hole founded architecture and entirely devoid of diagnostic artifacts in close association (Higham, forthcoming (a)). One reason why the foci of the late Saxon period are archaeologically obscure must lie in the high incidence of their reuse and successive redevelopment in the later Middle Ages, when the digging of great moats and the building of castles in stone was in fashion.

7

Postcript

If Earl Hugh managed his local interests through a network of minsters and monasteries, baronies and sergeancies, Earl Edwin had apparently been supported by a not entirely dissimilar following, which included the bishop and his men, the dean and clerks of St Werburgh's and numerous officers and thegns. The principal difference between them may well have been the far better documentation which survives for the later period (Barraclough 1988; Thacker 1991). The distinctive character and strong regional identity of Cheshire may have suffered severely in the Conquest itself but it was rapidly reasserted. In the days of the Norman earls, the Lyme was held to constitute a boundary not between one shire and another but between Cheshire and England. The dominant role of Earl Edwin's Chester-centric establishment in north-west Mercia was, however, a casualty of King William's new dispositions and there is every reason to think this deliberate.

Of Cheshire's boundaries, only the western frontier with Wales remained volatile. This was not a product of the Norman Conquest, since it had clearly been subjected to successive alterations as recently as the Confessor's reign, but Norman lords were quick to exploit Welsh discord. The political fall-out of King Gruffydd's fall in 1063 was still at its height in the 1070s, when the kings of Gwynedd and Powys both fell victim to internecine warfare. With native leadership riven by feud, Earls Roger of Montgomery and Hugh of Chester, and Robert of Rhuddlan were able to make deep inroads into northern Wales. The Domesday record of

Shropshire and Cheshire reflects their progress to 1086. Opportunities for conquest were much reduced after 1094, when Gruffydd ap Cynan established control of Gwynedd. Gruffydd was of the line of Rhodri Mawr, and his house was to rule north Wales until Edward I's destruction of Llywelyn the Last in 1282.

The death of Henry I in 1135 and England's long slide into anarchy diverted Marcher lords from Welsh events and provided Gruffydd and his son Owain with the opportunity to push Norman control back towards the borders of later medieval Cheshire (Lloyd 1939; Davies 1987). By 1167, King Owain (1137–70) had recaptured the Norman castles of Basingwerk, Rhuddlan, Deganwy and Tegeigl (Englefield) and Norman control of Mold and Hawarden was threatened. Further south, Welsh lordship was restored to Powys, which, under Llywelyn ap Gruffydd (1203–40), included all Maelor. Indeed, it is only at this stage that the name Maelor Saesneg is documented for that southern part of *Dudestan* Hundred beyond the Wych Brook (Palmer and Owen 1910). One consequence of the Welsh resurgence was a 'Welshification' of pre-existing names, many of which were of Old English origin, or the replacement of major foci with English names by alternates with names formed in Welsh.

When Edward I came to reorganise his Welsh conquests in 1284, under the Statute of Rhuddlan, he preferred to unite the territories of Englefield and Maelor Saesneg as detached portions of a single shire based on Flint, rather than restore any part to Cheshire. Excepting only Marford and Hoseley (also attached to Flint), the bulk of what had been *Exestan* Hundred was incorporated in Denbighshire.

It was at this stage that Cheshire was ultimately defined towards the west. The boundary chosen in the thirteenth century differed little from that postulated above on the basis of slender but much earlier evidence, separating the northern territory of the Cornovii from the Deceangli or Ordovices, then the *Wrocen sǣte* from Powys. It represents a retreat from the Mercian frontier on Wat's Dyke, now entirely outside Cheshire, but that line seems to have been long-contested by the Welsh kings with long memories of an ill-documented English usurpation of eastern Powys. The solution of total conquest had been attempted before, most notably by Mercian kings in the late eighth and early ninth centuries. On this occasion it proved to be the final solution. One result of the permanent conquest of Wales effected by King Edward I was to confine the most northerly of the marcher shires of England within borders far tighter than those associated with earlier but less decisive victories.

There is a good case for arguing that Cheshire's northern boundary on the Mersey was a major frontier with a history stretching back from Domesday for at least a millennium. It was certainly the frontier between Mercia and Northumbria. Earlier it was presumably the border between the two great Anglian 'overkingships' from which they evolved, snaking between what were probably for long years British tributaries both north (? British Makerfield, perhaps) and south (*Wrocen sæte*). The same river was probably a provincial boundary in the Roman period and a tribal frontier of high status even earlier.

Cheshire's border with Derbyshire seems more artificial, cutting as it does through an extensive region with a shared hundredal name which, in 1086, transcended the shire boundary. If the medieval hundreds of Macclesfield, High Peak, Wirksworth and Totmonslow constituted the Mercian province – formerly the tributary kingship – of the *Pecsæte*, then it is possible to guess at the boundary of the *Wrocen sæte* in this area, which perhaps departed little from the western borders of *Hamestan* Hundred. That hundred seems to have been extensively wooded and the district, woodland-originating name of Lyme may have been of considerable antiquity. This well-wooded and very marginal terrain probably acted as a frontier zone between the *Wrocen sæte* (perhaps even the Cornovii) and their eastern neighbours.

Cheshire's southern boundary was less ancient, coming into existence only with the shiring of the tenth century, but even there the boundaries chosen were probably based on pre-existing systems of lordship, parochial responsibility and territorial organisation. Along the borders of Cheshire, Shropshire and Staffordshire, exceptional concentrations of woodland-type township-names combine with the south-western edge of the Lyme to suggest that here was a large area of common grazing, woodland and waste which was peripheral to several communities and served both as common grazing lands and to divide their other interests. With some apparent horse-trading, this area of under-utilised terrain emerged as the frontier zone of the three shires during the tenth century.

Within the shire, the Domesday hundreds were extensively reorganised in the Norman period. Only one hundred name present in Domesday Book survived the process – Bucklow – and even this was now an amalgam of *Tunendune* and Domesday Bucklow. Ruloe and Rushton were combined to form a hundred which approximated to Eddisbury Forest, was given that name and met at the forest court on Eddisbury Hill, so perhaps resurrecting the tenth-century *burh* and the focal point of Iron Age central Cheshire. Willaston reverted to Wirral – apparently the earlier name – and *Dudestan* was converted to Broxton, with some rearrangement of the boundary between them which brought back to the northern hundred some, but not all, of its apparent earlier losses. *Warmundestrou* and *Hamestan* took the names of the places where meetings occurred; so Nantwich and Macclesfield. Yet even these drastic changes conceal considerable territorial continuity. With very specific exceptions, the boundaries of the medieval hundreds differed little from the hundreds or paired hundreds of late Saxon Cheshire, from which they had been formed.

It was modern, not medieval, reorganisation which brought this process of territorial evolution to an abrupt end, with the removal of county boroughs from the shire and the subsequent wholesale redrawing of county boundaries in 1974, with scant respect for what was being changed. For many, the sharp pencils of twentieth-century bureaucrats condemned to a creeping death the sense of belonging that was at the core of the social identity of an ancient shire community. Those same government officials were perhaps fortunate that the military reputation and instinct for direct action which had so long distinguished the medieval shire had by then long since dissipated.

References

Aldhelm (1884) *Epistola ad Gerontium*, in *Sancti Aldhelmi Opera Quae Extant*, ed. J. A. Giles, London.

– Alldridge, N. J. (1981) 'Aspects of the topography of Early Medieval Chester', *Journal of the Chester Archaeological Society*, **64**, 5–31.

Allen, D. F. (1963) *Sylloge of Coins of the British Isles: The Coins of the Coritani*, London.

Anderson, O. S. (1934) *The English Hundred-Names*, Lund.

– Annales Cambriae (1980), in *Nennius: British History and the Welsh Annals*, ed. J. Morris, Chichester, 85–91.

Antonine Itinerary (1929), in *Itineraria Romana*, ed. O. Cuntz, I, Leipzig.

Asser (1986) *Life of King Alfred*, in *Alfred the Great*, ed. S. Keynes and M. Lapidge, London.

Axon, W. E. A. (1884) *Cheshire Gleanings*, Manchester and London.

Aylett, P. (forthcoming) 'Tatton 1800–1958: Rising status. Rising Debt', in *Tatton: The History and Prehistory of one Cheshire Township*, ed. N. J. Higham, Chester.

Bailey, R. N. and Cramp, R. (1988) *The British Academy Corpus of Anglo-Saxon Stone Sculpture in England*, II: *Cumberland, Westmorland and Lancashire North of the Sands*, Oxford.

Barker, P. (1975) 'Excavations on the site of the Baths Basilica at Wroxeter, 1966–74: An Interim Report', *Britannia*, **6**, 106–17.

Barker, P. (1979) 'The latest occupation of the site of the Baths Basilica at Wroxeter', in *The End of Roman Britain*, ed. P. J. Casey, BAR, British Series, 71, Oxford, 175–81.

Barker, P. (ed.) (1990) *From Roman* Viroconium *to Medieval Wroxeter*, Worcester.

Barnatt, J. (1986) 'Bronze Age Remains on the East Moors of the Peak District', *Derbyshire Archaeological Journal*, **106**, 18–106.

Barnatt, J., Carver, N. and Pierpoint, S. J. (1980) 'A long barrow on Longstone Moor, Derbyshire', *Derbyshire Archaeological Journal*, **100**, 17.

Barraclough, G. (ed.) (1988) *The Charters of the Anglo-Norman Earls of Chester, c. 1071–1237*, Gloucester.

Barrow, G. W. S. (1973) *The Kingdom of the Scots*, London.

Bartley, D. D., Jones, I. P. and Smith, R. T. (1990) 'Studies in the Flandrian vegetational history of the Craven District of Yorkshire: the lowlands', *Journal of Ecology*, **78**, 611–32.

– Bartrum, P. C. (ed.) (1966) *Early Welsh Genealogical Tracts*, Cardiff.

Bassett, S. (1989) 'Lincoln and the Anglo-Saxon see of Lindsey', Anglo-Saxon England, **18**, 1–32.

Bassett, S. (1990) 'The Roman and Medieval landscape of Wroxeter', in *Roman* Viroconium *to Medieval Wroxeter*, ed. P. Barker, Worcester, 10–12.

– Bassett, S. (1992) 'Church and diocese in the West Midlands: the transition from British to Anglo-Saxon control', in *Pastoral Care Before the Parish*, ed. J. Blair and R. Sharpe, Leicester, 13–40.

Bede (1969) *Historia Ecclesiastic*: Bede, *Ecclesiastical History of the English People*, ed. B. Colgrave and R. A. B. Mynors, Oxford.

Beresford, M. and Finberg, H. P. R. (1973) *English Medieval Boroughs: A Hand-list*, Newton Abbott.

Birch, W. de Gray (1885–87), *Cartularium Saxonicum*, 3 vols, London.

Birks, H. J. B. (1965a) 'Late-glacial deposits at Bagmere, Cheshire, and Chat Moss, Lancashire', *New Phytologist*, **64**, 270–85.

Birks, H. J. B. (1965b) 'Pollen analytical investigations at Holcroft Moss, Lancashire, and Lindow Moss, Cheshire', *Journal of Ecology*, **53**, 299–314.

Birley, E. (1948) 'The Status of Roman Chester', *Journal of the Chester Archaeological Society*, **36**, 173–7.

Blair, J. (1985) 'Secular Minsters in Domesday Book', in *Domesday Book: A Reassessment*, ed. P. Sawyer, London, 104–42.

Blair, J. (1987) 'The Local Church in Domesday Book and Before', in *Domesday Studies*, ed. J. C. Holt, Woodbridge, 265–78.

Blair, J. (ed.) (1988) *Minsters and Parish Churches. The Local Church in Transition 950–1200*, Oxford.

Blockley, K. (1985) 'Excavations at Prestatyn', *Archaeology in Wales*, **24**, 29.

Blockley, K. (1986) 'A Roman Fort at Prestatyn? Fact or Fiction', *Archaeology in Clwyd*, **8**, 4–5.

Blockley, K. (1989) 'Excavations on the Romano-British settlement at Ffrith, Clwyd, 1967–9', *Journal of the Flintshire Historical Society*, **32**, 135–65.

Bonsall, C. (1981) 'The coastal factor in the mesolithic settlement of North West Europe', in *Mesolithikum in Europa*, ed. B. Gramsch, *VEB Deutscher Verlag der Wissenschaften*, 451.

Booth, P. H. W. (1981) *The Financial Administration of the lordship and county of Chester, 1272–1377*, Manchester.

Booth, P. H. W. and Dodd, J. P. (1979) 'The Manor and Fields of

References

Frodsham', *Transactions of the Historical Society of Lancashire and Cheshire*, **128**, 27–57.

Booth, P. H. W. and Jones, R. N. (1979) 'Burton in Wirral: From Domesday to Dormitory, Part II', *Cheshire History*, **4**, 28–42.

Boulton, G. S. and Worsley, P. (1965) 'Late Weichselian glaciation in the Cheshire-Shropshire basin', *Nature*, **207**, 704–6.

Branigan, K., Horsley J. and Horsley, C., with contributions from Birss, R. and Hunt, C. (1986) 'Two Roman lead pigs from Carsington', *Derbyshire Archaeological Journal*, **106**, 5–17.

Brassil, K. (1987) 'Tandderwen, Denbigh: a Dark Age Cemetery in the middle of Dyffryn Clwyd', *Archaeology in Clwyd*, **9**, 6–8.

Britnell, J. (1991) 'Settlement and industry in north-east Wales', in *Conquest, Co-existence and Change: Recent Work in Roman Wales*, ed. B. C. Burnham and J. L. Davies, *Trivium*, **25**, Lampeter, 130–7.

Brook, D. (1992) 'The Early Christian church east and west of Offa's Dyke', in *The Early Church in Wales and the West*, ed. N. Edwards and A. Lane, Oxford, 77–89.

— Bromwich, R. (ed.) (1961) *Trioedd Ynys Prydein*, Cardiff.

Brooks, D. A. (1986) 'A review of the evidence for continuity in British towns in the fifth and sixth centuries', *Oxford Journal of Archaeology*, **5**, 77–102.

Brooks, N. (1984) *The Early History of the Church of Canterbury*, Leicester.

Brooks, N. (1989) 'The formation of the Mercian kingdom', in *The Origins of Anglo-Saxon Kingdoms*, Leicester, 159–70.

Brown, A., Leaning, J. B. and Little, J. H. (1975) 'Excavations at Halton Brow, Runcorn, 1967', *Journal of the Chester Archaeological Society*, **58**, 85–92.

Brownbill, J. (1899) 'Cheshire in Domesday Book', *Transactions of the Historical Society of Lancashire and Cheshire*, **15**, 1–25.

Buchanan, M. Jermy, K. E. and Petch, D. F. (1975) 'Watling Street in the grounds of Eaton Hall: excavations north of Garden Lodge, 1970–1', *Journal of the Chester Archaeological Society*, **58**, 1–14.

Bu'lock, J. D. (1958) 'Pre-Norman Crosses of West Cheshire and the Norse Settlements around the Irish Sea', *Transactions of the Lancashire and Cheshire Antiquarian Society*, **68**, 1–11.

Bu'lock, J. D. (1960) 'Celtic, Saxon and Scandinavian Settlement at Meols in Wirral', *Transactions of the Historical Society of Lancashire and Cheshire*, **112**, 1–28.

Bu'lock, J. D. (1970) *Pre Conquest Cheshire*, Chester.

— Camden, W. (1586) *Remains Concerning Britain*, ed. R. D. Dunn, Toronto, 1984.

— Camden, W. (1610) *Britain, or a chorographical description of England, Scotland and the ilands adioyning*, trans. P. Holland, London.

Cameron, K. (1968) 'Eccles in English place-names', in *Christianity in Roman Britain*, ed. M. W. Barley and R. P. C. Hanson, Leicester, 87–92.

Campbell, A. (ed.) (1938) *The Battle of Brunanburh*, London.

Campbell, A. (ed.) (1962) *The Chronicle of Æthelweard*, London.

Cane, T. and Higham, N. J. (forthcoming) 'Hunter-Gatherers', in *Tatton: The History and Prehistory of One Cheshire Township*, Chester.

Carrington, P. (1985a) 'The Roman Advance into the north western Midlands before AD 71', *Journal of the Chester Archaeological Society*, **68**, 5–22.

Carrington, P. (1985b) 'The earliest evidence for lead mining in Flintshire', *Cheshire Archaeological Bulletin*, **10**, 102–5.

Casey, P. J. (1989) 'Coin Evidence and the end of Roman Wales', Archaeological Journal, **146**, 320–9.

Chambers, F. M. and Wilshaw, I. W. (1991) *A Reconstruction of the Postglacial History of Tatton Park, Cheshire, from Valley Mire Sediments*, Keele.

Chibnall, M. (ed.) (1969) *The Ecclesiastical History of Orderic Vitalis*, vol. 2, Oxford.

Clayton, K. M. (1979) 'The Midlands and Southern Pennines', in *Eastern and Central England*, ed. A. Straw and K. Clayton, London, 143–231.

Cocroft, W. D., Everson, P., Jecock, M. and Wilson-North, W. R. (1989) 'Castle Ditch Hillfort, Eddisbury, Cheshire, Reconsidered: The excavations of 1935–38 in the light of recent field survey', in *From Cornwall to Caithness: Some Aspects of British Field Archaeology, Papers presented to Norman V. Quinnell*, ed. M. Bowden, D. Mackay and P. Topping, Oxford, 129–36.

Collingwood, R. G. and Wright, R. P. (1965) *Roman Inscriptions in Britain, I, Inscriptions on Stone*, Oxford.

Coombs, D. G. and Thompson, F. H. (1979) 'Excavation of the hillfort of Mam Tor, Derbyshire, 1965–69', *Derbyshire Archaeological Journal*, **99**, 7–51.

Cowell, R. W. (1990) 'Current Prehistoric work on Merseyside: Greasley and other Prehistoric sites', *Council for British Archaeology, Group 5 Newsletter*, **60**, 3–4.

Cowell, R. W. (1992) 'Prehistoric Survey in North Cheshire', *Cheshire Past*, **1**, 6–7.

Cox, B. (1975–77) 'Place-Names of the earliest English records', *Journal of the English Place-Name Society*, **8**, 12–66.

Croom, J. (1988) 'The Fragmentation of the Minster *Parochiae* of South-East Shropshire', in *Pastoral Care Before the Parish*, ed. J. Blair and R. Sharpe, 67–82.

Crowe, C. (1982) 'A note on a Celtic Head in the Churchyard at Rostherne', *Transactions of the Lancashire and Cheshire Antiquarian Society*, **81**, 131–2.

Cunliffe, B. (1978) *Iron Age Communities in Britain*, 2nd edn, London.

Cunliffe, B. (1983) *Danebury: Anatomy of an Iron Age Hillfort*, London.

Cunliffe, B. (ed.) (1981) *Coinage and Society in Britain and Gaul: Some Current Problems*, London.

Dalton, R., Fox, H. and Jones, P. (1988) *Classic Landforms of the White Peak*, Sheffield.

References

Dalton, R., Fox, H. and Jones, P. (1990) *Classic Landforms of the Dark Peak*, Sheffield.

Davey, P. J. (1973) *Chester Northgate Brewery. Phase One, Interim Report*, Liverpool.

Davies, J. L. (1983) 'Coinage and Settlement in Roman Wales and the Marches: some observations', *Archaeologia Cambrensis*, **132**, 78–94.

Davies, R. R. (1987) *Conquest, Coexistence and Change: Wales 1063–1415*, Oxford.

Davies, W. and Vierck, H. (1974) 'The contexts of the Tribal Hidage: social aggregates and settlement patterns', *Frühmittelalterliche Studien*, **8**, 223–93.

Davnall, S. A. (1985) 'The Development of the Parochial System in Mid-Cheshire, 1086–1292', Unpublished M.A. thesis, University of Manchester.

Dodgson, J. McN. (1957) 'The background of Brunanburh', *Saga Book of the Viking Club*, **14, part 4**, 303–16.

Dodgson, J. McN. (1966/67–) *The Place-Names of Cheshire* (in progress), Cambridge.

Dodgson, J. McN. (1968) 'Place-Names and Street-Names of Chester', *Journal of the Chester Archaeological Society*, **55**, 29–61.

Dodgson, J. McN. (1967) 'The English Arrival in Cheshire', *Transactions of the Historical Society of Lancashire and Cheshire*, **119**, 1–37.

Dolley, R. H. M. (1955) 'The Mint of Chester, I', *Journal of the Chester and North Wales Architectural, Archaeological and Historical Society*, **42**, 4–5.

Dolley, R. H. M. and Blunt, C. E. (1961) 'The Chronology of the Coins of Alfred the Great', in *Anglo-Saxon Coins, presented to F. M. Stenton*, ed. R. H. M. Dolley, London, 77–95.

Dool, J. and Hughes, R. G. (1976) 'Two Roman pigs of lead from Derbyshire', *Derbyshire Archaeological Journal*, **96**, 15–16.

Dornier, A. (1982) 'The province of Valentia', *Britannia*, **13**, 253–60.

Dumville, D. N. (1989) 'The Tribal Hidage: an introduction to its texts and their history', in *Origins of English Kingdoms*, ed. S. Bassett, Leicester, appendix I.

Dumville, D. N. (1992) *Wessex and England from Alfred to Edgar*, Woodbridge.

Edwards, N. and Lane, A. (ed.) (1988) *Early Medieval Settlement in Wales*, Cardiff.

Esmonde Cleary, A. S. (1989) *The Ending of Roman Britain*, London.

Evans, J. G. (ed.) (1911) *Poetry from the Red Book of Hergest*, Llanbedrog.

Fellows-Jensen, G. (1983) 'Scandinavian Settlement in the Isle of Man and North-West England: the place-name evidence', in *The Viking Age in the Isle of Man*, ed. C. Fell, London, 37–52.

Fellows-Jensen, G. (1985) *Scandinavian Settlement Names in the North-West*, Copenhagen.

Fellows-Jensen, G. (1992) 'Scandinavian Place-Names of the Irish Sea

Province', in *Viking Treasure from the North West: The Cuerdale Hoard in its context*, ed. J. Graham-Campbell, Liverpool, 31–42.

Finberg, H. P. R. (1964) *Lucerna: Studies in some problems in the early history of England*, London.

Fleming, R. (1987) 'Domesday Book and the Tenurial Revolution', in *Anglo-Norman Studies*, **9**, ed. R. A. Brown, 87–102.

Foot, S. (1992) 'Anglo-Saxon Minsters: a review of terminology', in *Pastoral Care before the Parish*, ed. J. Blair and R. Sharpe, Leicester, 212–25.

Forde-Johnston, J. (1962) 'The Iron Age Hillforts of Lancashire and Cheshire', Transactions of the Lancashire and Cheshire Antiquarian Society, **72**, 9–46.

Fox, Sir C. (1955) *Offa's Dyke: A Field Survey of the western frontier works of Mercia in the seventh and eighth centuries*, London.

Frere, S. S. (1978) *Britannia*, 2nd edn, London.

Garton, D. (1987) 'A pilot archaeological field survey of Tintwhistle Moor, North Derbyshire', *Derbyshire Archaeological Journal*, **107**, 5–12.

Garton, D. and Beswick, P. (1983) 'The Survey and Excavation of a Neolithic Settlement Area at Mount Pleasant, Kenslow', *Derbyshire Archaeological Journal*, **103**, 7–40.

Gastrell, F. (1845) *Notitia Cestriensis, or historical notices of the diocese of Chester*, ed. F. R. Raines, Manchester.

Gelling, M. (1988), *Signposts to the Past*, 2nd edn, Chichester.

Gelling, M. (1989) 'The early history of western Mercia', in *The Origins of Anglo-Saxon Kingdoms*, ed. S. Bassett, Leicester, 184–201.

Gelling, M. with Foxall, H. D. G. (1990) *The Place-Names of Shropshire*, I, Nottingham.

Giles, J. A. (ed.) (1876) *William of Malmesbury's Chronicle of the Kings of England*, London.

Goudie, A. (1990) *The Landforms of England and Wales*, Oxford.

Green, M. J. (1982) 'Tanarus, Taranis, and the Chester Altar', *Journal of the Chester Archaeological Society*, **65**, 37–44.

Greene, P. (1989) *Norton Priory: The Archaeology of a medieval religious house*, Cambridge.

Guilbert, G. (1976) 'Moel y Gaer (Rosesmor) 1972–1973: An Area Excavation in the Interior', in *Hillforts: Later Prehistoric Earthworks in Britain and Ireland*, ed. D. W. Harding, London, 303–317.

Hamilton, N. E. S. A. (ed.) (1870) *Willelmi Malmesbiriensis monachi de gestis pontificum Anglorum libri quinque*, London.

Harris, B. E. (1979) 'Administrative History', in *A History of the County of Chester*, III, ed. B. E. Harris, London, 1–97.

Hart, C. (1976) *Archaeological Survey of Wormhill: A Peakland Parish under threat*, Buxton.

Hart, C. (1981) *North Derbyshire Archaeological Survey*, Chesterfield.

Hart, C. R. (1975) *The Early Charters of Northern England and the North Midlands*, Leicester.

Hartley, B. R. and Fitts, L. (1988) *The Brigantes*, Gloucester.

References

Hartley, B. R. and Kaine, K. F. (1954) 'Roman Dock and Buildings', *Journal of the Chester and North Wales Architectural, Archaeological and Historical Society*, **41**, 15–37.

Hartley, K. F. and Webster, P. V. (1973) 'The Romano-British pottery kilns near Wilderspool', *Archaeological Journal*, **130**, 77–103.

Harvey, S. P. J. (1976) 'Evidence for settlement study: Domesday Book', in *Medieval Settlement*, ed. P. H. Sawyer, London, 195–9.

Haselgrove, C. (1978) *Supplementary Gazetteer of Find-spots of Celtic Coins in Britain*, London.

Hawkins, E. (ed.) (1848) *The Holy Lyfe and History of Saynt Werburge, very fruteful for all christen people to rede*, Manchester.

Hennessy, W. M. (ed.) (1887) *Annals of Ulster*, Dublin.

Hewitt, W. (1923) 'Marl and marling in Cheshire', *Proceedings of the Liverpool Geological Society*, **13**, i, 24–8.

Hibbert, F. A., Switzur, V. R. and West, R. G. (1971) 'Radiocarbon dating of Flandrian pollen zones at Red Moss, Lancashire', *Proceedings of the Royal Society, London, B*, **177**, 161–76.

Hicks, S. P. (1971) 'Pollen-analytical evidence for the effect of prehistoric agriculture on the vegetation of North Derbyshire', *New Phytologist*, **70**, 647–67.

Higham, N. J. (1982) Bucklow Hundred: The Domesday Survey and the rural community', *Cheshire Archaeological Bulletin*, **8**, 15–21.

Higham, N. J. (1986) *The Northern Counties*, Harlow.

Higham, N. J. (1987a) 'Landscape and land use in northern England: a survey of agricultural potential *c*. 500 BC–AD 1000', Landscape History, **9**, 35–44.

Higham, N. J. (1987b) 'Brigantia Revisited', *Northern History*, **23**, 1–19.

Higham, N. J. (1988a) 'The Cheshire *Burhs* and the Mercian Frontier to 924', *Transactions of the Antiquarian Society of Lancashire and Cheshire*, **85**, 193–221.

Higham, N. J. (1988b) 'The Cheshire Landholdings of Earl Morcar in 1066', *Transactions of the Historical Society of Lancashire and Cheshire*, **137**, 139–47.

Higham, N. J. (1988c) 'Dispersed Settlement in Medieval Cheshire: Some Causal Factors', *Annual Report of the Medieval Settlement Research Group*, **2**, 9–10.

Higham, N. J. (1990) 'Settlement, Land Use and Domesday Ploughlands', *Landscape History*, **12**, 33–44.

– Higham, N. J. (1991) 'Old Light on the Dark-Age landscape: the description of Britain in the *De Excidio Britanniae* of Gildas', *Journal of Historical Geography*, **17**, 4, 363–72.

Higham, N. J. (1992a) *Rome, Britain and the Anglo-Saxons*, London.

Higham, N. J. (1992b) 'King Cearl, the Battle of Chester and the origins of the Mercian' overkingship', *Midland History*, **17**, 1–15.

Higham, N. J. (1992c) 'Medieval "Overkingship" in Wales: the earliest evidence', *Welsh History Review*, **16**, 2, 145–59.

Higham, N. J. (1992d) 'Northumbria, Mercia and the Irish Sea Norse, 893–926', in *Viking Treasure from the North West: The Cuerdale*

Hoard in its Context, ed. J. Graham-Campbell, Liverpool, 21–30.

Higham, N. J. (1993) *The Kingdom of Northumbria: AD 350–1100*, Gloucester.

Higham, N. J. (forthcoming (a)) *Tatton: The History and Prehistory of one Cheshire township*, Chester.

Higham, N. J. (forthcoming (b)) 'The Historical Context of the Tribal Hidage', in *The Burghal Hidage*, ed. D. H. Hill and A. R. Rumble, Manchester.

Higham, N. J. and Jones, G. D. B. (1975) 'Frontiers forts and farmers: Cumbrian aerial survey, 1974–5', *Archaeological Journal*, **132**, 16–53.

Hill, D. H. (1969) 'The Burghal Hidage: the establishment of a text', *Medieval Archaeology*, **13**, 84–92.

Hill, D. H. (1976) 'Problems associated with the *Burh* of Thelwall on the Mersey', in *The Archaeology of Warrington's Past*, ed. S. Grealey, Warrington, 34–7.

Hill, D. H. (1977) 'Offa's and Wat's Dykes: Some Aspects of Recent Work, 1972–1976', *Transactions of the Lancashire and Cheshire Antiquarian Society*, **79**, 21–33.

Hill, D. H. (1981) *Atlas of Anglo-Saxon England*, Oxford.

Hill, D. H. and Rumble, A. R. (ed.) (forthcoming) *The Burghal Hidage*, Manchester.

Hinchliffe, J. and Williams, J. H., with Williams, F. (1992) *Roman Warrington: Excavations at Wilderspool 1966–9 and 1976*, Manchester.

Historia Brittonum (1980), in *Nennius: British History and the Welsh Annals*, ed. J. Morris, Chichester, 50–84.

Hooke, D. (1981) *Anglo-Saxon Landscapes of the West Midlands: the Charter Evidence*, BAR, British Series, 95, Oxford.

Hooke, D. (1983) *The Landscape of Anglo-Saxon Staffordshire: The Charter Evidence*, Keele.

Hough, P. R. (1982) 'Beeston Castle', *Cheshire Archaeological Bulletin*, **8**, 22–30.

Hough, P. R. (1984) 'Beeston Castle', *Current Archaeology*, **91**, 245–9.

Hughes, E. M. (1984) 'A Roman Road between Hatton and High Legh, Cheshire', *Cheshire History*, **13**, 13–18.

Hume, A. (1863) *Ancient Meols: or, some account of the Antiquities found near Dove Point, on the sea-shore of Cheshire*, London.

Ingham, A. (1920) *Cheshire: Its traditions and history*, Edinburgh.

Jackson, K. H. (1953) *Language and History in Early Britain*, Edinburgh.

Jackson, K. H. (1969) 'Romano-British names in the Antonine Itinerary', appendix to Rivet, A. L. F. 'The British section of the Antonine Itinerary', *Britannia*, **1**, 34–82.

Jackson, K. H. (1982) 'Varia: II. Gildas and the names of the British Princes', *Cambridge Medieval Celtic Studies*, **3**, 30–40.

Jacobi, R. M. (1978) 'Northern England in the 8th Millennium BC: an essay', in *The Early Post-Glacial Settlement of Northern Europe*, ed. P. A. Mellars, London, 295–332.

Jacobi, R. M., Tallis, J. H. and Mellars, P. A. (1976) 'The southern

Pennine Mesolithic and the archaeological record', *Journal of Archaeological Science*, **3**, 307–20.

James, H. (1992) 'Early Cemeteries in Wales', in *The Early Church in Wales and the West*, ed. N. Edwards and A. Lane, Oxford, 90–103.

James, S. (1984) 'Britain and the late Roman Army', in *Military and Civilian in Roman Britain*, ed. T. F. C. Blagg, and A. C. King, BAR, British Series, 136, Oxford, 161–86.

Jarrett, M. G. and Mann, J. C. (1968) 'The Tribes of Roman Wales', *Welsh History Review*, **4**, 161–71.

Jermy, K. E. (1965) 'King Street – a Roman road in central Cheshire', *Journal of the Chester and North Wales Archaeological Society*, **52**, 23–5.

Jobey, G. (1978) 'Iron Age and Roman-British Settlements on Kennel Hall Knowe, North Tynedale, Northumberland', *Archaeologia Aeliana*, 5th series, **6**, 1–28.

Jolliffe, J. E. A. (1926) 'Northumbrian Institutions', *English Historical Review*, **161**, 1–42.

— Jones, F. (1954) *The Holy Wells of Wales*, Cardiff.

Jones, G. D. B. (1991) 'Searching for Caradog', in *Conquest, Coexistence and Change: Recent Work in Roman Wales*, ed. B. C. Burnham and J. L. Davies, *Trivium*, **25**, Lampeter, 57–64.

Jones, G. D. B. and Mattingly D. (1990) *An Atlas of Roman Britain*, Oxford.

Jones, G. R. J. (1976) 'Multiple estates and early settlement', in *Medieval Settlement*, ed. P. H. Sawyer, Chichester, 15–40.

Jowett, A. and Charlesworth, J. K. (1929) 'The glacial geology of the Derbyshire Dome and the western slopes of the Southern Pennines', *Quarterly Journal of the Geographical Society*, **85**, 307–34.

Kain, R. J. P. and Holt, H. M. E. (1983) 'Farming in Cheshire circa 1840: some evidence from the tithe files', *Transactions of the Lancashire and Cheshire Antiquarian Society*, **82**, 22–57.

— Kapelle, W. E. (1979) *The Norman Conquest of the North*, London.

Kenyon, D. (1986a) 'Notes on Lancashire Place-Names, I: the early names', *Journal of the English Place-Name Society*, **18**, 13–37.

Kenyon, D. (1986b) 'The antiquity of **ham** place-names in Lancashire and Cheshire', *Nomina*, **10**, 5–10.

Kenyon, D. (1991) *The Origins of Lancashire*, Manchester.

Keynes, S. and Lapidge, M. (1986) *Alfred the Great*, London.

Kirby, D. P. (1991) *The Earliest English Kings*, London.

Laing, J. and Laing, L. (1983) 'A Mediterranean trade with Wirral in the Iron Age', *Cheshire Archaeological Bulletin*, **9**, 6–8.

Laing, J. and Laing, L. (undated) *The Dark Ages of West Cheshire*, Chester.

Laing, L. (1976) 'Some pagan finds from Deeside', *Journal of the Chester Archaeological Society*, **59**, 50–1.

Lamb, H. H. (1972–77) *Climate, Past, Present and Future*, London.

Lewis, C. P. (1985) 'English and Norman government and lordship in the Welsh borders, 1039–1087', unpublished D. Phil. thesis, Oxford University.

Lewis, C. P. (1991a) 'An Introduction to the Lancashire Domesday', in *The Lancashire Domesday*, ed. A. Williams and G. H. Martin, London, 1–41.

— Lewis, C. P. (1991b) 'The Formation of the Honor of Chester, 1066– 1100', in *The Earldom of Chester and its Charters*, ed. A. T. Thacker, Chester, 37–68.

Lloyd, Sir J. E. (1939) *A History of Wales*, 3rd edn, I, London.

Longley, D. (1979a) *Prehistoric Sites in Cheshire*, unpublished report on behalf of the Department of the Environment, Chester.

Longley, D. (1979b) 'Aerial Archaeology in Cheshire, I', *Cheshire Archaeological Bulletin*, **6**, 4–9.

Longley, D. (1979c) 'Stray finds, prehistoric settlement and land use in Cheshire', *Cheshire Archaeological Bulletin*, **6**, 84–7.

Longley, D. (1987) 'Prehistory', in *Victoria History of Cheshire*, I, ed. B. E. Harris, assisted by A. T. Thacker, London, 36–114.

Lynch, F. (1969) 'The Megalithic tombs of North Wales', in *Megalithic Enquiries in the West of Britain*, ed. T. G. E. Powell, J. X. W. P. Corcoran, F. Lynch and J. G. Scott, Liverpool, 107–48.

Lynch, F. (ed.) (1984) 'Report on excavations of a Bronze Age Barrow at Llong near Mold', *Journal of the Flintshire Historical Society*, **31**, 13–28.

McNeil, R. (1982a) 'Church Lawton: Burial Mound (Church Lawton North)', *Cheshire Archaeological Bulletin*, **8**, 46–7.

McNeil, R. (1982b) 'Church Lawton: Burial Mound (Church Lawton South)', *Cheshire Archaeological Bulletin*, **8**, 47–9.

McNeil, R. (1985) 'Nantwich – St Anne's Lane. Roman brine tank', *Cheshire Archaeological Bulletin*, **10**, 70–1.

— McNeil, R. (1987) *Halton Castle – A Visual Treasure*, Liverpool.

McPeake, J. (1978a) 'The First Century AD', in *New Evidence for Roman Chester*, ed. T. J. Strickland and P. J. Davey, Liverpool, 9–16.

McPeake, J. (1978b) 'The End of the Affair', in *New Evidence for Roman Chester*, ed. T. J. Strickland and P. J. Davey, Liverpool, 41–4.

McPeake, J. C., Bulmer, M. and Rutter, J. A. (1980) 'Excavations in the garden of No. 1. Abbey Green, Chester, 1975–7: Interim Report', *Journal of the Chester Archaeological Society*, **63**, 15–37.

Manley, J. (1985) 'Early Medieval Radio-Carbon Dates and Plant re-mains from Rhuddlan, Clwyd', *Archaeologia Cambrensis*, **134**, 106–19.

Marsden, B. (1977) *Burial Mounds of Derbyshire*, privately circulated.

Marsden, B. (1982) 'Excavations at the Minning Low Chambered Cairn (Ballidon I), Ballidon, Derbyshire', *Derbyshire Archaeological Journal*, **102**, 8–22.

Marshall, S. (1975) 'The Bow Stones of Lyme Handley', *Transactions of the Lancashire and Cheshire Antiquarian Society*, **78**, 65–74.

Mason, D. J. P. (1976) 'Chester: the evolution and adaptation of its landscape', *Journal of the Chester Archaeological Society*, **59**, 14–23.

Mason, D. J. P. (1978) 'The Extra-Mural Area', in *New Evidence for Roman Chester*, ed. T. J. Strickland and P. J. Davey, Liverpool, 29–40.

Mason, D. J. P. (1980) *Excavations at Chester: 11–15 Castle Street and Neighbouring Sites 1974–8: A Possible Roman Posting House (Mansio)*, Chester.

Mason, D. J. P. (1983) 'Eaton-by-Tarporley: Excavations at the Roman villa, 1982', *Chester Archaeological Bulletin*, **9**, 67–73.

Mason, D. J. P. (1985a) 'The Status of Roman Chester: a reply', *Journal of the Chester Archaeological Society*, **68**, 53–7.

Mason, D. J. P. (1985b) *Excavations at Chester: 26–42 Lower Bridge Street 1974–6. The Dark Age and Saxon Periods*, Chester.

Mason, D. J. P. (1986) 'The *Prata Legionis* at Chester', *Jounal of the Chester Archaeological Society*, **69**, 19–43.

Mason, D. J. P. (1987) 'Chester: the *Canabae Legionis*', *Britannia*, **18**, 143–68.

Mason, D. J. P. (1988a) 'The Roman Site at Heronbridge, near Chester, Cheshire: Aspects of Civilian Settlement in the vicinity of Legionary Fortresses in Britain and beyond', *Archaeological Journal*, **145**, 123–57.

Mason, D. J. P. (1988b) '*Prata Legionis* in Britain', *Britannia*, **19**, 163–89.

Maund, K. L. (1989) 'The Welsh Alliances of Earl Ælfgar of Mercia and his family in the mid-Eleventh Century', *Anglo-Norman Studies*, **11**, 181–90.

Mayer, A. (1990) 'Fieldwalking in Cheshire', *Lithics*, **11**, 48–50.

Meaney, A. (1964) *A Gazetteer of Anglo-Saxon Burial Sites*, London.

Millett, M. (1990) *The Romanization of Britain*, Cambridge.

Moffett, C. (1990) 'The Anglo-Saxon Church of St Andrew at Wroxeter', in *From Roman* Viroconium *to Medieval Wroxeter*, ed. P. Barker, Worcester, 8–9.

Mommsen, T. (ed.) (1892) *Monumenta Germaniae Historica: Chronica Minora*, Berlin.

Morgan, P. (ed.) (1978) *Domesday Book: Cheshire*, Chichester.

Morris, C. (ed) (1982) *The Illustrated Journeys of Celia Fiennes*, London and Exeter.

Morris, E. (1985) 'Prehistoric Salt Distributions: Two Case Studies from Western Britain', *Bulletin of the Board for Celtic Studies*, **32**, 336–79.

Morris, J. (1973) *The Age of Arthur*, Chichester.

Morris, J. (ed.) (1976) *Domesday Book: Staffordshire*, Chichester.

Morris, R. (1989) *Churches in the Landscape*, London.

Musson, C. R. (1976) 'Excavations at the Breiddin 1969–1973', in *Hill-forts: Later Prehistoric Earthworks in Britain and Ireland*, ed. D. W. Harding, London, 293–302.

Musson, C. R. with Britnell, W. J. and Smith, A. G. (1991) *The Breiddin Hillfort. A later Prehistoric settlement in the Welsh Marches*, London.

Nash, D. (1987) *Coinage in the Celtic World*, London.

Nash-Williams, V. E. (1950) *The Early Christian Monuments of Wales*, Cardiff.

Nevell, M. (1991) 'A Field survey of High Legh Parish, pt. I: Prehistoric and Roman Evidence', *Archaeology North West*, **2**, 16–19.

Nevell, M. (1992) *Tameside before 1066*, Tameside.

Newstead, R. (1935) 'Roman Chester: the extra-mural settlement at Saltney', *Liverpool Annals of Archaeology and Anthropology* **22**, 3–18.

Newstead, R. (1939) 'Records of Archaeological Finds', *Journal of the Chester Archaeological Society*, **33**, 5–117.

Newstead, R. (1948) 'Records of Archaeological finds', *Journal of the Chester Archaeological Society*, **36**, 49–172.

Newstead, R. and Droop, J. P. (1932) 'The Roman Amphitheatre at Chester', *Journal of the Chester Archaeological Society*, **29/30**, 1–40.

Newstead R. and Droop, J. P. (1936) 'Excavations in the Deanery Field and Abbey Green', *Journal of the Flintshire Historical Society*, **23**, 3–50.

Newstead, R. and Droop, J. P. (1937) 'A Roman Camp at Halton, Cheshire', *Liverpool Annals of Archaeology*, **24**, 165–8.

Notitia Dignitatum (1876) ed. O. Soeck, Berlin.

O'Leary, T. J. and Davey, P. J. (1976–77) 'Excavations at Pentre Farm, Flint', *Journal of the Flintshire Historical Society*, **27**, 138–51.

Ormerod, G. (1882), *A History of the County Palatine and City of Chester*, revised and enlarged by T. Helsby, 2nd edn, 3 vols, London.

Owen, H. W. (1987) 'English Place-Names and Welsh Stress-Patterns', Nomina, **11**, 99–114.

Oxley, J. (1982) 'Nantwich: an eleventh century salt town and its origins', *Transactions of the Historical Society of Lancashire and Cheshire*, **131**, 1–20.

Ozanne, A. (1962–63) 'The Peak Dwellers', *Medieval Archaeology*, **6/7**, 15–52.

Palmer, A. N. and Owen, E. (1910) *A History of Ancient Tenures of Land in North Wales and the Marches*, 2nd edn, Wrexham.

Parry, M. L. (1978) *Climatic Change, Agriculture and Settlement*, Folkestone.

Petch, D. F. (1975) 'Excavations in Eaton Road, Eccleston, Chester, 1972', *Journal of the Chester Archaeological Society*, **58**, 15–39.

Petch, D. F. (1987) 'The Roman Period', in *Victoria History of Cheshire*, I, ed. B. E. Harris assisted by A. T. Thacker, London, 115–236.

Phillips, A. D. M. (1987) 'Agricultural Land Use and Cropping in Cheshire around 1840: some evidence from Cropping Books', *Transactions of the Lancashire and Cheshire Antiquarian Society*, **84**, 46–63.

Phillips, A. D. M. (1989) *The Underdraining of Farmland in England during the Nineteenth Century*, Cambridge.

Phillips, C. B. and Smith, J. H. (forthcoming) *The North-West from AD 1550*, Harlow.

Postles, D. (1986) 'The Bordars of Domesday Derbyshire', *Derbyshire Archaeological Journal*, **106**, 123–6.

References

Pretty, K. (1989) 'Defining the Magonsaete', in *Origins of Anglo-Saxon Kingdoms*, ed. S. Bassett, Leicester, 171–83.

Ptolemy (1883–1901) *Claudii Ptolemaei Geographia*, ed. C. Muller, 2 vols, Paris.

Radner, J. N. (ed). (1978) *Fragmentary Annals of Ireland*, Dublin.

Ravenna Cosmography (1940) *Ravennatis Anonymi Cosmographia*, ed. J. Schnetz, *Romana*, **2**.

Redknap, M. (1991) *The Christian Celts: Treasures of Late Celtic Wales*, Cardiff.

Reece, R. (1980) 'Town and Country: the end of Roman Britain', *World Archaeology*, **12**, **1**, 77–92.

Renaud, F. (1876) *The Ancient Parish of Prestbury in Cheshire*, Manchester.

Richards, M. (1969) *Welsh Administrative and Territorial Units*, Cardiff.

Riley, D. (1980) *Early Landscape from the Air*, Sheffield.

Rivet, A. L. F. and Smith, C. (1979) *The Place-Names of Roman Britain*, London.

Roberts, T. (1992) 'Welsh ecclesiastical place-names and archaeology', in *The Early Church in Wales and the West*, ed. N. Edwards and A. Lane, Oxford, 41–4.

Roffe, D. (1986) 'The Origins of Derbyshire', *Derbyshire Archaeological Journal*, **106**, 102–22.

Room, R. E. (1968) 'Excavations at the Roman site at Ffrith, Flintshire', *Journal of the Flintshire Historical Society*, **23**, 82–4.

Ross, A. (1967) *Pagan Celtic Britain*, London.

Rowley, G. (1975) 'Excavation of a circle at New Farm, Henbury', *Transactions of the Lancashire and Cheshire Antiquarian Society*, **78**, 79–80.

Rutherford Davis, K. (1982) *Britons and Saxons: The Chiltern Region 400–700*, Chichester.

Salway, P. (1981) *Roman Britain*, Oxford.

Sawyer, P. H. (1979) *Charters of Burton Abbey*, London.

Sawyer, P. H. (1985) '1066–1086: A Tenurial Revolution?' in *Domesday Book: A Reassessment*, ed. P. H. Sawyer, London, 71–85.

Sawyer, P. H. (1987) 'The Cheshire Domesday', in *The Victoria History of Cheshire*, I, ed. B. E. Harris, assisted by A. T. Thacker, London, 293–307.

Schoenwetter, J. (1982) 'Environmental Archaeology of the Peckforton Hills', *Cheshire Archaeological Bulletin*, **8**, 10–11.

Shimwell, D. M. (1985) 'The distribution and origins of the lowland mosses', in *The geomorphology of North-West England*, ed. R. H. Johnson, Manchester, 299–312.

Shotter, D. C. A. (1979) 'The Evidence of coin-loss and the Roman Occupation of North West England', in *The Changing Past*, ed. N. J. Higham, Manchester, 1–14.

Sims-Williams, P. (1990) *Religion and Literature in Western England, 600–800*, Cambridge.

Slofstra, J. (1983) 'An Anthropological Approach to the study of Romanization Processes', in *Roman and Native in the Low Countries*, ed. R. Brandt and J. Slofstra, BAR, International Series, 184, Oxford, 71–104.

Smart, V. (1986) 'Scandinavians, Celts, and Germans in Anglo-Saxon England: the evidence of moneyers' names', in *Anglo-Saxon Monetary History*, ed. M. Blackburn, Leicester, 171–84.

Smith, B. and George, T. Neville (1961) *British Regional Geology, North Wales*, London.

Smith, L. P. (1975) *The Agricultural Climate of England and Wales*, London.

Smith, W. and Webb, W. (1656) *The Vale-Royall of England*, published by D. King, London.

Stanford, S. C. (1984) 'The Wrekin Hillfort Excavations 1973', *Archaeological Journal*, **141**, 61–90.

Stead, I. M., Bourke, J. B. and Brothwell, D. (1986) *Lindow Man: The Body in the Bog*, London.

Stenton, Sir F. M. (1971) *Anglo-Saxon England*, 3rd edn, Oxford.

Stephens, G. R. (1985a) 'The Roman Aqueduct at Chester', *Journal of the Chester Archaeological Society*, **68**, 59–70.

Stephens, G. R. (1985b) 'Military Aqueducts in Roman Britain', *Archaeological Journal*, **142**, 216–36.

Stevens, C. E. (1940) 'The British sections of the *Notitia Dignitatum*', *Archaeological Journal*, **97**, 125–54.

Strickland, T. J. (1978) 'The Fortress in the second and third centuries', in *New Work on Roman Chester*, ed. T. J. Strickland and P. J. Davey, Liverpool, 25–8.

Strickland, T. J. (1980) 'First Century Deva: some evidence reconsidered in the light of recent archaeological discoveries', *Journal of the Chester Archaeological Society*, **63**, 5–14.

Strickland, T. J. (1982) 'The defences of Roman Chester: A note on discoveries made on the North Wall, 1982', *Journal of the Chester Archaeological Society*, **65**, 25–36.

Strickland, T. J. (1983) 'The defences of Roman Chester: discoveries made on the East wall', *Journal of the Chester Archaeological Society*, **66**, 5–11.

Strickland, T. J. and Davey, P. J. (ed.) (1978) *New Evidence for Roman Chester*, Liverpool.

Sylvester, D. (1960) 'The manor and the Cheshire Landscape', *Transactions of the Lancashire and Cheshire Antiquarian Society*, **70**, 1–15.

Sylvester, D. (1967) 'Parish and township in Cheshire and North East Wales', *Journal of the Chester Archaeological Society*, **54**, 23–36.

Tacitus, C. (1970) *Annals*, ed. and trans. J. Jackson, 5 vols, London.

Tait, J. (ed.) (1916) *The Domesday Survey of Cheshire*, Manchester.

Tait, J. (ed.) (1920) *The Chartulary or Register of the Abbey of St Werburgh, Chester*, I, Manchester.

Tallis, J. H. (1973a) 'Studies on southern Pennine Peats, V. Direct Observations on peat erosion and peat hydrology at Featherbed Moss, Derbyshire', *Journal of Ecology*, **61**, 1–22.

Tallis, J. H. (1973b) 'The Terrestrialization of Lake Basins in North

Cheshire, with special reference to the development of a "Schwing-moor" structure', *Journal of Ecology*, **61**, 537–67.

Tallis, J. H. and Switzur, V. R. (1990) 'Forest and Moorland in the South Pennine uplands in the mid-Flandrian Period: II. The Hillslope Forests', *Journal of Ecology*, **78**, 857–83.

— Taylor, J. (1966) *The Universal Chronicle of Ranulf Higden*, Oxford.

Terrett, I. B. (1948) 'The Domesday Woodland of Cheshire', *Transactions of the Historical Society of Lancashire and Cheshire*, **100**, 1–8.

Terrett, I. B. (1962) 'Cheshire', in *The Domesday Geography of northern England*, ed. H. C. Darby and I. S. Maxwell, Cambridge.

Thacker, A. T. (1982) 'Chester and Gloucester: Early Ecclesiastical Organisation in two Mercian Burghs', *Northern History*, **18**, 199–211.

Thacker, A. T. (1985) 'Kings, Saints, and Monasteries in Pre-Viking Mercia', *Midland History*, **10**, 1–25.

Thacker, A. T. (1987) 'Anglo-Saxon Cheshire', in *Victoria History of Cheshire*, I, ed. B. E. Harris, assisted by A. T. Thacker, London, 237–92.

Thacker, A. T. (ed.) (1991) *The Earldom of Chester and its Charters*, Chester.

Thacker, A. T. (forthcoming) 'Early Medieval Chester', in *Victoria History of Cheshire*, V, ed. A. T. Thacker, London.

Thomas, A. C. (1971) *The Early Christian Archaeology of North Britain*, Oxford.

Thomas, A. C. (1981) *Christianity in Roman Britain to AD 500*, London.

Thompson, E. A. (1979) 'Gildas and the History of Roman Britain', *Britannia*, **10**, 203–26.

Thompson, E. A. (1984) *St Germanus of Auxerre and the end of Roman Britain*, Woodbridge.

Thompson, F. H. (1965) *Roman Cheshire*, Chester.

Thompson, F. H. (1967) 'Excavations at Castle Hill, Oldcastle near Malpas, 1957', *Journal of the Chester Archaeological Society*, **54**, 5–8.

Thompson, F. H. (1969) 'Excavations at Linenhall Street, Chester, 1961–2', *Journal of the Chester Archaeological Society*, **56**, 1–22.

Thorn, F. and Thorn, C. (ed.) (1986) *Domesday Book: Shropshire*, Chichester.

— Thorpe, L. (ed. and trans.) (1978) *Gerald of Wales: Journey through Wales/The Description of Wales*, London.

Todd, M. (1970) 'The Small Towns of Roman Britain', *Britannia*, **1**, 114–30.

Toulmin Smith, L. (ed.) (1906–10) *The Itinerary of John Leland*, 5 vols, London.

Turner, R. C. (1985) 'The Bridgemere bronze hoard', *Cheshire Archaeological Bulletin*, **10**, 7–10.

Varley, W. J. (1935) 'Maiden Castle, Bickerton. Preliminary Excavations 1934', *University of Liverpool Annals of Anthropology and Archaeology*, **22**, 97–110.

Varley, W. J. (1936) 'Further Excavations at Maiden Castle, Bickerton,

1935', *University of Liverpool Annals of Anthropology and Archaeology*, **23**, 101–12.

Varley, W. J. (1950) 'Excavations of the Castle Ditch, Eddisbury, 1935–38', *Transactions of the Historical Society of Lancashire and Cheshire*, **102**, 1–68.

Victoria County History (1970) *Staffordshire*, III, London.

Waddelove, A. C. and Waddelove, E. (1983) 'Watling Street south of Chester', *Journal of the Chester Archaeological Society*, **66**, 13–22.

Waddelove, E. (1983) 'The Roman Road between *Varis* and *Canovium*', *Archaeologia Cambrensis*, **132**, 95–106.

Wainwright, F. T. (1950) 'Cledemutha', *English Historical Review*, **65**, 203–12.

Wainwright, F. T. (1975) *Scandinavian England*, Chichester.

Wallace, P. T. (1986) 'The English presence in Viking Dublin', in *Anglo-Saxon Monetary History*, ed. M. Blackburn, Leicester, 201–21.

Watkin, W. Thompson (1974) *Roman Cheshire*, 2nd edn, Wakefield (first published 1886).

Webster, G. (1953) 'The lead-mining industry in North Wales in Roman times', *Flintshire Historical Society Publications*, **13**, 5–33.

Webster, G. (1991) *The Cornovii*, 2nd edn, Gloucester.

White, R. (1978) 'New Light on the origins of the Kingdom of Gwynedd', in *Astudiaethau ar yr Hengerdd*, ed. R. Bromwich and R. B. Jones, Cardiff.

White, R. (1990) 'Excavations on the site of the Baths Basilica', in *From Roman Viroconium to Medieval Wroxeter*, ed. P. Barker, Worcester, 3–7.

Wittick, G. Clement (1982) 'Roman lead-mining on Mendip and in North Wales: a reapprasial', *Britannia*, **13**, 113–23.

Williams, A. (1982) '*Princeps Merciorum Gentis*: the family, career and connections of Ælfhere, Ealdorman of Mercia, 956–83', *Anglo-Saxon England*, **10**, 143–72.

Williams, A. (1986) ' "Cockles amongst the wheat": Danes and English in the western Midlands in the first half of the eleventh century', *Midland History*, **11**, 1–22.

Williams, I. (1931–33) 'Marwnad Cynddylan', *Bulletin of the Board of Celtic Studies*, **6**, 134–41.

Williams, I. (1935) *Canu Llywarch Hen*, London.

Williams, S. (1985) *Diocletian and the Roman Recovery*, London.

Williams, S. R. (1984/85) 'Aerial Archaeology in Cheshire during 1984', *Cheshire Archaeological Bulletin*, **10**, 11–18.

Williamson, T. (1984) 'The Roman Countryside: Settlement and Agriculture in North West Essex', *Britannia*, **15**, 225–30.

Williamson, T. (1987) 'Early co-axial field systems on the East Anglian boulder clays', *Proceedings of the Prehistoric Society*, **53**, 419–32.

Wilson, D. (1981) 'Withington', *Current Archaeology*, **76**, 155.

Wilson, D. (1988) 'Excavation of a round barrow at Twemlow, Cheshire', *Archaeological Journal*, **145**, 397–8.

References

— Winterbottom, M. (ed.) (1978) *Gildas: The Ruin of Britain and other works*, Chichester.

Wood, M. (1978–80) 'Brunanburh Revisited', *Saga-Book of the Viking Club*, **20**, 200–17.

— Wood, M. (1983) 'The Making of King Æthelstan's Empire: an English Charlemagne?', in *Ideal and Reality in Frankish and Anglo-Saxon Society*, ed. P. Wormald, Oxford, 250–72.

Worsley, P. (1970) 'The Cheshire–Shropshire lowlands', in *The glaciations of Wales and adjoining regions*, ed. C. A. Lewis, London, 83–106.

Worthington, M. (1986) 'The Wat's Dyke – a comment on the work of Sir Cyril Fox in Clwyd', *Archaeology in Clwyd*, **8**, 14–16.

Wright, R. P. and Jackson, K. H. (1986) 'A late inscription from Wroxeter', *Antiquaries Journal*, **48**, 296–300.

— Yorke, B. (1990) *Kings and Kingdoms of Early Anglo-Saxon England*, London.

Index

Plates are denoted by bold type.
For alphabetical purposes Æ is treated as A.

Abbreviations

abp. archbishop
bp. bishop
DB. Domesday Book
ea. ealdorman
e. earl
k. king
r. river

139, 145–6, 148, 178, 180–1, 214
Dunham (Mascy), 164
Dunham (Thornton-le-Moors), 151
Dunning, 147, 153
dykes, 99–101, 103, 212

Eadric 'the wild', 190
Eadric Streona, 184
Ealdgyth, Queen, 187, 189, 190
ealdormen, of Mercia, 182–4
earls, of Mercia, 123, 129, 135, 148–9, 151, 153, 172, 174, 178, 180, 186–91, 198–201
earls, Norman, of Chester, 131, 154, 175, 191, 203–5, 208–9
see Hugh, *e.*
Eastham, 108, 132, 179, 192, 208
Eaton-by-Tarporley, Roman villa, 52–3, 58, 62, 146, 151
Eaton-on-Dee, 180, 198
Eccleston, 43, 78, 80–1, 94, 193
Eddisbury, 54, 153
Castle Hill, 24, 111, **3**
Hundred, 214
Eddisbury Hill, Rainow, 24, 111
Edgar, *k.*, 119, 121, 123–4, 150, 160, 182, 184
Edward I, 103, 212–13
Edward the Confessor, 186–8, 191
Edward the Elder, 110–19, 124, 175–6
Edward, thegn, 158–9, 161, 194, 196, 208–9
Edwin, *e.* of Mercia, 103, 148–9, 152, 172, 184, 186–91, 194, 199–202, 208
Edwin, thegn, 135, 193, 208
Elmet, 70, 91
Elton, 151
enclosures
Domesday, 140, 153, 172
Roman, 54–9
English
immigration, 94–5
'overkingship', 69, 74, 84–92, 103, 106, 110–13, 187
Englefield, 72, 212

environment, 1–15, 22
estates, 119, 127–81
of bishop, 133
of crown, 103, 108, 117, 139–40, 143, 149, 152, 160, 176, 180, 182, 184
Ethelred, *ea.*, 106–8, 110–11, 143, 175
Ethelred, *k.* of the Mercians, 99, 129
Ethelred, II, *k.*, 124, 174, 182, 184
ethnicity, 77–8
Exestan Hundred, 117, 133–4, 181, 187–8, 193, 212
Eyton, 101

farming, 13–15
medieval, 123, 156, 162–3, 202–7
Mercian, 121, 138, 145
neolithic, 16–17
prehistoric, 24–5, 48
Roman, 48, 52–9
sub-Roman, 66
Farndon, 37, 79–81, 83, 119, 124, 127, 133–4, 138–40, 179, 205, 209
Ffrith, lead-working, 43–4, 51
fields, 54–5, 202–7
Fiennes, Celia, 12–13
fisheries, 14, 152–3, 194–8
Flaxmere, 12
Flintshire, 22, 212
flint tools, 15–17, 19
Frankby, 107
Frodsham, 108, 152–5, 172, 179, 181, 205, 208–9
frontier
character of Cheshire, 61, 125, 175
of Mercia with Wales, 84, 86, 98–104, 110, 115–19, 211–12
of Mercia with Northumbria, 111, 116, 155
see also Mersey, *r.*
of Norman control, 201, 211–13